The Visitor's Guide
to
SCOTLAND: THE LOWLANDS

INDEX TO 1:50 000 MAPS OF GREAT BRITAIN

Shading indicates maps used in this guide.

THE
VISITOR'S GUIDE TO
SCOTLAND:
THE LOWLANDS

RON SCHOLES
&
ROGER SMITH

MPC

HUNTER
PUBLISHING INC

Published by:
Moorland Publishing Co Ltd,
Moor Farm Road,
Airfield Estate,
Ashbourne,
Derbyshire DE6 1HD
England

© Roger Smith & Ron Scholes 1990

British Library Cataloguing in Publication Data:
Smith, R.
   The visitor's guide to the
   Lowlands of Scotland.
   1. Scotland. Lowlands - Visitor's
   guides
   I. Title II. Scholes, R.
   914.11'04858

ISBN 0 86190 381 1 (paperback)

Colour and black & white
origination by:
Scantrans, Singapore

Printed in the UK by:
Richard Clay Ltd, Bungay, Suffolk

Cover photograph: *Peebles*
(Ron Scholes).

All illustrations were supplied by the author.

Published in the USA by:
Hunter Publishing Inc,
300 Raritan Center Parkway,
CN 94, Edison, NJ 08818
ISBN 1 55650 262 1 (USA)

CONTENTS

Key to Symbols Used in Text Margin and on Maps

 Recommended walk

 Parkland

 Archaeological site

 Nature reserve/Animal interest

 Birdlife

 Garden

 Golf facilities

 Sports facilities

 Skiing facilities

 Horse riding

 Church/Ecclesiastical site

 Building of interest

 Castle/Fortification

 Museum/Art gallery

 Beautiful view/Scenery, Natural phenomenon

 Other place of interest

 Sailing

 Interesting railway

 Fishing

 Industrial archaeology

Key to Maps

 Main road

 Motorway

 River

Town/City

● Town/Village

Lake/Reservoir

- —-— Country Boundary

INTRODUCTION

Scotland can geographically be divided into three clear parts. The northern area is separated from the middle section by the Great Glen, a major geological fault occupied by the Caledonian Canal. The middle section is separated from the southern area by the firths of Clyde and Forth. South of this line, the area stretching as far as the border is known as the Lowlands of Scotland. 'Lowlands', however, is not completely descriptive, for large parts of the region are very hilly. The mountainous heartland of Galloway, with its rugged granite outcrops, is like a scenic combination of the Trossachs and the Cairngorms.

There is a marvellous variety of beautiful landscapes in southwest Scotland. The high Carrick Hills, which sweep down to the rocky shoreline of southern Ayrshire; the wild, bare moors of the Rhins; the dairy farming land of the Machars; the wide, shining sands of the Solway Coast. In the Firth of Clyde, the Isle of Arran dominates the scene, its lofty and jagged mountain outline beckoning the visitor across from the mainland.

Then there are the cities, with their wealth of interest, and beauty of a different kind. Glasgow is a city of dramatic contrasts and visual excitement, 1990's European City of Culture, with its imposing Victorian buildings and delightful parks. The nearby Clyde Valley offers impressive waterfalls and the unique industrial village of New Lanark.

Edinburgh has always been a major attraction to visitors to Scotland. It is a renowned centre for the arts, is rich in history, and has a mini-wilderness in its centre, while the nearby Pentland Hills offer beautiful scenery and good walking.

Transport

The M6 and A74 give easy access from the south, and can be left either by the A7 up to Hawick or by the A708 Moffat/Selkirk road. The A68 will take you from Newcastle over Carter Bar to Jedburgh in well under 2 hours. A little further east, the A697 winds up through Wooler to cross the Tweed into Scotland at historic Coldstream, and on the east coast the A1 — the Great North Road itself — takes a longer but very beautiful route, keeping close to the sea all the way.

There are main rail lines to west and east still, though the smaller border lines and the scenic Waverley route are sadly gone, no doubt for ever. The western line carries regular services from Glasgow down through Carlisle, and the east coast has the express Edinburgh-London route. There are local services to Dunbar, North Berwick, Musselburgh, Drem, Longniddry and Prestonpans. For other areas of the eastern section of the Scottish Lowlands, visitors may alight at either Berwick, Carlisle or Edinburgh.

Lowlands, Border and Western Scottish buses still provide a good network, and excellent comprehensive timetables are available. It repays a bit of careful study to maximise connections. For example, Lothian Regional Public Transport operate a 'Busline' telephone service which gives information on all bus timetables within Lothian Region. The area, finally, is ideally suited to the slower means of travel — cycling and walking. Apart from the few trunk routes, the roads are generally quiet, and great for touring cyclists. Inexpensive accommodation with a friendly welcome is not hard to find, and there is no shortage either of refreshment places or distractions calling for a stop during the day's pedalling.

Accommodation

Accommodation generally is unlikely to be a problem to the Lowlands and Borders visitor. All grades can be found, from good hotels with excellent cuisine to the many comfortable bed-and-breakfast houses. Wherever you stay, the welcome will be warm and you will be well looked after.

There are a number of self-catering schemes in the region, offering either cottages or caravans, and there are many youth hostels. See Further Information for details. The one at Broadmeadows is a piece of history; it was the first hostel opened by the SYHA in 1931 and has been going strong ever since.

Information about accommodation can either be had in advance, using one of the several excellent guides available, or locally at a Tourist Information Centre. These are to be found at all main centres of population, and a list is given in Further Information.

Some of these information centres operate a 'book-a-bed-ahead' service, through which you can secure accommodation in the price range of your choice for a small fee. This is a useful service but it is not essential in the borders — a reflection of the fact that the area could do with more visitors.

Recreation

For the active visitor, there is plenty of choice. The walking, of course, is first-class, whether your taste is for coastlines or high hills. A waymarked long-distance route, the Southern Uplands Way, was opened in 1984. It stretches from Portpatrick near Stranraer to St Abb's Head on the Berwickshire coast, a distance of 212 miles (340km). Suggestions for shorter walks are given in the text.

The Borders Regional Council countryside rangers operate a programme of guided walks in the summer months, and several hotels cater specially for the walker. The youth hostel network is also an ideal framework for a walking (or cycling) holiday.

Pony-trekking thrives; the Southern Upland hills and quiet by-ways are absolutely ideal for travel on horseback, and a leaflet on the subject can be obtained from the Regional Tourist Board or from the Scottish Tourist Board. All classes and ages are catered for.

Another principal recreation is, not surprisingly, fishing. The Tweed and its tributaries are famous game fishing waters, not least because the entire water system is free from any industrial pollution. No fewer than sixteen different species of fish have been noted here.

Full information for all fishing, is available locally, or via the Tourist Information Centres.

There are also many golf courses in the region, both 18- and 9-hole. Many of these are delightfully scenic and all of them welcome visitors. Some hotels arrange special golf weeks.

Other recreational possibilities include sailing on St Mary's Loch and off the Berwickshire coast, and orienteering at any one of several permanent courses operated by the Forestry Commission in conjunction with local clubs. The upper headwaters of the main river valleys, and many acres of moorland and hill slopes, are now clothed with extensive forests. The River Tweed winds down from Tweedsmuir to Melrose, and at every turn soft woodland colours of larch and spruce blanket the steep slopes, blending with the valley

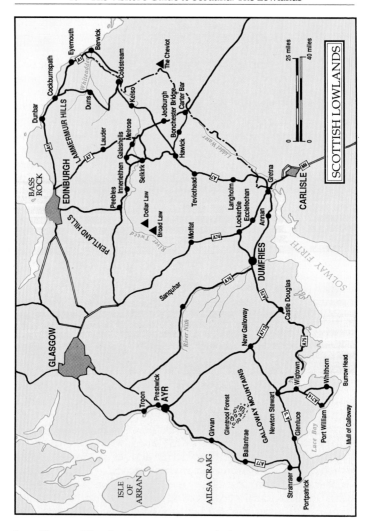

SCOTTISH LOWLANDS

broadleaves. The closely-growing trees hide the courses of myriads of small streams that chuckle and race their way down the hill flanks to join the mighty Tweed.

Although there are stands of Scots Pine surviving, once the descendants of a great natural forest, the modern commercial planta-

The rolling hills of the Scottish Lowlands

The Lowlands in winter

tions have created dense woodlands of close-pressing larch, spruce and lodge-pole pine that now obscure many a once-fine view. The forests on the other hand, provide employment for many thousands of people and supply raw materials for the building, newsprint and chemical industries.

Forestry also gives diverse habitats for wildlife, and the woodland is home to a large number of animals and birds. Roe deer are common, and red squirrels, badgers, foxes and other smaller mammals are often seen. Several species of rare birds of prey are becoming established.

Over the years the Forestry Commission has learned from its early mistakes, and now provides visitors with miles of forest tracks and paths, and in some parts forest drives, picnic areas, interesting nature trails and bird-watching locations.

Festivals

For those who prefer a less strenuous holiday the choice is just as wide. One of the great features of the region is the series of Common Ridings and festivals held at all principal towns. There are twelve main ridings and celebrations, running more or less one a week from early June to mid-August. They have their origins in the need to define and protect common land and many of them celebrate historical incidents. All are colourful spectacles and although they are celebrations for the local community, they are also prime attractions for visitors.

Apart from these annual events, other festivals with specific themes such as fishing, golf or Borders life are arranged by the regional or district councils each year. Then, of course, there is the biggest festival of all, the Edinburgh Festival.

Climate

Weather is an important consideration for any visitor, so what can be expected in the Scottish Lowlands? The eastern part of the region is generally drier than the west, as it true for the whole of Scotland — the western hills catch the rain borne on the prevailing south-westerly winds first. On the other hand, the west is a little warmer overall than the east. Scotland's east coast, including Berwickshire and East Lothian, has some glorious sandy beaches, but it does suffer from rather too much east wind, and also on occasion from 'haar' — a sea fog that can blanket the coast in a cold mist while 20 miles inland is glorious sunshine.

The south-east coast is, however, still among the sunniest places in Scotland from May to July, recording an average 6-6$^1/_2$ hours per day of bright sunshine. These (particularly May and early June) are the months when good settled spells are most likely.

Records taken over the whole holiday period from May to September show that eastern areas of Scotland often record less than 250mm (10in) of rain during this time, so you will be unlucky if you get a long spell of wet weather. Showers can never be ruled out of course, but the scenery is often at its most dramatic and rewarding in these conditions, with the quality of the light constantly changing — a challenge for the photographer.

The autumn period can also have advantages. The weather is quite often dry, there are fewer visitors overall (so that roads are less crowded) and the trees are in brilliant colouring along the river valleys. The air on the hills is invigorating, and a walking holiday in the Scottish Lowlands and Borders in September or October could have much to commend it.

Extremes of temperature are rare in the region, although temperatures of -20°C have been recorded. The weather station at Eskdalemuir also holds the unenviable record of the most concentrated period of rain ever recorded in Scotland — 3$^1/_2$in in one hour, on 26 June 1953.

One blessing is that the region is much less prone to the irritations of the midge than more northerly parts of Scotland. This little pest can be a real menace in summer in the western highlands, but you are unlikely to suffer too badly in the Lowlands and Borders.

The Scottish Lowlands and Border country has plenty of space for everyone. It is a welcoming region, with no shortage of things to see and do, and no shortage either of glorious countryside to wander in or ride through. This book aims to give a broad picture of what is available and will hopefully tempt you to try for yourself this often neglected part of Scotland.

1

THE BORDER AND THE CHEVIOT HILLS

A border could perhaps be defined as a historical accident that has become historical fact. The border between Scotland and England as now defined makes some odd-looking twists and turns, at one point heading south-east when its basic alignment is south-west to north-east. This chapter will start on the east coast and trace the border across, having a look at the land and places immediately to either side of it.

The first surprise is that **Berwick-on-Tweed** is not in Scotland, but in England. It sits on the north bank of the Tweed, and should surely belong to Berwick*shire* but it is firmly in Northumberland, England, despite being a burgh not a borough.

None the less, it would be unusual for anyone to pass over the Tweed there without the definite feeling of crossing a border. Bridges have always been important to Berwick. There was a timber bridge here for centuries before the oldest structure still standing; the James VI bridge was built in the early years of the seventeenth century. For its time, it is a marvellous piece of work, with fifteen arches and a total span of 1,164ft (361m) of river.

No less spectacular, and certainly more obvious to the modern traveller, is the Royal Border Bridge which carries the railway into the town. Designed by Robert Stephenson, son of George of *Rocket* fame, it has no fewer than twenty-five tall arches, spans just over 2,000ft (620m) and was opened by Queen Victoria in 1850. You get an excellent view of it from the third Berwick bridge, carrying the A1 road. This is a mere youngster; it was completed in 1928, and reflects modern engineering design in that the number of arches has been

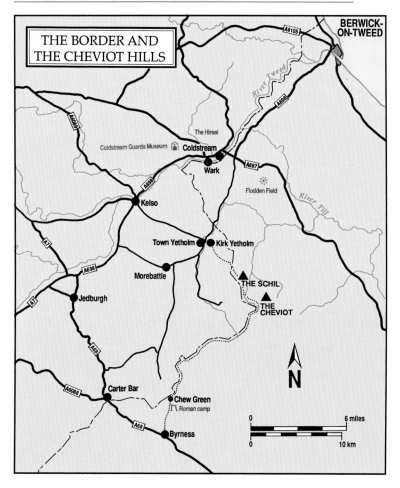

THE BORDER AND
THE CHEVIOT HILLS

BERWICK-ON-TWEED

reduced to three.

A feature of Berwick is the impressive Town Wall, one of the most complete in Britain. It encloses the old town and gives a real impression of a fortified burgh if you walk round it.

A town that has seen so many battles should have a castle; and so it has, even though it is not very impressive. The railway is partly to blame for that, for when Berwick station was built in the nineteenth century, a goodly chunk of the castle ruins were cleared to make way for it. Enough remains to impress on the visitor the strength of its position, on a high bluff above the river.

The border line meets the coast 3 miles north of Berwick and describes a swinging loop to the west of the town, meeting the Tweed at Gainslaw. After this, river and border run together as far as Carham, west of Coldstream. This is all low-lying, rich, agricultural land, though the hills are never out of sight completely. On the Scottish side, the area is called the Merse, and is covered more fully in the chapter on Berwickshire.

After Berwick, the next river crossing point is the Union Bridge at **Horncliffe**, best approached by a minor road from the A698. It is worth going to see, for this was the first suspension bridge in Britain to carry vehicular traffic when it was opened in 1820. It was designed by Captain Sir Samuel Brown and was opened as a toll-bridge. The tollhouse, on the English side, was demolished in 1955 and replaced by a small forecourt made up of the cottage's foundations. The bridge is listed as an ancient monument.

With the Union and Coldstream bridges, Norham Bridge is administered by the Tweed Bridges Trust. The Trust was formed in 1884, at the time when Norham became the third 'border bridge' over the Tweed, replacing an older timber structure. It carries B6470 across the river to **Ladykirk**. The church here was built in the late fifteenth century at the order of James IV of Scotland as a thank-offering for a narrow escape from drowning in the Tweed. It was built entirely of stone to avoid the risk of fire, presumably with those Border raiders in mind!

Fifteen miles from Berwick, and still on the Tweed, is the first true Border town, **Coldstream**. Before the border reaches there, however, the Tweed has been joined by the Till, crossed by the Tudor bridge at Twizel. At Coldstream is another of the Tweed Border Bridges. Coldstream Bridge was built by John Smeaton (who gained more fame as a lighthouse-builder), and completed in 1766 at a cost of £6,000. The small stone building on the Scottish side of the bridge, built as a tollhouse, became far better known as a marriage-house which rivalled the one at Gretna in popularity. The practice was stopped by an Act of Parliament in 1856. Downstream of the bridge is a small dam or 'cauld' with a gap at its south end to allow fish free run.

At the entrance to the main street is the monument to Charles Marjoribanks, first MP for Berwickshire after the Reform Act of 1832. Off Market Square, near the river, is the Coldstream Guards Museum. The original company of Guards was raised in this area by

General Monk in 1659; they marched to London in 34 days and helped to restore order and the monarchy, following the death of Oliver Cromwell. The close association between Guards and town has been maintained ever since; the museum houses many exhibits illustrating the history of the regiment, and also the scroll commemorating the occasion in August 1968 when the regiment was honoured with the Freedom of the Burgh. The colours of the second Battalion are laid up in the parish church, together with a side drum and a bugle.

Another interesting old building is The Dovecot, facing the Leet Water. It dates from the late eighteenth century. Penitents' Walk, which runs along the Leet to the Tweed, and Nuns' Walk which joins it, are reminders that there was once a Cistercian priory here. Nothing remains but these two names.

If you take the walk, you are likely to see fishermen trying their luck; if you wish to join them, you will be welcome to do so in season. Visitors' permits for trout and coarse fishing are available locally at very reasonable rates. Enquire at the Tourist Information Centre at Henderson Park. Other facilities for visitors include a caravan and camp site nicely sited by the river and more than adequate hotel and guest house accommodation.

A couple of miles from Coldstream, off the A697, is **The Hirsel**, the seat of the Home family and presently the home of Lord Home, the former Prime Minister. The house itself is not open to the public, but the grounds are open all the year round. There is a wildfowl sanctuary and a very wide variety of bird life in the splendid woods. Nature trails are laid out, and the estate interpretation centre will be glad to give visitors further details. Flower displays of particular interest include daffodils in April and rhododendrons in June.

Whilst in the Coldstream area, a short excursion into England will give a fuller picture of Border history. No visitor to the area should leave without a trip to Flodden Field, where the site of the battle is marked by a simple stone cross. Flodden has been described as 'the worst defeat ever inflicted on a Scots army'.

A little way west of Coldstream, on the English bank of the river, is **Wark**, where a mighty castle once stood. This place was the origin of the Order of the Garter, which really did begin as its name suggests. Edward III was staying in the castle, and during a ball he was dancing with the lady of the house, the Countess of Salisbury, when one of her garters came loose and fell upon the floor. Edward picked it up and checked the assembly's mirth by saying with dignity *honi soit qui mal y pense* — the words chosen as the motto of

Halter Burn at the end of the Pennine Way

the Order.

Four miles west of Coldstream, the border takes an abrupt turn south-east, away from Tweed, as if drawn by magnetism to the high Cheviot Hills. At the point where it turns, **Birgham**, a treaty was signed in 1290, reaffirming the independence of the Scots.

The border crosses the valley of the Bowmont Water before climbing Coldsmouth Hill and linking the summits of White Law, Black Hag, The Schil, and Auchope Cairn, at 2,382ft (738m) its highest point. Bowmont Water divides the twin villages of **Town Yetholm** and **Kirk Yetholm**, which in earlier times were gipsy strongholds. There is a nature reserve run by the Scottish Wildlife Trust at Yetholm Loch, but access is by permit only.

No permits are needed to walk the Pennine Way, which was the first designated long distance footpath in Britain. Most people walk it south to north, starting at Edale in the Peak District National Park, and so finishing their 270-mile journey at Kirk Yetholm. Their first port of call is frequently the Border Hotel, where a free celebratory drink, courtesy of the guidebook writer A. Wainwright, has been the custom since the path opened. Originally you got a pint on Mr Wainwright, but so many people now walk the route that the bounty

Kirk Yetholm

has been reduced to a half. There are only two conditions — you must have walked the whole route, and you must be carrying Wainwright's *Pennine Way Companion* when you enter the pub. So, one way and another, you don't really get your drink for nothing.

Using the Wainwright guidebook, with its superb maps and line drawings, or any other similarly detailed guide, you can reverse the modern pilgrims' triumphant finish, and walk southwards from Kirk Yetholm towards the border. It is a splendid outing, however far you go; over the hill and up the valley to Burnhead, then round the slopes of The Curr and up again to meet the border on The Schil, with Cheviot itself looming up to the south-east. To The Schil NT869223, and back is about 12 miles, but you can retrace your steps at any point and still have a most enjoyable walk.

This last stage of the Pennine Way is generally reckoned to be the toughest, if you are trying to do it in one day. The last previous habitation is at Byrness, and the path follows the border all the way from Coquet Head to The Schil. The full distance from Byrness to Kirk Yetholm is not much short of 30 miles, with a goodly amount of climbing and some rough and boggy ground to traverse.

If you prefer being carried by four sturdy legs rather than using

U your own two, there is a trekking centre at **Belford**, high in the Bowmont Valley. Beginners are catered for, and the proprietors will also advise on walks in the area.

The border line stays almost on the watershed all the way along this stretch, now running south-westwards. It passes the dramatic gash of the Hen Hole on its way to within a mile of Cheviot summit —a diversion most Pennine Wayfarers seem to take, despite its being one of the most notoriously nasty bits of peat bog in Britain. For those for whom the struggle becomes a bit too much and Kirk Yetholm is just out of reach, there is a shelter (an old railway wagon), NT875202 on the ridge leading to Auchope Cairn which can be used as an emergency bothy.

The hills are crossed by a number of tracks and droving routes and, further south-west by Coquet Head, by the Roman Road named Dere Street, which leaves the impressive site of the camp at Chew Green heading north towards Kelso. Dere Street can be followed for many miles by the dedicated walker, though access from public roads is not easy. Just on the Scottish side of the border, and just east π of Dere Street, is the fort on Woden Law, a pre-Roman stronghold that was overrun by Agricola's army in AD80.

Just on the English side, by Coquet Head, and on the Pennine π Way, is Chew Green, an impressive Roman camp and an important staging-post on Dere Street. So, with a northwards twist, the border reaches its highest main road crossing at **Carter Bar**. At over 1,300ft (396m) it makes a dramatic entry point into Scotland for any traveller. As you crest the rise after the long climb from Catcleugh Reservoir, a great panorama of hills unfolds before you, with the triple peaks of Eildon prominent. In the summer months there is a tourist information point, a tea-bar, and often a lone piper here to mark your crossing.

From Carter Bar the line heads due south-west again, over Carter Fell and through the vast coniferous spread of Kielder Forest, one of the largest man-made forests in Europe. With the construction of Kielder Water a wide range of recreational possibilities has been opened up. On the Scottish side the forest is called Wauchope. This is all part of the Border Forest Park. Four and a half miles (7.2km) south of Bonchester Bridge on the B6357 is Piet's Nest, a picnic place and car park set among Scots pines. There are fine open views from here.

The next place where a motorable road crosses the border is the grimly-named **Deadwater**. It is on the line of another Roman road, the Wheel Causeway. Deadwater is a true watershed — within half a mile of it you will find the Deadwater Burn, which runs into Kielder Water, and thus to the Tyne and the North Sea, and Liddel Water, which runs down the beautiful Liddesdale to the Esk and so to the Solway Firth.

The borderline runs with Kershope Burn through another large area of forest, now with Cumbria to the south, to join Liddel Water at Kershopefoot. The modest height of Carby Hill, 875ft (268m) provides an excellent viewpoint. The grassy top is occupied by the remains of an ancient settlement, once defended by a circular barrier of stones. There are wide-ranging views down Liddesdale and the Esk to the Solway. To the east, in Cumbria, the coniferous regiments of Kershope Forest march resolutely away to the purpled slopes of Christianbury Crags. Beyond the horizon, and out of sight, spread the enormous tracts of Kielder Forest in Northumberland. The border stays with Liddel until that river joins the Esk. This area is out of the hills and on less easily defendable land — the 'Debatable Land' — and the borderline in these parts was consequently in dispute much later than elsewhere. This was Armstrong country — probably the toughest and boldest of all the Border families in the fifteenth and early sixteenth centuries.

It would be logical for the border to follow the Esk to the sea, but of course it does not. Following a treaty made in 1552, it veers due west for about 5 miles (8km) to join the much smaller River Sark. The line between the two waters was marked by the Scots Dike, an earthen embankment and ditch constructed to mark a definite border between the two kingdoms. The Scots Dike can still be made out near the A7, some 2 miles (3.2km) south of Canonbie.

The border follows the winding Sark, passing the site of the battle of Solway Moss, to Gretna and the sea. It is the end of a 110 mile (176km) journey, a wandering journey indeed when the straight-line distance from Gretna to Berwick is only 70 miles (112km).

Gretna's main claim to fame is as the place where run away marriages once took place. Up to 1940, it was possible for eloping couples to be married by declaration, and the smithy at Gretna Green was the first place many of them reached after crossing the border. The marriage trade has ceased now that a residential qualification has been introduced, but many souvenirs and curios are on show at the museum at the smithy.

Crossing the border has always been a significant event, whether for romantic, martial, or peaceful reasons. Having traced it from coast to coast, the Border counties will now be explored in more detail.

2

ANNANDALE AND ESKDALE DISTRICT

T his area will be covered from east to west, starting down by the border and working upwards to a point where it is logical to hand over to the next area to be covered, Tweeddale. The first 'way in' is therefore the A7 road, which crosses the border at the Scots Dike, already mentioned, and heads more or less due north towards Hawick. As far as Langholm, the first town of any size, it follows the fine valley of the River Esk.

Langholm is, in appearance, a true Border town. It sits in a narrow valley and has among its prominent buildings the mills one expects to find further north on the Tweed. At one time it was said that the most expensive suiting cloth in the world was produced here. Langholm is divided into a New Town (Meikleholm, built in the 1770s to a regular pattern) and an Old Town, the original burgh under the Dukes of Buccleuch. As three rivers join here, there are several fine bridges. At least one of them had as an apprentice workman Thomas Telford. The man destined to become such a great engineer was born in Westerkirk, in Eskdale. An obelisk has been erected in his memory on a hilltop above the town.

Also from Westerkirk was one General Sir John Malcolm, a distinguished soldier who became governor of Bombay and is buried in Westminster Abbey. There is a 100-ft tower to his memory on the summit of Whita Hill above the town; an excellent short walk giving fine views southwards to the border. Sir John had three brothers who were all knighted, and there is a statue to the one who chose the Navy, and duly became an admiral, beside the Town Hall. Another of Langholm's sons to achieve fame in recent times was the

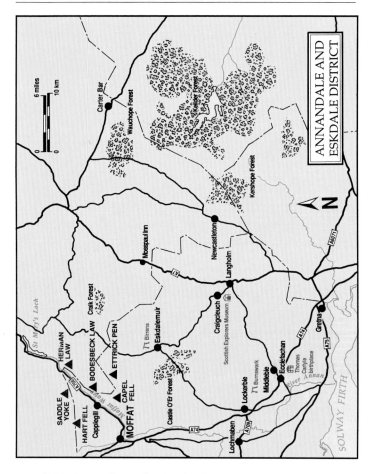

poet C.M. Grieve, better known by his pseudonym Hugh MacDiarmid.

At Langholm the first Common Riding is encountered; this one traditionally takes place on the last Friday in July. An odd feature of the day is that the colours worn by the Cornet for his ride are those of the winner of the Epsom Derby each year. This practice has been carried on for 100 years but its origins are not known. If you are in Langholm for the Riding, be prepared for an early start. The day's events begin at 5am with a procession led by a flute band, up to Whita

Hill, where a hound trail race is held, starting at 6.30am. This is a most exciting spectacle, with the hounds following a scent previously laid, and great competition to find the winner. The Langholm Classic, as it is known, is considered the top event of its kind in the Borders.

At 8.30am the Cornet takes the Town Standard round the old and new towns for the first Fair Crying, when the riding is announced to all and sundry. There follows the gallop up the Kirkwynd to Whitta Yett and Castle Craigs, where the fair is cried again. On returning to the town the horsemen are met by school children carrying heather besoms, and everyone goes to the Market Place for another crying. The horsemen then ford the River Ewes to Castleholm, where the race known as Cornet's Chase is run.

There is no let-up in the afternoon — more horse racing, foot races and other sports, wrestling, and highland dancing are all enjoyed and in the evening (for those with energy left!) there is an open air dance, including the Common Riding Polka led by the principals. Finally, the Cornet returns the Town Standard and the festivities are over. An exhausting day, but one not to be forgotten by either visitor or resident. MacDiarmid's poem on the Langholm Common Riding conveys perfectly the spirit of the annual celebrations:

> 'Drums in the Walligate, pipes in the air,
> Come and hear the cryin' o' the Fair.
> A' as it used to be, when I was a loon
> On Common-ridin' Day in the Mickle Toon.

 On a hillside 2 miles (3.2km) north-east of Langholm on the by-road to Newcastleton, is a striking memorial sculpture to the twentieth-century Scots poet. Two miles (3.2km) north-west of Langholm on the B709 is a fine mansion that houses a most interesting and fascinating collection of artifacts from all over the world. This is the Scottish Explorers' Museum at Craigcleuch.

The A7 continues up the valley of the Ewes, passing some charmingly-named places — Unthank, Crude Hill, Castlewink, and Butter Hill among them — to cross into Roxburgh at the watershed where the Mosspaul Inn stands. This ancient coaching inn is one of the objectives of the riders who follow the Hawick Cornet on his ride outs during the annual Common Riding ceremony at the beginning of June each year. There is a fine walk from the inn up to Wisp Hill, NY387993, on the west of the road. It is a pretty steep ascent, but nowhere difficult. From Wisp Hill, either turn south to Whin Fell or north to Comb Hill before returning to the starting point.

The next valley is Eskdale, which strikes off north-westwards from Langholm and runs for 20 miles in typical rolling Border hills through country where the sheep and the conifers far outnumber the people. The very large parish of Eskdalemuir and Westerkirk counts less than a thousand people today, though the number of ruined farms and steadings tell that it was not always so.

The road (B709) follows the Esk through Westerkirk into Castle O'er Forest. On the B723, which joins it, there is a picnic site provided by the Forestry Commission, and you can walk into the forest for a little way if you wish. Further up the valley is **Eskdalemuir**, where a weather station has been faithfully recording excesses of various kinds for a good many years. Some of the lowest temperatures suffered each winter usually come from here, and in June 1953 Eskdalemuir was in the news again — not for a heatwave, unfortunately, but because no less than $3^1/_2$in of rain fell in an hour — far more than usually descends in a month! There is a plaque on a bridge nearby marking this feat, the previous bridge having been swept away by the force of the rapidly rising floodwater.

In the valley of the White Esk, near to Eskdalemuir, the keen-eyed traveller may spot the coloured roof of the Samye Ling Tibetan Monastery rising above the trees. Also, look for the prayer flags in the grounds of this religious retreat. The Tibetan Centre, which attracts people from all over the world, was founded in 1967 by three Tibetan monks who were forced to leave their monasteries when the Chinese invaded their country. The exterior of the temple is now complete, and the interior has been painted in traditional style by an old Tibetan monk artist.

Returning to the A74, the next town northwards is **Ecclefechan**. The odd-looking name actually has a very logical root — the church *(eaglais)* of St Fechan, a sixth-century Celtic missionary. In the little town is the Arched House, birthplace of Thomas Carlyle and now owned by the National Trust for Scotland, holding a collection of his manuscripts and letters. Carlyle is buried in the kirkyard in Ecclefechan.

A little way north of Ecclefechan, near **Middlebie**, are two substantial reminders of Roman times. Birrens is a fort which has been extensively excavated. The ditches and ramparts are clearly visible. Burnswark is thought to have been used as a training ground for siege warfare; on a clear day, it has fine views over the Solway estuary.

Six miles to the north of Ecclefechan is the market town of **Lockerbie**, with a population of just under 3,000. It has a 9-hole golf course and facilities for bowls and tennis. The cattle market is one of

Samye Ling Tibetan Monastery, near Eskdalemuir

the most important in the area. Lamb Hill, above the town, is named from the Lockerbie Lamb Sales, which began here in the seventeenth century. So profitable were these sales that the town was able to buy Lamb Hill as public ground — and have £10,000 over to build the fine town hall. Lockerbie was tragically in the news at the end of 1988 when an airliner en route to America was blown up over the town. Loss of life was great and included townspe)ple as well as the airline passengers.

Glaswegians will find an echo of their city 3 miles south-east of Lockerbie at Castlemilk, the seat of the Jardine family. The present house dates from 1866. Travelling north-west for the same distance from the town, another Jardine stronghold can be seen at Spedlins. This fifteenth-century pele tower has a prison cell within the thickness of one of the walls — a horrid place to be incarcerated.

From Lockerbie, the A74 passes through pleasant country in the valley of the River Annan for a further 15 miles to reach the turn-off for **Moffat** — a true Border town, despite its position at the very edge of the region. Mineral springs were discovered here in the mid-eighteenth century, and Moffat became a fashionable place to visit. It still has a slightly genteel air with several fine town houses with

Valley of Moffat Water

The former Spa Building, Moffat

large gardens. In the centre of the town is the handsome square; and in the centre of the square is the Colvin Fountain, surmounted by its famous ram. It proclaims clearly that this is sheep country.

The town park offers bowls and tennis, and there is an 18-hole golf course on the outskirts, but above all Moffat is a centre for walking. To the north and east are splendid hills, and two longish excursions will give the flavour of the area very well.

The first walk leaves the town due north, following the valley of the Birnock Water by Archbank, NT091068. Walk up this valley for about 4 miles, with the bulk of Swatte Fell looming ever nearer. It is a straightforward ascent by the left-hand of the two streams at the head of the valley. Once on the ridge, follow it round the head of the valley which contains Auchencat Burn and so gain Hart Fell, NT114136. The summit has a triangulation pillar and stone shelter.

From Hart Fell, head first north then east, keeping to the high ground over Hartfell Rig and then southwards onto Priest Craig and Saddle Yoke. Look down to your right into the deep gash of the Blackshope Valley and feel for the runners who have to make that descent, and then climb the equally steep slope opposite, during the annual Moffat Hill Race, run in early October.

To end the walk, either take the hill runners' route, though more slowly, and then use the track alongside Blackshope Burn to the main road; or continue along the ridge from Saddle Yoke, descending a little less steeply. Either way, you will reach the A708 at or near Capplegill. Unless you have transport waiting here, the walk is best done (in summer) on a Thursday, when the Harrier bus service passes this way going to Moffat (timetables from the regional tourist board or enquire locally). The walk is about 12 miles (19.32km) with a fair amount of climbing, and as in poor visibility the navigation could be tricky, keep it for a good day.

The second walk also demands a good day. This one starts from Capplegill, NT143096 (buses from Moffat) and crosses the Moffat Water, through Bodesbeck, to follow the track that leads over the Potburn Pass into the Ettrick Valley. Do not, however, go down with the track, but turn left at the pass and climb smartly up for 600ft (186m) on to Bodesbeck Law.

From here it is a genuine highway, keeping to the ridge (also the regional boundary) over Bell Craig, Mirk Side, and Andrewhinney Hill to Herman Law — a superb ridge walk of 6 miles (9.66km) with stunning views. From Herman Law head east north-eastwards to Peniestone Knowe and on to the right of way over Pikestone Rig. The path descends to Loch of the Lowes and follows the lake shore to

Tibbie Shiels' Inn by St Mary's Loch—a splendid place to end a walk, especially if the inn is open! If it is not, there is a café nearby beside the monument to James Hogg. This glorious walk is about $12^1/_2$ miles (20km), but could take up a full day with no difficulty at all, so splendid is the country and so wide are the views.

Another right of way is the Captain's Road from Crosscleuch, NT243204, slightly east of Tibbie Shiels' Inn. The path climbs round the shoulder of Earl's Hill and follows the Hopehouse Burn to Hopehouse in the valley of the Ettrick Water, a distance of 5 miles (8km). If you are following these linear walks don't forget to arrange return transport.

Having seen the Grey Mare's Tail from above, it is worth a look from below, taking the A708 Selkirk road from Moffat to the car park at the foot of the Tail Burn. The fall and the surrounding hills are in the care of the National Trust for Scotland, having been purchased in 1962. Loch Skeen sits in a perfect example of a hanging valley or high corrie, scooped out by the forces of ice during the last Ice Age.

From the car park by the roadside, NT187146, a path is signposted up the east side of the fall to the loch. Please follow the marked route — this is a very steep hillside and there have been some nasty accidents here. The path has had a lot of work done on it in recent years and the most eroded parts are now bypassed or have steps. Take your time going up to the loch — it is very steep! — and enjoy the widening views across the valley. You might like to extend the walk westwards from Loch Skeen up on to the summit of White Coomb, a grassy plateau at nearly 2,700ft (837m). You can either return the way you came or go down the ridge south-westwards to Carrifran, for a walk of about 5 miles (8km) in matchless surroundings.

One more notable landscape feature demands attention before the route passes into Tweeddale District. Take the A701 road north out of Moffat and climb up to the watershed at over 1,300ft (403m). Just over the rise is the source of the Tweed; on this side the eye is irresistibly drawn to the great scoop known as the Devil's Beef Tub. This too was formed by glacial action, and is hardly less dramatic than Loch Skeen.

By the roadside is a stone commemorating John Hunter, a Covenanter shot here by Douglas's Dragoons in 1685. His grave is in Tweedsmuir churchyard. With this rather grim reminder of a troubled past, leave Dumfries and Galloway and re-enter Borders Region, into Tweeddale District by the side of the infant Tweed.

Grey Mare's Tail

St Mary's Loch

Loch Skeen

3

TWEEDDALE DISTRICT

Leaving the Devil and his Beef Tub behind, the traveller on the A701 crosses the watershed and enters Tweeddale District. Within a couple of miles, the shallow basin on the right (east) of the road gives up the source of the Tweed, third longest river in Scotland at 90 miles (145km). By the side of the road is a small memorial to a sad event — the death of the driver and guard of the Edinburgh mail coach in a fearsome blizzard in February 1831.

The road runs down through a great deal of young forest and the infant Tweed is soon joined by enough side burns to give it shape and power. Not surprisingly, some of this water-power has been harnessed, and at the small village of **Tweedsmuir** a side-road leads into a wild landscape and up to three reservoirs — Talla, Fruid, and the Megget Reservoir which was completed in 1983. Whatever one thinks of altering the countryside in this way, it makes a wonderfully scenic drive, and at the high point of the road is the Megget Stone, an ancient boundary marker.

Megget Stone is an alternative start to Tweedsmuir for the 5 mile (8km) walk to Broad Law, at 2,754ft (840m), the highest point in the Borders. It is a straightforward walk over easy ground, mostly well-cropped grass and broad ridges. The walk goes over Cairn Law and the oddly-named Porridge Cairn, and the return can be made in any one of three ways — either back to your starting point if you are self-driven, or, if you have an obliging driver, by extending it and making it a rather more satisfying outing.

There is a radio station at the summit of Broad Law, and a surfaced track leads all the way up to it from Tweedsmuir. You can use this for your descent route, or you can make a very pleasant loop by continuing north-eastwards from Broad Law over Cramalt Craig and Dun Law, dropping down to the path that leads from the Manor Valley to St Mary's Loch and walking down to the Tibbie Shiels' Inn on the lochside.

If you decide to go down to Tweedsmuir, your companion could wait for you at the Crook Inn, just north of the village. This is one of the oldest Border inns, and has been a meeting-place for travellers since 1604. In the seventeenth century the inn was the scene of many a secret Covenanters' meeting and later gave inspiration to Robert Burns for his poem *Willie Wastle's Wife*, written in the old kitchen, which is now the bar. John Buchan, born nearby, used the area as background for several of his books, and took the title of Lord Tweedsmuir when he was ennobled in later life.

The John Buchan Centre has been established at **Broughton** on the A701, 6 miles (9.6km) east of Biggar. This village was the happy haunt of Buchan's childhood days. The former church building where he often attended services now houses some of his own and family belongings and other memorabilia. There is a display of books and photographs illustrating John Buchan's career and achievements.

More recently, the inn saw a piece of Scottish mountaineering history enacted; it was the chosen location for the first-ever meet of the Scottish Mountaineering Club in 1891. Members braved the ascent of Broad Law — a humble beginning for a club which has achieved so much in the ensuing decades.

From the village of **Coulter**, on the A702, take the minor road south for some 2 miles (3.2km) to Birthwood. Walk up the valley of the Culter Water to Culter Waterhead Reservoir. From here there are many points of access on to the tops and hill ridges. The ridges encircling the reservoir make an excellent round walk of 10 miles (16km).

A linear walk of 14 miles (22.4km) begins at **Crawford** in the Clyde Valley. Follow the minor road by the Camps Water to Camps Reservoir. Continue along the western side of the reservoir and then northward up Grains Burn. At a point where the track turns east, head northward up Linn Burn to the col between Windgate Bank and Hudderstone (some maps mark it as Heatherstane Law). Descend steeply to the south-east corner of Cowgill Upper Reservoir and follow the road alongside Cow Gill to Birthwood and down to Coulter.

Ten miles or so north of Tweedsmuir, a right turn leads to the village of **Drumelzier**, pronounced Drumeelyer, one of the many reputed resting places of the magician Merlin. It was also the scene

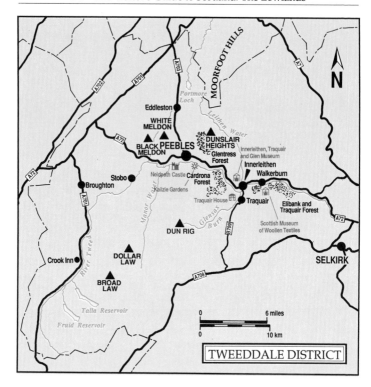

TWEEDDALE DISTRICT

of a prediction come true, in 1603. The prediction was one of many made during his long life (1225-1307) by Thomas the Rhymer, actually Thomas Learmounth of Earlston. He said:

> When Tweed and Powsail meet at Merlin's grave,
> Scotland and England shall one monarch have.

On the day when James VI of Scotland was crowned in London as James I of England, it is reported that the Tweed rose to an extraordinary level and ran into the Powsail Burn. It has never happened since. On a rocky knoll just north of the village is another reminder of history — the ruins of Tinnis Castle, blown up during one of the frequent border feuds between families — in this case the Tweedies and Flemings.

 A little further along the road is a more tranquil scene — the arboretum at **Dawyck**. The gardens were first developed by the

Traquair House, near Peebles

Naesmyth family, who lived at Dawyck until 1897, when it was acquired by Colonel F.R.S. Balfour. He carried out a great deal of planting, planning and development, work which was continued by his son, Lieutenant-Colonel A.N. Balfour, who handed the gardens into the care of the Royal Botanic Society of Edinburgh in 1979.

The B712 road continues past Stobo Castle, now a very expensive health clinic, and running beside the Tweed all the way, joins A72 for the final 4 miles through beautiful woods and into the county town, Peebles. Just before reaching the town you cannot fail to notice the dramatic outline of **Neidpath Castle** on the right, superbly set on a bluff high above the river. The castle is an outstanding example of a Borders pele tower and is well worth a visit.

So to the Royal Burgh of **Peebles** — a comely town indeed. Peebles received its royal charter from David II in 1367, but it was settled long before that, and there was a stronghold here in the twelfth century — natural enough, given the town's position at the confluence of five valleys and with a ford across the Tweed.

Peebles today has a population of about 6,000, and no shortage of facilities for the visitor. The Tourist Information Centre, just off the High Street and clearly signposted, is open from Easter to mid-October.

Many of Peebles' more interesting buildings are associated with famous sons of the town, and a Town Trail was laid out as a contribution to European Architectural Heritage Year. A leaflet is available from the Tourist Information Centre or local shops. A good place to start is Chambers Institution, near the Tourist Information Centre. The building dates from the sixteenth century but was extensively modernised in the nineteenth, by which time it was in the hands of the Chambers family, founders of the Edinburgh publishing company famous for their dictionaries and encyclopaedias. William Chambers gave the building to the burgh of Peebles and it has been used as a civic centre, meeting place and museum ever since.

Walking west along the attractive High Street, you pass the County and Tontine Hotels, both buildings of character and history. The County's eighteenth-century façade conceals a much older interior with a vaulted room, thick-walled for security. The Tontine (the name derives from the method of investment used to fund the property) dates from 1808 and has an elegant dining room with a music gallery.

A little further along on the left is the entrance to Parliament Square — so called after an emergency session held here in 1346. The steps leading down from the square are called the Stinking Stair, probably from the smell arising from a tannery once sited at the bottom.

Across the street is Bank House, once the home of John Buchan and still housing the firm of writers (solicitors) which bears his name. The street has as its handsome endpiece Peebles Old Parish Church, built on the site of the medieval Peebles Castle and the centrepiece of some of the Beltane Festival ceremonies.

A right turn across the burn known as The Cuddy, a walk along Biggiesknowe (a name corrupted from Bridge House Knowe) and a left turn lead to the thirteenth-century Cross Kirk with its atmosphere of serenity, despite the busy town around it. The church was built by order of King Alexander III after the discovery of a magnificent cross on the site, and rumour has it that St Nicholas is buried here. The church is now a listed monument and is open to view.

In the third week of June — midsummer — Peebles comes alive for the Beltane Festival, inaugurated in 1897 to mark the Diamond Jubilee of Queen Victoria but really a revival of a very much older tradition.

Peebles is an ideal centre for walking or fishing holidays. Details of the latter can be obtained from local tackle shops or the addresses given in the Further Information section, and there are beats enough to satisfy the most energetic angler. The walking can be sampled either along or around Glensax, a very beautiful valley south of the town. The more straightforward walk goes out through Gallowhill and turns right, through the Haystoun estate and on to the track in Glensax. Follow the track for about 3 miles (4.83km) to Glensax Lodge, NT265341, which has lost some of its former splendour but is still used by shooting parties. Return to Peebles the same way — even though the route is retraced, it is never boring with such splendid hill scenery around.

To sample those hills, a strenuous but by no means difficult circuit starts the same way. Instead of turning right through Haystoun, NT259384, go straight on through the pretty Gipsy Glen and up on to the old droving road that climbs the ridge east of Glensax. At the start of the climb the walls either side of the track show how wide it was when it was regularly used by cattle on their way to the markets of England.

Follow the ridge over Kailzie Hill and Birkscairn Hill, with superb views over Tweeddale, and keep to the high ground, following old fence posts, all the way up to Dun Rig, NT254316, whose survey pillar is, at 2,434ft (742m), the high point of the walk. It gives a fine panorama of the Border hills, from the Eildons to Broad Law. Work round the head of the Glensax Burn and on to Hundleshope Heights. Keep to the right-hand ridge on the descent and drop down into Glensax to pick up the clear track along the glen, through Haystoun, and so back to the town. This is a circuit of about 12 miles (19.32km), and makes a most invigorating spring or autumn walk.

A shorter walk with much to commend it starts at Tweed Bridge. Walk west along the river and turn up the hill at the waymark, a little way before the wood. Turn right up a road and follow it when it becomes a track, turning first left then right to a stile. Follow the path round the edge of South Park Wood — a very interesting place for birdlife. On rejoining the road, walk downhill and turn right over Old Manor Bridge, built in 1703. The return path follows the river bank all the way, passing under a splendid railway bridge (now

Peebles

disused) and below the frowning bluff on which Neidpath Castle stands. The walk is about $4^1/_2$ miles and makes a very pleasant outing for a summer evening.

From the Manor Bridge, a minor road leads south for 9 miles (14.49km) into the beautiful Manor Valley. It is a splendidly scenic drive, passing another tower at Castlehill and a fort at Glenrath romantically named Macbeth's Castle. From the road end there are numerous walking possibilities; an outline of two will give the flavour.

West of the valley, the ascent of Dollar Law is steep but without difficulty, following the edge of a forestry plantation up the ridge to the survey pillar, at 2,683ft (818m) second only in height in the Borders to Broad Law. To the east, a clear track leads through the hills (really more south than east), under Bitch Craig and in 6 miles (10km) down to Glengaber on the back road that follows the Megget Water down to St Mary's Loch. There is an inn at the end of this walk; so it could be done both ways in a day with a pleasant break in between.

Another, shorter walk well worth doing from Peebles takes the road through Kingsmuir to its end at Tantah, NT246392. Past the farm and through a gate, a clear path winds up on to Cademuir, site of a Celtic fort. It is an easy walk but the rewards are great in terms of the view. The Tweed winds far below; across it to north and east are the Moorfoot Hills, while to the south and west the hills of Manor and Megget stand out. In autumn, with the heather at its best, it makes a glorious scene.

The back road from Peebles to Innerleithen (B7062) yields two treasures to the visitor. First, 3 miles (4.83km) from Peebles, is **Kailzie** (pronounced Kailey). The name derives from an old word Kelioch or Kaillow, meaning a wooded glen, and first appears in records in 1296. After being in the hands of the Tweedie family for several centuries, the property passed through a number of owners before the present owner, Mrs Richard, took it over in 1962. At that time the old house was demolished and Mrs Richard conceived the idea of developing and improving the gardens. They now provide a wide variety of habitats.

The Wild Garden is at its best in the spring, when daffodils and bluebells provide a magnificent carpet of colour. The 'Major's Walk' is rich in plants, including primulas, polyanthus, and more azaleas and rhododendrons. A Cupressus walk leads to the duck pond, from where there are fine views across the Tweed. There are over twenty varieties of duck in the pond. Not far away is the pheasantry, with a dozen varieties of these colourful game birds; two recent arrivals are Iranian eagle owls.

The plant centre has many interesting plants and shrubs for sale as well as preserves made on the estate. Part of the old stable block has been carefully converted into an attractive tearoom, an interesting note being that the doors were brought here from St Andrew's church in Peebles when it was demolished in 1980. Next door to the tearoom is a small art gallery featuring the work of local artists. As well as the attractions of the gardens and woods, there are holiday cottages to let throughout the year.

Four miles further east is the entrance to **Traquair,** the oldest continually inhabited house in Scotland — its first charter was granted by Alexander I in 1107. The house has changed little in appearance since the seventeenth century, but you will not use the original entrance through the Bear Gates. They were locked after Prince Charlie passed through here in 1745, and tradition has it that they will not be reopened until the Stuarts are restored to the throne of Britain. The house contains a number of relics relating to the Stuarts, including the cradle of James VI, and many other treasures and works of art.

The present laird, Mr Peter Maxwell Stuart, brews Traquair Ale in the eighteenth-century brewhouse, sited below the chapel, and powerful stuff it is, too. Traquair is a centre for craft workers with a number of outbuildings having been converted for use by potters, weavers, woodworkers and others.

There are woodland and riverside walks laid out and the tea- room, in a 1745 cottage in the walled garden, provides refreshments. Traquair deserves at least half a day to itself. Your stay may be inadvertently extended if you take in the maze!

Between Kailzie and Traquair, Cardrona Forest offers a picnic area and a choice of three forestry walks, all of them clearly signposted. On the east side of the forest are the rather overgrown ruins of a pele tower.

Traquair village is the start of one of the Borders' best-known walks, the drove road over Minch Moor to Selkirk. The route climbs up through mature forest to pass the 'Cheese Well', where an offering of cheese is said to placate the fairies and thus safeguard the traveller. The route winds on over Brown Knowe and Broomy Law to the distinctive triple cairn of the Three Brethren. From here there are three choices of route. Straight on leads down Long Philip Burn to the outskirts of Selkirk (if you can pass Philipburn House, a hotel noted for its fine cuisine). A left turn goes down through Yair Forest to the A707 at Yair, and a right turn leads to Broadmeadows. This was the route taken by walkers in May 1931 preceding the opening of

Scotland's first youth hostel, at Broadmeadows, a walk repeated in May 1981 to mark the SYHA's Golden Jubilee.

From Traquair it is a short mile along the road to the mill town of **Innerleithen**, whose patron saint, St Ronan, has a well dedicated to him on the hill north of the town. The name was actually popularised by Sir Walter Scott, who published a novel of that name in 1824. It led to Innerleithen having a long period of popularity as a spa, visited for its mineral waters. St Ronan's Games are still held here each year, in July. On the final day there is a firework display on Caerlee Hill and a modern 'saint' throws an effigy of the Devil onto a bonfire — the Cleikum ceremony. The emblems used in that ceremony, along with many other items relating to the history and traditions of the area, can be seen in the Innerleithen, Traquair and Glen Museum, housed in the former Burgh Council offices. In 1990, it is hoped to provide a new Interpretive Centre at St Ronan's Wells, housing objects and photographs associated with the history of the wells, and recreating the atmosphere of the late nineteenth-century spa. The wells are situated in a site of great tranquility and beauty, and the visitor can still sample the water at the original stone cisterns.

One of the streets in Innerlethen is called Strand. A walk around the town also reveals a Bond Street, Morningside, and a Piccadilly — idiosyncrasies of the last Earl of Traquair. Of note, too, is Caerlee Mill behind Chapel Street. It was established in 1790 by Alexander Brodie in order to give employment to the young of the area and to make use of the plentiful supply of excellent wool available locally. Other factories and mills followed, and Innerleithen is still renowned as a centre for knitwear and woollen yarn.

Two miles east of Innerleithen is the smaller town of **Walkerburn**, where no visitor should fail to stop at the Scottish Museum of Woollen Textiles in the Tweedvale Mill complex. The progress of the industry is recreated from the early days of hand spinning and weaving up to factory production and modern high speed machinery. There are evocative early photographs and a fascinating display of plants and flowers which were traditionally used to produce dyes. Produce can be bought at the mill shop and refreshments are available.

The Tweed Valley Hotel, at the east end of the town, is a notable base for sporting holidays. The angler, walker, and hunter are all well catered for, and the cuisine is more than sufficient both in quality and quantity for the needs of the hungriest holidaymaker.

As this is almost the eastern boundary of Tweeddale District, go back a little to Innerleithen and the start of one of the loveliest walks

*Springtime at
Neidpath Castle*

in the Borders. It's a longish 15 miles (24.15km) and will occupy a full
day, but it can easily be shortened. The walk starts by turning north
along the little road directly opposite the B709. Turn left over a stile
in the woods, and on reaching the radio mast at St Ronan's Well, turn
right for the sharp pull up to Lee Pen, NT326386. It is a climb which
will tax anyone, but the views are opening up all the time, giving
plenty of good reasons for stopping.

Lee Pen, at 1,647ft (502m), is not the peak it appears to be as you
climb, but the abrupt end of a long ridge leading north-west over
Black Knowe, Black Law (trig pillar, 1,765ft, 538m) and on to the high
TV booster mast at Dunslair Heights 1,975ft (602m). If you go no
further, you will have enjoyed a splendid walk, with wide views
south over the Tweed Valley and north across the Moorfoot Hills.
There is a fair amount of forestry development taking place in these
hills, but the ridge itself is clear.

The Moorfoot Hills consist of five hills of 2,000ft (610m) and above, and several others slightly less than 2,000ft. The long range of hills assumes a south-east direction, and affords splendid views overlooking the Tweed Valley. The highest point is Windlestraw Law, 2,162ft (659m).

Motorists will enjoy the B709 road as it climbs up through the Moorfoot Hills north from Innerleithen reaching a height of 1,250ft (381m). An excellent round trip can be made down the valley of the Heriot Water, then south following the twisting Gala Water, and returning to Innerleithen along the banks of the River Tweed.

An enjoyable $10^1/_2$ mile (16.8km) walk can be taken in the Moorfoot Hills. From the south side of Gladhouse Reservoir, NT 295 525, walk up the valley of the River South Esk, and follow the eastern tributary to the summit of Blackhope Scar, 2,137ft (651m). Follow the ridge round the head of the Esk valley, taking in Emly Bank and Bowbeat Hill, 2,050ft (625m), and head north to Jeffries Corse, 2,004ft (611m). Descend to Gladhouse Cottage, and return to the starting point.

Dunslair Heights is the top of Glentress Forest (oddly named — the small settlement of Glentress is miles away in the valley of the Leithen Water) and it is a simple matter to cut short the walk here by dropping down through the forest, either to the car park at Horsbrugh or to Peebles. There are several forest walks in Glentress, starting from the forestry office at Horsbrugh, which is on the A72 about 2 miles east of Peebles. There is also a forest wayfaring course — a non-competitive version of orienteering. Glentress is one of the more mature of the Borders forests and, as well as being very pleasant to walk through, has been used for a number of orienteering championship events.

It is well worthwhile to carry on along the ridge from Dunslair, as the best of the walk is in its second part. It follows the forestry fence over the sharp knob of Makeness Kipps and the undulations of Cardon Law and Hog Knowes on to the broad back of Dundreich, a very fine hill and, at 2,043ft (623m), the high point of the walk in every way. From here, on a clear day, there is a marvellous view northwards taking in the whole of Edinburgh, the Pentland Hills, and the Firth of Forth. Gladhouse Reservoir, a major wintering-ground for waterbirds, is visible a little east of north.

Descend westwards from Dundreich to hit the track running south from Portmore Loch (which is private ground) and follow it through the farmstead at Boreland to the main road just north of Eddleston. There is a very good teashop here, the Scots Pine, and there are hourly buses from Eddleston back to Peebles or Innerleithen.

Looking east from Dundreich across the valley of the South Esk (a much shorter river than the one of the same name in Angus) the eye is drawn to Blackhope Scar, at 2,138ft (652m) the highest point in Lothian Region. (Only just — the summit is right on the boundary.) To the east again is the northward continuation of the B709 from Innerleithen to Heriot, a drive well worth taking for its scenic quality. There are also any number of possible walks on either side of the valley. But before following this road, it is worth travelling east from Innerleithen to Blackhaugh, NT 424 383, where there is a pedestrian right of way up the Caddow Valley to Scroof. After that, continue up the ridge to the east and descend to Lugate Water, then proceed over Stagehall Hill and down to Stow in the valley of the Gala Water. This walk covers 8$^1/_2$ miles (13.6km).

Leaving Innerleithen towards Heriot, and passing one of a number of fairly remarkable small golf courses in the Borders, there is a good view across the town to the point known as St Ronan's Well (see p42). Then the road climbs steadily with fine hills to either side following the Leithen Water as far as Dod Hill, where it turns right to run alongside the equally attractive Glentress Water. From the steading of Glentress a splendid walk leads up to the ridge of Windlestraw Law, NT371431, with the oddly-named Deaf Heights available as an extension for the energetic. Across the valley to the west, Whitehope Law is a sharper pull but is worth the effort for its views.

The road climbs to 1,194ft (364m) at the watershed, NT347464, — a useful starting-point for the ascent of Blackhope Scar, if you wish to take that hill on its own. It is a fairly tough climb over rough ground, and a slightly easier alternative is to go round to the steading at Blackhope and follow the Blackhope Water up, diverting either side of it in due course to gain the ridges leading to the Scar.

On the downhill run, the road keeps by Dewar Burn until that watercourse becomes Heriot Water — a lonely run past a number of isolated houses and farms, before meeting the A7 at the village of Heriot. Return south here, across the Tweed, to leave Tweeddale District and enter the old county of Selkirkshire.

4

ETTRICK AND LAUDERDALE DISTRICT

Geographically, Ettrick and Lauderdale, in part the old county of Selkirkshire, is a most odd shape. Its boundaries take many a twist and turn, reflecting the turns of history and fortune which have divided and joined the communities and estates it contains over hundreds of years. It is a county rich in scenery, historic houses, monastic ruins, and with plenty of opportunities for visitors, be they of an enquiring mind or seeking energetic recreation.

Staying with the A72 from Peebles, pass through the neat village of **Clovenfords**, with a fine statue of Sir Walter Scott outside the hotel, to reach **Galashiels** on Gala Water. With a population of just over 12,000, 'Gala' as it is always known is second only to Hawick in size among the Border towns, and would no doubt see itself as being superior in every other respect. It certainly warrants a long stay.

Gala hosts one of the famous seven-a-side Rugby tournaments in April each year, and its festival, the Braw Lads Gathering, is held in late June or early July. It has been a weaving town for at least 700 years, but its modern growth can be traced back to 1790, when George Mercer built the first real factory in Scotland here. It does not survive, but Valley Mill, behind Market Street, does and is a fine example of nineteenth-century mill architecture. This was the home of Scottish Tweed — not, as many think, named after the river, but from a slip of the pen when a clerk transcribed the word twill (pronounced 'tweel') and put a 'd' at the end.

The Scottish College of Textiles was established in Gala in 1909 and still thrives. There are several mill shops, selling tartans, tweeds, wools and other knitted materials. Of equal interest is the Tweed-

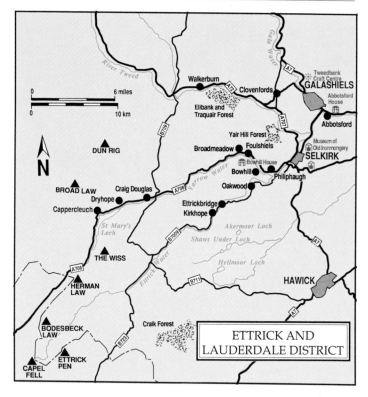

ETTRICK AND
LAUDERDALE DISTRICT

bank Craft Centre across the water, where a number of craft workers operate and can be seen.

Galashiels has a 9-hole golf course at Torwoodlee and a full 18-hole course at Ladhope. Both are open to visitors. Fishing is available on both Tweed and Gala waters; details, and any gear you might need, are available from the long-established tackle and sports shop of J. & A. Turnbull in Bank Street. Permits for single or multiple days' fishing can be obtained here. Pony trekking is available at the Galashiels Riding Centre at Netherbarns, on the Selkirk road. Horses can be supplied for day treks or longer periods, and advice on where to ride. Horses can also be hired for the Braw Lads Gathering, which was established in 1930, and takes its name from a well-known poem by Robert Burns (also a fine song). The events associated with the Gathering stretch over a week in late June.

At the war memorial is the statue of the Reiver, a famous landmark. Here too is the clock tower, where the bells play the old air 'Gala Water' every evening at eight o'clock. This is the air to which Burns wrote the poem 'Braw, Braw Lads', in 1793. Burns has a statue at the foot of Lawyer's Brae, and there is inevitably one of Sir Walter Scott, in St John Street.

Scott is, however, principally associated with the lovely house of **Abbotsford**, where he lived from 1811 to his death in 1832. The house is much grander now than it was when Scott bought it — and so is its name, for it was previously known as Cartley or Clarty Hole, meaning 'a dirty place'! The house is a lasting monument to the man. It contains many treasures Scott collected in his lifetime, including Rob Roy's gun, the keys from the Old Tolbooth (gaol) in Edinburgh, and some fine antique furniture. The library is very fine and among its many rare and magnificent books is the first volume ever to be printed in Australia — a unique work indeed.

Abbotsford is hard against the Roxburghshire border, so turn south, down the A7, for the short journey beside Ettrick Water to the ancient burgh of **Selkirk**. It has been truly said that history has marked the town with an indelible stamp. Its abbey was founded in 1113 by the man who later became David I; it was already a famous hunting area for the nobility. William Wallace was proclaimed Guardian of Scotland here, and the town will be forever linked with the sad chapter of Flodden Field.

Sir Walter Scott was sheriff of Selkirk for 33 years, and his statue is prominent in the Market Place. Behind it is the courtroom, completed in 1803, and at certain times (enquire locally) you can see his bench, chair, and robing-room. There are also copies of the burgh's ancient charters, and letters from Robert Burns, James Hogg, and other notables. A portrait of Scott hangs above the bench. The curfew bell rings from the tower at 8pm each night.

On the west side of the Market Place is the fascinating Museum of Old Ironmongery (in Halliwell's Close) with a wonderful collection of household utensils from times past, in a beautifully restored eighteenth-century town house. Nearby, next to the post office, is Robert Douglas's bakery, where the baker made the original Selkirk bannock. Douglas used only the finest ingredients — if the best was not available, he did not bake.

Kirk Wynd contains the ruin of the old parish church, and from here there is a lovely view over the Ettrick Water to the hills beyond. The road bridge at the south end of the town was washed away in a flash flood in 1978 and had to be rebuilt. Off Kirk Wynd is Back Row, the oldest part of the town but now with a modern housing development which won a Civic Trust award in 1971. Local materials were used and the character of the old town has been carefully preserved.

The public library, in Chapel Street, contains another excellent museum, this time featuring local history. The building was originally the town gaol. It was acquired in 1883 by Thomas Craig-Brown, a former provost of Selkirk and a noted historian. He had the building refurbished and gave it to the town as a free library. Among the exhibits in the museum is the banner captured from the English at Flodden by one Fletcher, the only Selkirk man to return from the battle alive. According to the story, when he reached the Market Place he could find no words to tell the crowd of the battle. He merely cast the banner on the cobbles in anguish and despair. The casting is a central feature of Selkirk Common Riding, held in June each year.

Flodden is not the only battle commemorated in Selkirk. Just across the river from the town is Philiphaugh, where the royalist forces led by Montrose were defeated in a bloody encounter by Lesley's Covenanting Army in 1645. A hundred years later, Prince Charlie passed this way, stopping in Selkirk for the souters to fit his men with good shoes for their ill-fated march south into England.

There is a fine walk from here of $6^1/_2$ miles (10.4km) up Long Philip Burn to the Three Brethren. It's a steady climb, but the path is clear all the way. You can either return by the same route, or turn left at the cairn for Broadmeadows. The youth hostel here was the first to be opened in Scotland, in May 1931, and still offers simple accommodation to the traveller, young or old.

Across the A708 from Broadmeadows is **Bowhill**, seat of the Duke of Buccleuch. The house dates mainly from the early nineteenth century and contains many magnificent works of art, including the *Madonna and the Yarnwinder*, the only painting by Leonardo da Vinci still in private hands in this country. There are many fine examples of seventeenth- and eighteenth-century furniture and clocks, including a remarkable longcase clock made in 1780 in Fife. It plays eight different Scottish airs, but the mechanism is arranged so that the clock observes the Sabbath — from midnight Saturday to midnight Sunday it is silent!

The grounds are a perfect demonstration of the fact that farming, forestry, conservation, amenity and sport can all be reconciled. There are fine gardens, nature trails and woodland walks, an adventure playground for youngsters, and all the while the running of the estate goes on. Bowhill is well equipped for visitors, with ample car and coach parking (free), access for wheelchairs, gift shop and tea rooms. It should not be missed by anyone in the Selkirk area.

The Bowhill estate also runs a riding centre offering pony trekking for beginners, and trail riding for experienced riders, with treks of up to 5 hours escorted by experienced guides.

Not surprisingly, there is excellent fishing in the Selkirk area. The Ettrick Water offers trout fishing in season (1 April to 30 September), with tickets available for periods from a day up to a month. There is stillwater fishing for brown trout and rainbow trout on Lindean Reservoir during the same months, with 3-rod boats available. In both cases the firm of D. & H. McDonald, 9-11 High Street, Selkirk, will advise and issue permits.

On the A708, not far from Broadmeadows, is the hamlet of **Foulshiels**, the birthplace in 1771 of the noted explorer Mungo Park. He spent much time in Africa, particularly exploring the River Niger, with a spell as a doctor in Peebles between expeditions. He died in Africa in 1806; there is a statue of him in Selkirk High Street.

The A708 continues up the Yarrow Valley, a lovely drive at any time, particularly perhaps in spring, when the many trees are in fresh leaf. This valley was the home ground of James Hogg, a fine poet generally known as the Ettrick Shepherd, who was glorified in verse by Wordsworth. The church in the village of **Yarrow** dates back to 1640 and is worth a visit.

Passing the Gordon Arms Hotel, an excellent hostelry, the road winds on towards the lovely St Mary's Loch. Up a track running northwards into the hills from the east end of the loch is Dryhope Tower, a typical Border fortification doubling as a dwelling-place. It was the birthplace of Mary Scott, known as 'the flower of Yarrow', who married a noted reiver named Auld Wat of Harden in 1576. Sir Walter Scott is descended from her.

A little east of the Dryhope track, NT268246, a fine walk leads into the hills from **Craig Douglas**, part of an old droving track. The way is clear past Blackhouse, with its tower, and on to Muttonhall, following the Douglas Burn the whole time. The return walk is about 6 miles (10km); and there is an alternative way back south-west across the hill from Blackhouse to join the Dryhope track.

A minor road turns off at **Cappercleuch** and follows the valley of the Megget Water. The road climbs high and overlooks the Megget Reservoir which was completed in 1983. The Megget Dam is the highest impounded embankment dam in Scotland, constructed to supply water to Edinburgh. In the second stage of the scheme, additional water will be pumped from St Mary's Loch into the Megget Reservoir.

The Yarrow Valley, near Gordon Arms

St Mary's Loch must be one of the finest settings for sailing anywhere in Britain; the sailing club is at the west end of the loch, on the neck of land between it and the smaller Loch of the Lowes. Here too is the Tibbie Shiels' Inn, which has been giving comfort to travellers for two centuries and more. In this country of long attractive valleys, sparkling streams and smooth-sided hills, two famous native writers, Sir Walter Scott and James Hogg gleaned inspiration from these surroundings for their novels and poetry. They would regularly meet to make merry at the inn, to enjoy each other's company and to discuss their ideas. The old hostelry was kept by Isabella Richardson (maiden name Shiels) who took in guests to support her large family after the death of her husband. She was noted for her hospitality, candour and good humour.

The inn lies on the route of the Southern Upland Way, the coast to coast long-distance walk from Portpatrick to Cockburnspath. A commemoration plaque marks the official opening on 27 April 1984 with words from *A Boy's Song* by James Hogg, who was born in a farm cottage in Ettrick in 1770. His mother, Margaret Laidlaw, was a fine ballard-teller who was a great source of information on folklore. Sir Walter Scott used her fund of knowledge for his research on local tales and legends. The bronze statue of Hogg situated between St Mary's Loch and Loch of the Lowes, gazes out across the water with a seemingly wistful glance towards the Tibbie Shiels' Inn.

The Ettrick and Lauderdale boundary runs along the ridge on the north side of the Ettrick Valley (see also chapter 3) and round the head of the valley to turn north at Wind Fell, 2,180ft (664m). Ettrick Valley is also well worth exploring. At Ettrickhill is a tall sandstone monument commemorating the birthplace of James Hogg. He died in 1835 and is buried in Ettrick churchyard nearby. The grave of Tibbie Shiels', who died in 1878, aged 95 years, and her husband Robert Richardson, may be located to the west of the church tower. Also buried in the churchyard is James Hogg's grandfather, the famous local character Will o'Phaup. It can be reached on foot through the hills from the south end of Loch of the Lowes — a fine walk of 7 miles (11km) or so — but you would need an obliging chauffeur to pick you up. An alternative is to walk from the north end of the same loch by Earls Hill and Hopehouse Burn to Hopehouse, a few miles further down the Ettrick Valley (also about 7 miles of walking).

The B7009 winds its way down this beautiful valley back towards Selkirk. In the hills either side are any number of ruined towers, evidence of more unsettled times. They are marked on Ordnance Survey and Bartholomew maps, and many have tracks leading up to them which make fine short walks. **Ettrickbridge**, about 5 miles (8km) up-valley from the junction of Ettrick and Yarrow, is the home of Sir David Steel, Liberal Democrats MP and ex-leader of the Liberal Party, whose constituency is one of the largest in Britain as will be evident from its name — Roxburgh, Selkirk and Peebles.

It is a beautiful area indeed he has responsibility for, and the discerning visitor will seek out the less well known and remoter attractions, mostly unpublicised, well off the main roads and sometimes hard to reach. Blackhouse Tower has already been mentioned. Two other towers which can be seen are at Kirkhope and Oakwood. Kirkhope is set up on the hillside north of the village of Ettrickbridge, and makes an attractive short walk. It was home to the elder sons of the Scotts of Harden, and it was to here that Mary, the Flower of Yarrow, came as bride to Auld Wat.

Oakwood is a tall building now integrated into the farm steading of the same name, a mile or so up the Ettrick Valley from its junction with the Yarrow. It is one of a number of Border houses associated with the wizard Michael Scott. This strange thirteenth-century figure studied at several of the great universities of Europe and was for a time Astrologer Royal to the Emperor Frederick II before returning to England where he was knighted by Edward I. He died in 1292, and is supposed to have left a mighty book of magic buried somewhere in the grounds of Melrose Abbey.

The south-east corner of Ettrick and Lauderdale, between the Ettrick Valley and the A7, is little visited, but it contains many fine walks. It is criss-crossed by old tracks, and study of the Ordnance Survey map (1:50,000 sheets no 73 and 79) will reveal plenty of possibilities. Ettrick Bridge to Essenside, or southwards by Shaws Underloch to the Ale Water, or the valley of the Deloraine Burn are just three examples.

From all these walks you can look into the next district, Roxburgh, to the old towns of Melrose and Hawick, to the new administrative centre of Newtown St Boswells and always to the alluring triple peaks of the Eildon Hills, which dominate the area.

5

ROXBURGH DISTRICT

Roxburgh is one of the four districts that now make up Borders Region. Its modern boundaries are slightly different from those of the old shire which are followed in this chapter. The first stopping place, Melrose, is nowadays in the district of Ettrick and Lauderdale, but it is, just, a Roxburghshire town and it makes a worthy introduction to this chapter.

Melrose is small, with a population of only 2,000, but it is a very ancient settlement and its history is as rich as any place in Scotland. There is evidence that a chapel dedicated to St Cuthbert was here in the seventh century, and long before that the Romans were occupying the slopes of the Eildon Hills at their fort called *Trimontium*.

The heart and centrepiece of Melrose is the great abbey, a Cistercian foundation of 1136 in the reign of David I. Despite suffering repeatedly at the hands of English invading armies much remains, and the stonework is magnificent — tracery and flying buttresses in a reddish stone, with the highlight of it all perhaps the window in the north transept with its famous 'crown of thorns'.

There are some extraordinary examples of carving and statuary — a pig playing the bagpipes and a Virgin Mary with headless child among them. It is said that the head of the child fell on the arm of a man trying to demolish the statue during the Reformation, crippling him for life. Another piece depicts a mason with his chisel and mallet. The abbey is full of wonderful stories, many of them in the guide available at the entrance. One is that of Robert the Bruce, who was so grieved at the abbey's desecration in 1322 that he voted the enormous sum (for those days) of £2,000 for its restoration. The snag was that there was rather less than this amount in the entire Scots treasury! The restoration was nonetheless carried out, though per-

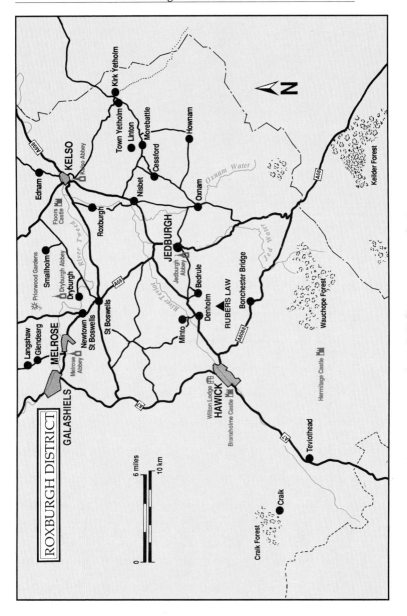

ROXBURGH DISTRICT

haps over a longer period of time than the king would have wished.

Robert Bruce has a further association with Melrose Abbey — his heart is buried here, its final resting place after long travels around Europe in a lead casket during the Crusades. In the side chapels are burial places for notable Border families, including Scotts, Pringles and Douglases.

Alongside the abbey, and certainly not to be missed, is the splendid Priorwood Garden, owned by the National Trust for Scotland since 1974. The garden specialises in plants that can be dried for display, and a selection of dried flowers, with pamphlets on how to use and prepare them, is always on sale at the shop. There is an orchard with a special 'Apples through the Ages' walk, and a picnic area. Each autumn a special sale of dried plants is held to raise money for the Trust.

The Borders Information Centre adjoins Priorwood, and staff here will be glad to help with any enquiries you may have regarding places of interest in the area, accommodation, food, etc. A wide range of tourist literature is available. For the active visitor, as well as many walks, there is a 9-hole golf course in a charming setting, and fishing on the Tweed for salmon, brown and sea trout. Information is available from Anglers Choice in High Street, and there is an unusual beat between Gattonside House and the suspension bridge; unusual in that it is controlled by the monks at St Aidans, Gattonside. There is no set fee; like the other Melrose beats, this is fly fishing only, with a limited number of rods, and a donation is asked to go to St Aidans' work with the mentally handicapped.

Melrose has its own festival and riding, held in mid-June. The principal, a bachelor of the town, is called the Melrosian and his 'kirking' on a Sunday morning marks the festival's opening. This is followed by a week of celebrations, including the Eildon Hill Race which is run on the final afternoon.

The Rugby Club at Melrose has a famous seven-a-side tournament held in April each year. Competition over the long day is fierce but fair, and there is always a great turnout for a splendid sporting occasion.

A short walk northwards from the abbey to the Tweed leads to the Chain Bridge linking the town with Gattonside. It was one of the first suspension bridges in Scotland, opened in October 1826; no more than eight people may be on it at any one time and it is an offence to make the bridge rock or swing. The riverside path on the south bank leads to Melrose Cauld, a rapid stretch of water made by the abbey monks to take water to their mill lade. A path leads on up to Weir Hill, with a fine view along the Tweed.

North again from here, up the valley of the Allan Water, are two more of the Border towers, at **Glendearg** and **Langshaw**. 'Glendearg', an odd name for this area, is in fact an invention Sir Walter Scott used in his book *The Monastery*. The true name of the place is Hillslap, but it is marked as Glendearg on all modern maps and the old name is almost forgotten. The tower, an L-shaped sixteenth-century building, can be seen by asking at the farm.

Just east of Melrose is **Newstead**, reputed to be the oldest continually inhabited village in Scotland. It lies on part of the site of the Roman fort of *Trimontium* and has been occupied ever since. The Romans are believed to have built a bridge over the Tweed here to carry Dere Street on towards Edinburgh. There is now little direct evidence of *Trimontium*, as the excavations were efficiently covered over, though there is a memorial in the form of an altar on the road from Newstead to Leaderfoot.

Before leaving the Melrose area, take a walk on the Eildon Hills. The highest point is only 1,385ft (420m) but they dominate the area; truly they are the jewel at the centre of the Borders. The Eildons have a long history and are rich in legend. It is said that King Arthur is buried here (one of many places in Britain carrying this legend) and that the wizard Michael Scott clove the hills into three, a nice story, but alas untrue. The Eildons were formed from volcanic activity millions of years ago; geologically they are a cluster of domes of plutonic rock standing above the old red sandstone, which can clearly be seen in the colour of the soil around Jedburgh in particular. They have undoubtedly been three hills for many thousands of years.

There is a signposted walk, called the Eildon Walk, starting from the square in Melrose. It is about 4 miles in length and on a clear day gives wonderful views. Walk along Dingleton Road for about 200yd (186m) to the signpost, then turn left and start a fairly steep climb, heading towards Eildon Hill North. At the top hedge, go half right, climbing towards the col between Hill North and Middle Hill. The latter is the highest of the three and is an easy climb. On its summit are a triangulation pillar and a mountain indicator — a brass plate inscribed with the names of many of the hills and points of interest. The indicator was erected in 1927 and was paid for by public subscription. It bears the dedication: 'To the memory of Sir Walter Scott. From this spot he was wont to view and point the glories of the Borderland'.

It is possible to make a short diversion to Wester Hill before returning over Middle Hill to go on to the summit of Hill North. Here an Iron Age hill fort was sited, extending to 39 acres at its peak. It must be remembered that at that time the hilltops would have risen above a dense forest covering most of the lower ground and would therefore have given a very commanding position.

The lines of defence can be seen on the ground, with their gateways, and also a number of small mounds which mark the sites of huts occupied at the time the hill fort was built. No fewer than 296 of these hut sites have been discovered, together with some pottery which must have been used by the inhabitants. The only inhabitants now are birds; the area has a richly varied fauna including pipits, snipe, grouse, skylarks, and other rarer varieties.

The view of the Cheviot Hills from here is particularly fine. After enjoying it to the full, take the path leading east and then north to the top of Eildontree Plantation, where it meets the path encircling the hill on its northern flank. The path now drops downhill quite steeply; part of this route is used by horses as well as people, and can be muddy at times.

The signposted route turns right at the road and left in a short while, going down to Newstead. A diversion to the right goes to the site of *Trimontium*; straight ahead leads to the Tweed and a very pleasant riverside walk back into Melrose; or turn left for a more direct route to the town.

Before finally leaving the Eildon Hills it may be useful to note that a detailed guide to the area is published by the Scottish Wildlife Trust and is available from local shops.

The route now heads for the next Borders abbey, Dryburgh; an interesting way of getting there is to take the back road, B6359, south for Bowden out of Melrose. **Bowden** is a pretty village with a green and an old church which still retains the 'laird's loft' where the lord of the manor and his family would sit during services. At one time this was a weaving village, but the coming of mills and machinery to the surrounding towns led to the demise of this true cottage industry.

The road to Bowden gives fine 'backside' views of the Eildon Hills; turn left out of the village on B6398 to keep those views as far as **Newton St Boswells**, where the headquarters of the Borders Regional Council is situated. A short mile down the A68 from here is the older village of **St Boswells**, actually named after an early Christian saint called Boisil, one of the first missionaries to reach lowland Scotland. The village has a very fine tree-ringed green where cricket is played in the summer months. It is also the scene of a gipsy fair in July each year. The gipsies now come in cars and

Scott's View, near Melrose

modern caravans rather than the horse-drawn variety, but the scene is still as colourful and you can have your fortune told if you wish.

It is possible to drive to **Dryburgh** from St Boswells but it is much more pleasant to approach the abbey on foot from the village, crossing the Tweed by a footbridge. Dryburgh was the second Border abbey to be established, not long after Melrose, and being away from any towns or main roads it has a marvellously peaceful atmosphere. Most of the existing remains date from the twelfth or thirteenth century, and the cloister buildings are still complete enough for visitors to imagine what the abbey was like when it was in daily use. Sir Walter Scott and Field Marshal Earl Haig are both buried here, and the abbey is open to view all year round.

Further pleasant exercise can be gained by following a riverside walk maintained by the regional council. The walk, about 4 miles (6.4km) in length, starts in Newtown St Boswells by the post office. Walk down Melbourne Place and look for the signpost on the left saying 'To the Glen'. This road changes to a track and leads to a small footbridge over a burn. The path leads on to the Tweed by the footbridge to Dryburgh. Do not cross the river but keep on the south bank.

Stay by the river until the path leaves it to go up to St Boswells. Follow the path up this little valley, cross the burn and walk back down the other side to reach the riverside golf course (9-hole, open to visitors). The path stays by the river all the way to Mertoun Bridge; go over the B6404 and carry on to a stile which leads into a wood near Benrig House.

Climb some steps beside a wall and follow the path left beside the graveyard; it eventually climbs again through a wood to Maxton church. There is a postbus back to Newtown from Maxton village, except on Sundays.

There are two more places to visit before moving on towards Kelso. The first is cheating a little, for it is just over the county boundary into Berwickshire, but it is far more logical to include it here. On B6356 between Dryburgh and Earlston is the great house of **Bemersyde**, the home of the Haig family for centuries. It was bought by the nation after World War I and given to the great soldier, who lived there until his death. His son, now in residence, is a serious painter whose work has been exhibited in galleries in Scotland, London and New York. Another branch of the family founded the well-known whisky distilling firm, and the former American Secretary of State, Alexander Haig, is also related. The house is open to the public at certain times.

Close to Bemersyde is 'Scott's View', a point where the writer often stopped his carriage to admire the panorama over the Tweed to the Eildon Hills. His horses got so accustomed to stopping there that on his last voyage of all, to be buried at Dryburgh, they stopped automatically at this point. A little nearer to Dryburgh, another notable Scotsman, William Wallace, is commemorated by a 21ft (6.5m) statue just off the road. The statue was commissioned by the eleventh Earl of Buchan, and was completed in 1814.

A little north of Bemersyde, a minor road leads east to the village of **Smailholm** (and back into Roxburghshire). This has a small church with a Scott memorial window, but the main attraction is a couple of miles away at the steading of Sandyknowe. It is Smailholm Tower, an outstanding example of its type, set on a rocky knoll. The tower is 57ft (17.67m) high and in a good state of preservation. This might not have been the case previously for in 1799 the tower was due to be demolished. It was saved by Sir Walter Scott who heard of the plans and pleaded with the owner to change his mind.

Following the road from Smailholm to Kelso will lead to the entrance to **Floors Castle**, home of the Duke and Duchess of Roxburghe and one of the great houses of the Borders. The house was built in 1721 by William Adam for the first Duke, on the site of an earlier building, and commands glorious views of the Tweed Valley and the distant Cheviots. The house has a roofscape as exotic as any in Britain, with fretting, corner towers and balustrades. Old maps show the name as 'Fleurs', French for flowers, and indeed Floors (or Fleurs) has been famous for its carnations for many years. The present walled garden, a little way west of the house, produces all the flowers, fruit and vegetables for the estate including such exotic varieties as melons, peaches and nectarines. There is a garden centre, opened in 1978, where produce and plants can be bought. A holly tree in the park is said to mark the spot where King James II of Scotland was accidentally killed by a bursting cannon in 1460.

Floors Castle itself contains an outstanding collection of French furniture from the seventeenth and eighteenth centuries, many fine paintings, and tapestries. More unusual exhibits include a fine collection of stuffed birds, including now extinct species such as the passenger pigeon, and (in the basement) a model of the castle made from matchsticks and icing sugar. It was made by a castle chef in 1851. The basement also contains a facsimile of the Kelso Charter, a superbly illuminated manuscript which granted lands to Benedictine monks. The original is on loan to the National Library of Edinburgh. Also on display is a letter written by Mary Queen of Scots in September 1566 summoning the Laird of Cessford to discuss a visit to Jedburgh. Pipe bands play at the castle during the summer.

So to **Kelso**, perfectly set at the junction of Teviot and Tweed and described by Scott as 'the most beautiful town in Scotland'. It is a busy market town with a population of around 5,000, and nowadays also hosts a number of firms manufacturing electronic equipment. Pride of the town is the abbey, established in 1128 when the name appears to have been 'Calchou'. At this time the town, set on the south bank of the river, was called Roxburgh, with a fine castle on the Marchmount. Who held Marchmount held the entrance to Scotland, it is said. It changed hands many times in the years between the twelfth and mid-seventeenth century; now there is virtually no trace of town or castle left.

The main remnant of the abbey is the western transpet, which served as the parish church until 1771, when a fall of part of the roof (which had only been added in 1649) caused it to be abandoned. The arcade on the south side of the abbey is the burial place of the dukes of Roxburghe; although this was not built until 1933, it does include a thirteenth-century ornamented doorway and a window of stained glass which is much older.

Smailholm Tower, near Kelso

Kelso town centre

Bridge over the River Tweed, Kelso

Behind the abbey is the old parish church, designed in an octagonal shape by local architect James Nisbet — he was perhaps following the advice of John Wesley, who maintained that an octagon was the best shape for a preacher to use. Behind the church in turn is the passageway known as the Butts, where bowmen used to practise their skills — Border archers were renowned for their accuracy in the Middle Ages.

On a bend of the Tweed is the fine bridge designed by John Rennie and built in 1803 to succeed an older structure swept away by floods. The present bridge has itself survived a number of notable floods, the most recent being in 1977 when the water level was 12ft (3.72m) above normal. Rennie used the Kelso bridge as a model for Waterloo Bridge in London, and when that was demolished in 1935, two of its elegant lamps were brought to Kelso to stand at the south end of the bridge over the Tweed after shining down on the Thames for over a hundred years.

The oldest surviving house in Kelso is in Abbey Row, not far from the bridge. It is Turret House, a seventeenth-century building that has been carefully restored and is used in the summer as a Tourist Information Centre. At the other end of Horsemarket and Woodmarket is the Square, with fine eighteenth- and nineteenth-century town houses, and the Town Hall, built in 1816 with funds provided by the people of Kelso. At one time the bell here rang at six in the morning to rouse the people for work and again at eight in the evening, when their labours could cease.

The Bull Ring, in the centre of the square, is just what it says — the point where bulls were tethered during markets. Markets, and shows, are now held in Springwood Park, across the river. There are three important shows in the month of July — Kelso Ram Sales, the biggest in Scotland; the Ponies of Britain show; and the Border Union Show, which for livestock and produce is second only to the Royal Highland Show itself.

Other sporting occasions include horse races at various times at Berrymoss on the north edge of the town, point-to-point meetings based at Friarshaugh in February and March, and cricket in Shedden Park — Kelso Cricket Club was the first to be formed in Scotland, in 1821, and is still going strong.

Kelso Civic Week is also held in July, and includes the ceremonies and rideouts presided over by the Kelso Laddie. The main rideouts are on the Friday (the Whipman's Ride) and on the Saturday, when the riders go all the way to Yetholm, practically on the border.

There is a pleasant signposted walk along the River Teviot from

Kelso to Kalemouth, a distance of about 6 miles. It can be started from the Kelso Bridge or from the ruins of Roxburgh Castle; on its way it passes through the modern Roxburgh village, a small place with a rather more peaceful history than its predecessor. There is a bus service (Eastern 420) back from Kalemouth, or you can use it to get there and then walk back to Kelso if you prefer.

Two miles north of Kelso is the village of **Ednam**, associated with two writers. The poet James Thomson (1700-1748) is commemorated by a monument on Ferny Hill; he wrote the words of *Rule Britannia* and many other works, including the major four-part *Seasons*. Henry France Lyte's words are often sung on Sundays throughout the land; he was a hymn-writer whose works include *Abide With Me* and *Praise, my Soul, the King of Heaven* and his life (1793-1847) is marked by a plaque on Ednam Bridge (one of the gathering points, incidentally, for the 1715 rising).

Turning south, take the A698 to the village of Crailing, with its ancient market cross, and turn right for **Nisbet**, beautifully sited among woods and below the slopes of Peniel Heugh. There were once several towers here, but no trace of them remains. Peniel Heugh is the site of the Wellington Monument, and is part of a most interesting estate with a tremendous range of activities for the visitor.

Lothian Estates have set up here a 'Conservation Concept' with a Woodland Centre entered from the A68 near its junction with B6400, west of Nisbet. The centre features an exhibition related to trees, woodwork and natural history — the theme changes from time to time. Slide/tape programmes on local conservation and nature themes can be seen, there is a large play area for children, and board games in two guises. A 'quiet room' offers tables for backgammon, chess and cribbage and giant boards can be used in another part of the centre to play Nine Men's Morris, draughts, etc. Rules for all games are available, and a family or group can stage a competition.

Refreshment facilities are available, very welcome after taking one of several fine woodland walks laid out on the estate. The longest walk is the Wellington Walk, about 3 miles, leading up to the monument on Peniel Heugh. This was started within 2 weeks of the Battle of Waterloo in June 1815, though the wooden top dates from 1867. The monument is 150ft high and there are 228 steps in a spiral staircase giving access to the viewing gallery. The tower can be climbed *only* by escorted parties — ask at the Woodland Centre for details.

Even if you cannot climb the tower, there is still a superb view from the hill, with the Eildon Hills and the Cheviots standing out on a clear day. The monument was built by the sixth Marquess of Lothian and the present holder of the title still has his home at Monteviot House on the estate (the house is not open to the public, though the gardens are occasionally). The house was started in 1740 and has been added to a number of times.

The whole estate is geared to visitors, while still remaining a working estate. It is a fascinating place where you could easily spend a whole day.

Next to **Jedburgh**, a town with a thousand years of history behind it; but although it takes care of the relics of its past, it lives firmly in the present and there are a number of light industrial sites. Jedburgh's pride is the abbey, miraculously well preserved in view of its extremely turbulent history. The earliest parts to have survived are at the east end. There is a fine rose window, and the north transept serves as the burial vault for the family of the Marquesses of Lothian.

From the abbey, with its superb outlook over a bend of Jed Water, it is a short step up to Castlegate and the Castle Jail, built in 1823 to a castellated design by Archibald Eliot, and now serving as a museum of local and social history, well worth a visit.

Prince Charlie stayed in a house in Castlegate, at the corner of Blackhills Close, on his way south in 1745 — his last stopping place

Jedburgh town centre

Jedburgh Abbey

in Scotland before crossing the Border on the ill-fated march to Derby. The exterior of the house has been restored. Two hundred years earlier, Mary stayed in Jedburgh when she came here, as queen, to hold a circuit court in 1566. She stayed at a fortified 'Bastle House' which now serves as a museum illustrating the living conditions of the time. Mary's bedroom can be seen, and there are some valuable relics in the Great Hall.

Jedburgh is pronounced 'Jethart' by the inhabitants, and its festival bears this name, the Jethart Callants; it is held at the beginning of July and lasts for two weeks.

There are several places of interest between Jedburgh and Hawick. **Denholm** has as its centrepiece the memorial to Dr John Leyden (1775-1811) who packed an impressive list of achievements into a short life. He was a shepherd's son but qualified as both a doctor and a minister before his study of Oriental languages took him to India and Malaya. He held office as a professor of languages in Bengal and served under Lord Minto in Calcutta before dying of fever in Java aged 36. His thatched cottage birthplace is in the village; another fine Denholm building is Westgate Hall, with its lintel dated 1663.

Minto has been mentioned; the village and hills after which the earldom was named is just north of Denholm. Minto House was the birthplace of Jean Elliot (1727-1805) who wrote a set of words for the pipe lament *The Flowers of the Forest*.

South of Denholm is **Rubers Law**, a fine viewpoint easily reached from the village, firstly along lanes, and then by a clear track up the north ridge of the hill. Although only 1,400ft (424m) it commands an impressive spread of country and the round trip of about 5 miles is well worth doing on a clear day.

Bedrule, on a minor road east of Denholm, has both old and new claims to fame despite its small size. In the Middle Ages there was a castle here, a Turnbull stronghold from where the fierce clan controlled the surrounding country. The castle was sited not far from the point where the modern church with its splendid heraldic ceiling now stands. Bedrule is the home of the Leadbetter stable of racing horses, and the 1979 Grand National winner, Rubstic, came from this stable.

As might be expected from the second part of its name, **Bonchester Bridge** has Roman connections. There was a fort on Bonchester Hill, on one of the routes north from the crossing at Carter Bar. Brown trout fishing is available on the Rule Water — permits from the Horse and Hounds Inn, in the village. If bowls is your game you can be sure of a comfortable session in Bonchester — an all-weather green has been set up here and is a popular attraction.

From Bonchester Bridge, the A6088 winds a twisty 7 miles northwest to join the A7, 2 miles east of Hawick, the largest of the Border burghs with a population of about 17,000. It is the administrative centre for the modern Roxburgh District. **Hawick** has an interest in beasts alive and dead; it has the longest-established auction mart in Britain, with several hundred thousand sheep and cattle passing through each year, and has been a knitwear centre for as long, with a reputation for both clothing and carpets.

Hawick today provides an excellent range of facilities for the visitor. There is an 18-hole golf course on Vertish Hill, a modern swimming pool and leisure centre, and in the beautiful 107-acre Wilton Lodge Park visitors can enjoy tennis, bowls, putting, or work out on the Jubilee Trim Track, opened in 1978. Or simply stroll among the many fine trees, or sit by the riverside watching others at play. Wilton Lodge itself contains a very well run museum giving a full picture of Border life, social, industrial and archaeological; and the Scott Gallery hosts travelling exhibitons of art, changing frequently.

From the west end of the park, where Langlands Bridge — preserving the name of former owners of the lodge — crosses the River Teviot, it is a pleasant riverside stroll back into town, reaching the Tourist Information Centre in Common Haugh. Recrossing the river leads you to St Mary's Church, rebuilt in 1764 on a grassy knoll above the Slitrig stream. There was a strange flood along here in 1767. The Teviot ran at its usual level, but in the space of only 2 hours, the Slitrig rose over 20ft (6m) and carried away fifteen houses and a mill. Fortunately no-one was killed. The flood is said to have been caused by fairies who lived in a pool at the source of the stream, high on Wyndburgh Hill, and were angered by a shepherd throwing stones into their mountain home. So be careful not to do likewise!

Further out along the Slitrig is the Motte, still something of a mystery. A conical mound about 25ft high (8m), it might be the base of a Norman fortification, or be much older. No-one knows for sure. Moat Park surrounds the Motte and is another enjoyable place to visit.

The Motte features in the ceremonies of the Hawick Common Riding, as does the impressive equestrian statue at the north end of High Street. It commemorates the Hornshole Raid of 1514, when Hawick youths partly redeemed the awful tragedy of Flodden by routing a band of English raiders and taking their flag back to Hawick. The Hawick Cornet bears a flag in exactly the same style — blue with a gold cross — during the Common Riding, which with all its rideouts lasts for over a month. There are rideouts each Saturday in May, to Bonchester Bridge, Lilliesleaf, Robertson, Mosspaul, and finally to Denholm, with shorter rides in midweek. Of all these, Mosspaul is the principal. It is a long day indeed, reaching the Border at the Mosspaul Inn via Skelfhill and Millstone Edge. The main Common Riding ceremonies and events take place on the first or second weekend in June.

Riders visiting Hawick for the festivities, or indeed at other times, might like to try the Hawick Circular, a 27 mile (43km) horse riding route using minor roads, tracks, and cross country sections. The route has been prepared to take full advantage of the glorious countryside around the town, and passage for riders has been made as easy as possible. The route makes a grand circuit round the old town, and it is interesting to note that half of its route is on land owned by Buccleuch Estates. A leaflet describing the route is available locally.

The route does not quite reach as far out as The Snoot, a beautifully-sited youth hostel on the Borthwick Water, 6 miles west of

Mary Queen of Scots'
House, Jedburgh

Hawick. From here the Scottish Youth Hostels Association run pony-trekking courses in the summer months, and it is also an excellent base for walkers — or indeed for fishermen, for a couple of miles further west again is Alemoor Loch, where brown trout can be fished in season (mid-March to early October). Permits can be obtained from several shops in Hawick. The smaller and more remote Hellmoor Loch can also be fished, as of course can the rivers in the area.

Hawick also boasts the 'Greens' — the famous rugby club based at Mansfield Park. They have supplied many Scottish internationals, and in common with other Border clubs have a seven-a-side tournament in the spring.

Roxburgh extends a good way south and west of Hawick, and the A7 follows the Teviot almost to the watershed. Three miles out of the town is **Branxholme**

Castle, which was the principal setting for Scott's *Lay of the Last Minstrel*, a lyrical work of great romantic power. It is still used as a private residence. Further upstream is the village of **Teviothead**, where Johnnie Armstrong lies buried. He was a renowned reiver and in 1530 was convicted of theft of cattle and ordered by James V to be hanged: Many songs and ballads commemorate him; the astronaut Neil Armstrong is a present-day descendant of another branch of the family. On the hill slopes west of Teviothead is the Riddell Monument, to the memory of Henry Scott Riddell (1798-1870). He was the minister at Teviothead and was renowned locally for his poetry. He, too, is buried in the churchyard here.

The monument makes a pleasant short walk, and there are numerous tracks on either side of the Teviot Valley leading up into the hills. One of them leads west to the village of **Craik**, a distance of about 7 miles (11.27km). The area has been extensively planted by the Forestry Commission, and a 3 mile (4.83km) forest walk starts from a picnic place beside the Borthwick Water at Craik. It leads to a waterfall at Wolfcleuchhead, where seats are provided for a rest before returning to the starting point. Pony trekking is also available — enquire locally or at the forest office.

Now swing east and north through the extensive tract of country between the towns and the border. First point of call is **Hermitage Castle**, a superbly evocative place now in the care of the Ancient Monument division, and open all year. The name arises from a monk, Brother William, who retired here to live a life of prayer in the twelfth century. The foundations of the chapel he founded can be seen near the castle.

Hermitage Castle is on the B6399, a splendid route into or out of Scotland if you have plenty of time — it is a narrow, twisty road and cannot be hurried. It is crossed at Roberts Linn Bridge by the Catrail, an earthwork dating from the Dark Ages. It can be walked from Roberts Linn to the minor road at Priesthaugh, a long 10 miles, but you will need to be met at the far end.

Railway buffs with a keen sense of exploration and nostalgia may care to locate the site of a remote railway station. Riccarton Junction was situated in the middle of nowhere. Here passengers who had travelled from Hexham and Newcastle-on-Tyne, through Bellingham and Kielder on the Border Counties line, changed at Riccarton Junction for trains on the 'Waverley Route' to Edinburgh or Carlisle. Midland Railway expresses ran from St Pancras to Edinburgh via the Settle and Carlisle line. The Border Counties line from Hexham to Riccarton Junction was closed in 1956. The main line suffered a similar fate on 6 January, 1969. It is a great pity that the attractive 'Waverley Route' was allowed to close down. If only the tremendous support had been forthcoming that had ultimately triumphed on the Settle-Carlisle line, then yet another marvallously scenic route may well have been retained.

Riccarton Junction, NY538978, was always a fascinating place, because it had no proper road access, and the railway community there was completely dependent on the railway for all services. Today, a forest track leaves the B6399 at NY532013 to Riccarton Junction. The distance there and back is $5^1/_2$ miles (8.8km). The platforms remain in solitary state waiting forlornly for the appearance of the next Waverley Express. It is a superb setting for a ghost-train scenario, often enhanced by swirling mist and driving rain. They don't create junctions like this any more!

At the east side of the extensive Wauchope Forest is Souden Kirk, on the A6088 road from Carter Bar to Hawick. It was excavated in 1910 and is dedicated to the memory of the Scots dead from the battle of Otterburn in 1388 (the battle the English call Chevy Chase, when Hotspur was routed by Douglas, who himself died in victory). An annual service of remembrance is held here. From the church it is a short but steep walk to Southdean Law, with a prehistoric fort and settlement on its summit and a fine view as well.

The next road east is the A68, and on its way to Jedburgh it passes near **Ferniehirst Castle**, with a long and troubled history, which now gives hospitality to visitors from many lands. It is a most unusual hostel with its magnificent staircases and great hall with a vast fireplace.

Not far from the hostel is Ferniehirst Mill Lodge, a centre for riding holidays. The riding here is not for beginners, but the standard of care of both people and horses is very high. In the summer months a 5-day Cheviot Trail Ride covers 100 miles; the horses stay at hill farms overnight while riders are ferried back to base.

East of Ferniehirst is the pretty village of **Oxnam**, with an attractive whitewashed church and a pottery where visitors can watch Peter Holland — the seventh generation of his family to follow this calling — making domestic and ornamental pots and earthenware, and perhaps leave with a souvenir.

The back road from Oxnam to Hownam is crossed by the Roman Dere Street, which can be walked from here to the camp at Chew Green, just into England. There are plans to turn this into a way-marked path linking the Pennine Way with the Southern Upland Way at Selkirk, a stretch of 25 miles (40km) through fine rolling country. **Hownam** is on the Kale Water, and much further up that stream, on Dere Street, is Woden Law. On its summit was a native fort guarding the border; it was overrun and demolished by the Roman army under Agricola in AD80, after which the Romans themselves built fortifications here, which it is believed were used largely for siege warfare training.

The back road from Hownam to Woden Law is part of an ancient highway known as The Street or Clattering Path. It too can be walked to the camp at Chew Green, but take care not to cross to the south side of the Coquet Valley, which is part of the extensive military training area in frequent use. The last points of call in Roxburghshire are Morebattle and Linton. **Morebattle** is not named after a fight, but was originally *Merebotle*, the town by the lake. The water in question was Lynton Loch, which extended over 1,000 acres before it was drained in 1832. The parish church, built in the mid-eighteenth century, stands on the site of an older building which was part of the estates of Glasgow Cathedral.

Linton today is a quiet place, but it was not always so. Not only was it the scene of numerous Border raids, but it had a resident monster. The Linton Worm was a dragon which lived in a cave on the north-east slope of Linton Hill near Greenlees Farm on today's maps. It terrorised the neighbourhood in the twelfth century, eating cattle and sheep and driving people from their homes with its scorching breath. You can see the dents said to have been made by its great coils on Wormiston Hill today.

Linton Church is also notable in its own way, for it is built on a hillock of pure sand, with no apparent solid foundations. Above the entrance is an ancient panel depicting the slaying of the Worm. From the church, a 4-mile walk leads along the minor road to Bankhead and up on to Linton Hill, returning the same way. Do please ask permission to go on the hill when you reach the farm — you are most unlikely to be refused. You are also most unlikely to find any dragons on Linton Hill today, and can enjoy in peace the splendid views, east to the Cheviot Hills and north into Berwickshire, the subject of the next chapter.

6

BERWICKSHIRE DISTRICT

B erwickshire District is in shape a squiggly rectangle, with the county town of Duns set right in the middle. The exploration of the county begins on its west side, travelling up the Leader Water through the village of Earlston to the royal and ancient burgh of **Lauder**. Despite its small size, with a population of under 1,000, this is the only royal burgh in Berwickshire, having held its charter since at least the fourteenth century.

Entering the town from the south, the tolbooth faces you in the main street. As the name indicates, its original purpose was the collection of tolls from people passing through. The ground floor was used as a gaol for many years. Names around Lauder such as Witches Knowe and Ducking Pool indicate the crimes of which some of those imprisoned here were accused. The upper floor was the council chamber, with a platform at the top of the stair from which proclamations could be made. There was previously a market cross in front of the building and a 'tron', an old weighing device for gauging the weight of goods for sale or toll purposes.

The parish church, on the south side of Market Place, is built on the plan of a Greek cross and has an octagonal bell-tower. It was designed by Sir William Bruce, architect to the king, in the 1670s.

Just to the east of Lauder is Thirlestane Castle, an outstanding example of a Border fortress and well worth a visit. It was in fact originally constructed as a fort, but in the sixteenth century was converted into a dwelling-house. It is an imposing red sandstone building with turrets, towers, balconies, and a splendid collection of furniture and paintings assembled by the Earls of Lauderdale over the years.

Another unusual attraction in Lauder is the Border Country Life

Museum, opened in 1982. Displays of photographs, old maps, farm machinery and furniture show the development of social and agricultural life in the region.

Lauder has its own Common Riding, held in early August. The riding fell out of custom in the nineteenth century, but was revived to mark the coronation of George V in 1910 and has been held ever since.

From its sources in the Lammermuir Hills the Leader Water has carved out an attractive valley through the Old Red sandstone as it flows south to join the Tweed. Lauderdale has a prosperous landscape of rich red sandy soils and mature woodlands. There are splendid walks all round Lauder, and study of the map will reveal numerous tracks leading off the main road which can be used to gain access to the hills on either side. A 5 mile (8km) walk leads up the Harry Burn just north of Lauder, heading west to Whitlaw and up on to Inchkeith Hill, and returning on a different track to Trabrown.

A longer walk, making a really fine day out, starts from the Carfraemill Hotel, at the junction of A68 and A697 about 4 miles (6.4km) north of Lauder. Take the minor road running due north alongside the Kelphope Burn, diverting on to a track after about half a mile to avoid some of the road walking. Rejoin the road and take the right fork through Tollishill for the track on to Crib Law, NT525598, at 1,680ft (509m) a splendid viewpoint for the Lammermuir Hills and north to Edinburgh and the Firth of Forth.

You can either return the same way for a round trip of 11 miles (18km) or extend the walk by striding out along the ridge eastwards for 2 miles (3km) to Seenes Law, NT557597, returning down the lovely valley of the Whalplaw Burn to Longcroft and the main road at Cleekhimin, half a mile south of Carfraemill (round trip 14 miles, 23km).

Turn east from Lauder and before heading for Duns take a diversion south-east on A6089 which leads to Greenknowe Tower and Gordon. The tower, half a mile north of the town, was built in 1581 on the site of an earlier building founded by the knight Aidan de Gordun. In the fifteenth century the line passed to the Seton family, whose coat of arms is carved over the door of the tower. The tower house was the favoured house-type of the landed gentry in James VI's Scotland. Greenknowe was used as a residence until about 1850. It is open to the public.

Gordon is a pleasant small town, having links with the clan of the same name which settled here before spreading its influence to the Highlands. Three miles south of Gordon, west of the main road, is

Mellerstain House, one of Scotland's finest Georgian mansions. It was built in the 1720s by William and Robert Adam for the Baillie family. The gardens were laid out in 1909 by Sir Reginald Blomfield and include many fine trees, avenues and a lake. Mellerstain is now the home of Lord and Lady Binning and the house contains a superb collection of paintings, including works by Van Dyck, Constable and Gainsborough, and magnificent Adam ceilings.

From Mellerstain a minor road leads east to Hume, passing Hume Castle, a good example of the early design of Border fortified houses, featuring a square enclosure or quadrangle with a tower at each corner. From Hume it is a short run north on B6364 to **Greenlaw**, which preceded Duns as the county town. The town contains a number of fine buildings, notably the imposing Town Hall, built in 1830, and the Castle Hotel from a year later. The church was built in 1675 and restored in the nineteenth century. The tower, which appears to be part of the church, is in fact separate from it and was used as a prison. There is trout fishing on the Blackadder from March to early October; permits from the post office or hotels in Greenlaw.

The A6105 road from Greenlaw to Duns passes two places of interest. Off the road to the south is **Marchmont House**, another Adam building from that fruitful period in the mid-eighteenth century. The house is now the home of Sir Robert and Lady McEwen and the gardens are open in the summer months. A little further on is the village of **Polwarth**, a place of rural quiet but with a curious and appealing custom from the past. Whenever a marriage was celebrated in the village, all the villagers would dance round the two old thorn trees on the green. The trees are still there although the dancing has long since ceased.

Duns was the county town of Berwickshire from 1903 until local government reorganisation in 1975 made it, instead, the administrative centre for Berwickshire District Council. The name derives from an old word for a hill fort, and the original settlement was on the slopes of Duns Law. In Newtown Street, together with the council offices, you will find the Jim Clark Memorial Room, a rather unusual type of museum. It commemorates the life and career of the racing driver who lived in Duns and was world champion in 1963 and again in 1965. He was killed in a crash in 1968, and the Memorial Room contains many of his trophies, with other mementoes of his career, donated by his parents.

Murray Street, on the other side of the square, leads to the public park, where bowls, tennis, and putting can be played. (For the golfer there is a 9-hole course on the outskirts of the town.) In the park, too,

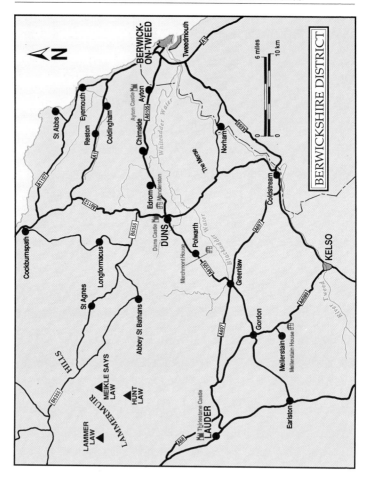

is a bronze statue of John Duns Scotus, scholar and theologian of the late thirteenth and early fourteenth century. It was presented to Duns by the Franciscan Order on the 700th anniversary of his birth in 1966.

Another son of Duns to achieve fame was Sir Joseph Paxton, who started his career as a gardener with the Duke of Devonshire at Chatsworth, in Derbyshire. He began to design buildings for horticultural purposes and went on to design the (original) famous

Crystal Palace in London, and many fine fountains. His books *Paxton's Flower Garden* and the *Pocket Botanical Dictionary* were best-sellers in their day.

Paxton would undoubtedly have approved of the creation of a nature reserve in the grounds of Duns Castle, just north of the town. The castle itself, the seat of the Hay family, is strictly private, but the reserve can be visited if you obtain a permit from the warden. From the car park on B6365 at the north end of the reserve, a nature trail leads round the reserve to the 'Hen Poo', a beautiful stretch of water providing an ideal habitat for many types of water fowl. In the woods you may see woodpeckers, pied flycatchers and redstarts, and mammals frequenting the reserve include roe deer, red squirrels and badgers.

Duns supplies the last of the twelve Border festivals, which takes place during the first full week in July.

A mile or so east of Duns is **Manderston**, one of the finest Edwardian country houses in Britain. A feature of particular interest is the 'downstairs' — the domestic quarters which are preserved to give a real insight into life in such a house 80 to 90 years ago. The stables too are splendidly preserved. In the house itself are magnificently decorated staterooms, a 'silver staircase' and fine furniture and hangings. The 56-acre park with its lake has formal and woodland gardens with walks laid out.

Further along A6105 is **Edrom**, where the church contains a fine Norman doorway. It is the only remnant of the original building, dating from about 1140; the church was rebuilt in 1732. In the manor house a school for cellists has been established, with pupils coming from many overseas countries to study here. At The Dun is Edrom Riding Centre, where horses can be hired for an hour or longer.

The next village eastwards is **Chirnside**, a T-shaped settlement with a long street running along the hill slope. The church is the oldest building in the village by some way; as with Edrom, a Norman doorway at the west end survives. At the east end of the village, a prehistoric grave was excavated in 1906 and was found to be that of a chieftain of the Beaker Folk. A cairn marks the site today. A plant in Chirnside makes the paper covers for tea bags.

Four more miles eastwards on B6355 from Chirnside is the pleasant village of **Ayton**, on the A1 and near to the Eye Water, on which trout fishing is available in season. Ayton has two interesting churches and a castle. The old church dates back to the twelfth century and bears an unusual dedication, to St Dionysius. It was the site of several meetings in the fourteenth and fifteenth centuries between Scottish and English parties to discuss truce and border-line arrangements. The church, now largely in ruins, lies to the east of the present parish church, built in 1864 in the Gothic style. The spire is 130ft (40m) high.

Ayton Castle is an imposing building of red sandstone, designed by James Gillespie Graham, who was also responsible for Brodick Castle on the Isle of Arran, which is markedly similar to Ayton. The castle was built for William Mitchell-Innes, who was at the time governor of the Bank of Scotland. It has been a family home ever since, except for a period in World War II when it was used as a school. The entrance hall, dining room and library all contain very fine Victorian decoration and furniture, with splendid painted ceilings.

Leaving the coast to the next chapter, turn north along the A1, following the Eye Water and the main east coast rail line and passing through **Reston**, where a fortnightly auction market is held throughout the year. Instead of continuing north, an interesting diversion can be made by turning left here, westwards along the northern edge of the Merse, the area of rich Berwickshire farmland between the coast and the hills. The B6438 leads through the scattered parish of Bonkyl or **Bunkle**, with several ruined castles of which Bunkle itself, half a mile west of Marygold village, is perhaps the best preserved. The name is thought to mean 'the place of the cell' and there has been a parish church since at least 1420. The present church, at Preston, is fairly recent, having been built in 1820.

Three miles west from Preston on B6355, a right turn on to a minor road leads to **Abbey St Bathans** in the valley of the Whiteadder Water. On the north-east slopes of Cockburn Law, before reaching the river, is the impressive Edin's Hall Broch, one of only ten such structures in the whole of Lowland Scotland. A good way of seeing the broch is to follow the walk from Abbey St Bathans waymarked by the regional council. The walk leaves the village heading east along the road; where the road meets the river, it crosses by the footbridge and climbs steeply through the wood (this valley contains almost a third of the oak woodland in the Borders region and is an important habitat for birds and wild flowers). Follow the track, now heading away from the river for a mile to the road, where you turn right for another mile to Elba Wood. The name does not come from the island in the Mediterranean but possibly from Gaelic words meaning a hill dwelling.

Turn right off the road and take the forest track to the river, crossing it by a footbridge near Elba Cottage. There was once a copper mine in this area, but it was abandoned in the 1820s. The walk continues on the south side of the river, gradually climbing on to Cockburn Law and the Broch. The return to Abbey St Bathans is made by walking north-west to the sharp bend in the road known locally as 'Toot Corner' — very apt! For a shorter walk follow the first route to the road, NT 781 622, and turn left. Walk to Moorhouse, bear left across the stile, and follow the path to Whare Burn. Walk downstream to the visitor centre, where there is a tearoom and a shop. There is also a youth hostel opposite the church.

There was a priory of Cistercian nuns in Abbey St Bathans in the late twelfth century. The priory was badly damaged during English raids in the sixteenth century but the east gable and north wall are still there, incorporated into the present church. The name itself is something of a mystery as it seems certain that the priory never attained abbey status. The gardens of Abbey House are sometimes open to the public — enquire locally. In the village there is a visitor centre, a trout farm and a car park.

Leave this peaceful spot the way you came in and turn right on the B6355, taking another small back road to the left where the road meets the Whiteadder at Ellem, to the hill village of **Longformacus**. The village contains a church with a long history, and is also an excellent centre for walks on the Lammermuir Hills. West from the village, a track leaves the road after half a mile, NT684569, and passes through Whinrig to Watch Water Reservoir, set in a valley amid fine hill scenery. The round trip is about 5 miles (8km). It could be extended by turning north from the reservoir to the Dye Water valley and regaining the road via Horseupcleugh, a distance of about 9 miles (14.4km), or 11 miles (17.71km) if you walk back along the road to Longformacus.

Two more hill walks will give the flavour of the Lammermuirs — a wide stretch of pretty empty country, but very satisfying walking terrain and with generally excellent views, northwards to Edinburgh and the Firth of Forth and eastwards to the sea. The first walk is circular, of about 9 miles (14.4km), and starts from St Agnes, just in Lothian Region on the B6355. Walk north along the track that follows the Bothwell Water up into the hills, to the point where the path crosses the West Burn to Beltondod. Turn left and climb on to Spartleton Edge. The return route descends past Gamelshiel Castle to the Whiteadder Reservoir. Bear left down the road past The Bell to the starting point. This outing should take no more than 5 hours; it is generally quite easy walking, though the navigation in the centre section would need a little care in poor visibility.

The second walk traverses the southern part of the Lammermuirs and is linear, so transport would have to be arranged at either end. It starts from Pyatshaw, on the A697 about 3 miles (5km) east of Lauder. Take the minor road running up the east bank of the Brunta Burn and cross the burn after half a mile on the track leading to Blythe. Just past Blythe, take the right fork and follow this path in a north-easterly direction, keeping to the higher ground over Nun Rig and crossing Blythe Edge to drop into the valley of the Dye Water at Byrecleugh.

Turn more north-westerly here to climb up to the Mutiny Stones and Long Cairn, an earthwork about 60yd (55.8m) in length and a good place for a break. The way from here is north, then north-east at a fork to pass Killpallet (now in Lothian Region) before reaching the road at Duddy Bank. This is a total distance of about 10 miles (16km); an energetic walker could extend the day by another 2 miles (3km), continuing on the track west of Faseny Water through Penshiel to meet the 'support party' at the west end of Whiteadder Reservoir, a pleasant place for them to wait.

Having glimpsed the coast on these walks, it is now time to consider its attractions in more detail.

7

THE COAST AND EAST LOTHIAN

The Berwickshire coast is rocky, dramatic in outline, and served by very few roads. It is not a place for the idling holidaymaker looking for a wide beach with the full facilities of a resort. It is still a working coast with a fishing fleet. Above all, it is a coast rarely visited and well worth exploring. Take a few days and work your way north along it before plunging into the heady whirl of Edinburgh.

The first settlement on the Scottish side — north, that is, of the piece of Scotland stolen by the English 500 years ago — is **Lamberton**, a tiny place on the landward side of the present A1. Its main claim to fame is that its church was the scene of the betrothal vow of James IV of Scotland and Margaret Tudor in 1503; the ruins of the church can be seen, but Habchester Fort, up on Lamberton Moor, is in private hands and cannot be viewed close to.

The first truly coastal settlement is **Burnmouth**, 3 miles north of Lamberton. Driving along the A1, or passing by in a train, you would not know there was a settlement here at all — it is so well hidden down its steep ravine. Nonetheless, there it is and it still remains active in lobster and crab fishing. It has seen its moments of history, despite its small size, being the first place in Scotland on the coast. Burnmouth was the scene of the signing of two of the many treaties between England and Scotland, in 1384 and 1497. It would not be chosen for events of such importance today!

Two miles north of Burnmouth, the Eye runs into the North Sea, forming as it does a natural harbour round which the town of **Eyemouth** has grown up. The first fishermen to exploit this facility are believed to have been Benedictine monks from Coldingham

Priory, in the thirteenth century. Eyemouth became a burgh in 1597 and was granted the status of a free port. From then until the late nineteenth century, haddock and herring fishing flourished with a fleet of upwards of thirty vessels. On 14 October 1881 there occurred here one of those terrible tragedies that seem to visit fishing communities everywhere.

A fleet of thirty vessels had gone out from Eyemouth, along with ships from other ports. A great storm blew up and the fleet turned for home. They were caught, and only a few of the ships managed to make the run into harbour without the sea tearing them apart or hurling them onto the rocks. Of the awful total of 191 men drowned that day, 129 were from Eyemouth. The town was left with over 100 widows and 350 children without fathers.

The centenary of the disaster was marked by various events in 1981, among them the opening of a fine new museum in the former Auld Kirk. The Tourist Information Centre is in the same building. The museum tells the story of the 1881 storm and includes a 15ft (4.65m) long tapestry depicting the disaster. It was sewn by local women, all of them descendants of men who were drowned that day, and it contains one million stitches. There are other exhibits showing how fishing has changed over the centuries and how the town itself has developed. The museum is also the start of Eyemouth Town Trail which links eight story-boards around the town and harbour.

Eyemouth harbour is still a busy place, with all the fascination of any port where boats are active. Fishing these days is mainly for white fish, prawns, lobster and crab. You can see fish being landed and auctioned, and if you are lucky, being filleted and smoked in traditional smokehouses. There is a boat building and repair yard across the harbour. The Eyemouth fishermen are not, legally, permitted to fish for salmon, as the seas outside the harbour limits are in legal terms considered to be part of the River Tweed. It makes little logical sense, but that is the way of it.

Eyemouth has a surprising range of facilities for the sportsperson. Sea angling is well established, with a thriving local club, and boats can be hired to fish for cod, mackerel, flounder, sole and haddock. There is coarse fishing on the Eye Water inland from the town. The town also has a 9-hole golf course, the only one on this stretch of coast. There is safe sea bathing and a modern indoor swimming pool. Sailing is growing in popularity. Bowls and tennis are available in season.

Well worth a visit are the gardens of Netherbyres, an eighteenth-century house just south of the town. The gardens are oval in shape and are walled; they are open in the summer months.

There is a splendid 4 mile (6.44km) coast walk from Eyemouth up to Coldingham and St Abbs, the next two villages northwards. The walk is waymarked and follows the cliff-top most of the way. At Coldingham Bay, either turn left into the village or walk on for an extra half a mile or so to St Abbs. There is a bus service between Coldingham and Eyemouth, or for a longer day the walk could simple be reversed — coastal scenery is always worth studying in both directions. On this walk there is a variety of birdlife, coastal plants such as sea pinks, sea bindweed and vipers bugloss, and exposed volcanic rock.

Coldingham village is so well tucked into its sheltered valley, fed by the Buskin Burn, that even from half a mile away it is not obvious that there is a settlement there at all. It was granted burgh status in 1638 and was at that time an important religious centre, with the Benedictine priory at its heart. The priory was founded in 1098 by Edgar, King of Scots, thus making it one of the oldest establishments of its kind in Scotland. Edgar's building, dedicated to St Cuthbert, was in fact erected on the site of an even older church, to St Mary. The tower stood 90ft (27.9m) at its full height; alas, like so many fine buildings of the Borders, it suffered repeated damage, notably by Cromwell in 1648. Public worship is still observed at the priory, which is open to visitors all the year round free of charge.

Coldingham has several hotels, a youth hostel, and facilities for caravans and tents. There is a small studio in the village where art classes are held each summer. Sea angling is available, as are skin-diving and sailing; trout can be fished on Coldingham Loch, 2 miles (3.2km) north. Numerous walks are possible from the village, one of the best leading back through St Abbs to St Abbs Head, a noted bird reserve.

St Abbs takes its name from Ebba, a sister of King Oswy of Northumbria. She founded a religious community here in the seventh century. A walk from the village to the headland is only about $1^1/_2$ miles (2.4km) but is not to be missed. The cliff scenery is among the most dramatic of the whole coast, rising to 310ft (96m) at St Abb's Head itself. Bird life abounds, and as well as a lighthouse there are a number of settlement sites dating from prehistoric times. If time is limited, drive to the reserve along a lane from Coldingham, to a car park near the headland.

St Abb's Head was purchased by the National Trust for Scotland in 1980 and is managed jointly with the Scottish Wildlife Trust. The reserve covers 192 acres of cliff and coastal area. It is an important

Eyemouth Harbour

breeding area for seabirds, as might be expected. The reserve is open all the year round and the ranger, who takes guided walks throughout the summer, will be pleased to tell you more about it. He can be contacted at Ranger's Cottage, Northfield Farm, St Abbs — groups planning to visit the reserve should always contact him in advance. The facilities available on the site include a visitor centre, where leaflets can be obtained, and a tearoom.

Three miles west of St Abbs Head is one of the most extraordinary ruins in all Scotland — **Fast Castle**, perched almost unbelievably on a stack, not even on the main cliff, and accessible only via a gangway after a cliff-face descent that would test the strongest nerve. Close by rise some of the highest sea cliffs on Britain's east coast. The ruin can be seen from above, and that may be enough for most people. Even to get so far requires a decent walk — the nearest road is the A1107, 2 miles (3km) away at Meikle Black Law. A round trip on foot from Coldingham to Fast Castle, using lanes via Lumsdaine and across the Dowlaw Burn, and then back to the road via Dowlaw itself, would cover about 6 miles (10km) and make an unusual and satisfying excursion. You would, of course, need a driver to collect you.

The coast winds on, round headlands and through bays with

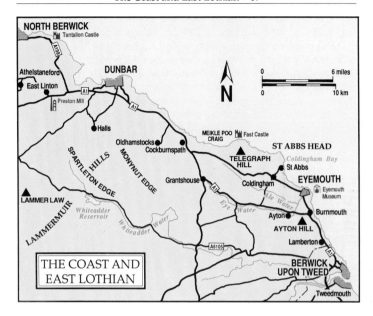

names that stay in the memory — Black Bull, Meikle Poo Crag, Pease Bay — to the tiny fishing settlement of **Cove**, with its secluded harbour. Cove is an example of a 'heugh-heid' (clifftop) fishing village. The harbour is too small to hold many houses, so they were built at the top of the cliff, on the nearest bit of flat ground. Cove harbour was built between 1770 and 1831 to designs by Sir John Hall; today it offers a beautiful spot for a bathe or a picnic. An interesting feature dates from the 1750s. There is a 164ft (50m) long tunnel driven through the sandstone that gives access to a private dwelling and the sandy shore. Cars are not allowed down the harbour road but must park at Cove village.

A mile or so inland is Cockburnspath (usually said as Co'path), on the A1 but alas, no longer with a railway station. There is a fine mercat cross with a rose and thistle emblem. Co'path is the eastern terminus for the Southern Upland Way long distance footpath, which begins its 212 mile (340km) journey across Galloway and the Borders' at Portpatrick, near Stranraer. Any walker covering the whole path should take the extra mile to reach the coast and thus truly walk sea to sea.

West of this coastal region, the Lothian plains stretch uninterruptedly inland as far as the Pentland Hills. The dramatic whale-backed hill of Traprain Law, which in geological terms is a laccolith — (a dome-like igneous mass which arches over the overlying sedimentary rocks) provides a magnificent viewpoint over the East Lothian countryside. Its summit was once the capital or Oppidum of the Votadini tribe. The 40-acre site was occupied for a period of a thousand years lasting until the Saxons came. In 1919, a treasure cache of silver was unearthed, and is now exhibited in the National Museum of Antiquities of Scotland in Edinburgh. A path climbs to the summit up the west end of the hill, rewarding the visitor with a tremendous all-round view.

East Lothian is the heart of one of the loveliest areas of the Scottish Lowlands. Here is some of the finest arable land in Scotland, and its landscape lies in horizontal planes of colour — green of grass, darker green of growing crops and dark and bright red ploughland. The tilled fields stretch with a final flourish right to the edge of the sea cliffs. There are many small towns and villages that dot this lovely countryside and the attractive coastline offers wonderful beaches with grassy dunes, sheltered bays, dramatic headlands and rocky foreshores that are rich in bird life and wild flowers. The visitor should have no difficulty in selecting from the great variety of things to do. For the golfing enthusiast, sixteen golf courses fringe the coast, from Musselburgh Links, one of the oldest golf courses in the world to Muirfield, with its famous championship courses. There are special weekly golf tickets available to visitors staying in Tourist Board registered accommodation.

East Lothian also offers sea and river angling, bird watching, hill walking, pony-trekking sand yachting, swimming and sailing. Being close to England it is hardly surprising that the area was for centuries a battleground. So it is rich in history with ruined castles at Tantallon, Hailes, Dunbar and Dirleton, and sites of some of the most famous battles between the Scots and the English.

Inland, East Lothian rises to the northern escarpment and moorland plateau of the Lammermuir Hills. There are long stretches of heather-covered ground with rolling summits and tawney-coloured grasslands unbroken by major rock outcrops. The surface is relatively dry forming easy walking conditions. The streams run off the moorland, mainly in a south-east direction into Berwickshire, including the Whiteadder, Bothwell and Monynut Waters. The Lammermuir Hills form a charming, quiet area of wide, empty horizons, narrow, almost secret valleys and attractive villages.

From the A1, near the district boundary, a country lane runs to the village of **Oldhamstocks**. The settlement consists of a single one-sided street of pantiled cottages overlooking the valley. There are wide grass verges, and a whitewashed church to complete the peaceful scene. A winding country lane twists and turns round the eastern slopes of Blackcastle Hill to reach the neighbouring village of Innerwick — a journey of 4 miles (6.4km). The old school buildings in Innerwick have been converted into a Field Studies Centre and there are pony-trekking facilities nearby at Braidwood. Between the two villages there is an interesting cleft through the hills in the form of the narrow valley of Aikengall. Its steep sides and gravel-covered bed illustrate a good example of a glacial channel gouged out by melt water.

An enjoyable $12^1/_2$ mile (20km) walk can be taken from Elmscleugh, NT 697 719. Take the track that climbs on to the moor overlooking Monynut Edge. Follow the track into the valley of the Monynut Water for just over 1 mile (1.6km), and then climb the opposite hillside and descend to Crichness in the valley of the Bothwell Water. Cross the stream and walk up the valley to Belton-dod. Climb up to Friardykes Dod, and soon bear right on the path to Boonslie, Weatherly and on to Woodhall. A short walk along the country lane brings one back to the starting point.

Garvald is a red sandstone village situated on the north-western slopes of the Lammermuirs and lying in the steep valley of the Papana Water. Its church dates partly from the twelfth century. On the hillside above the village the monks of the Cistercian order at Nunraw have moved into the new monastery of Sancta Maria. The monks, who are farmers as well as builders, have reclaimed the hill slopes, and sustain their order's custom of hospitality.

Gifford is an attractive village with a tree-bordered green, a wide main street and it still has its mercat cross in the square. The surrounding countryside is pleasantly wooded with the forests planted in the early eighteenth century as part of the enlightened attitude of landowners towards re-afforestation. Approaching the village through Bolton Muir Wood, the verges have been planted with rowan and birch and backed by beech trees to create a mass of colour in autumn. The village was once the home of several small industries, and at least three livestock fairs were held there each year. In the eighteenth century, paper for the Bank of Scotland notes was made there. Gifford's present church was built 1708-10 and it contains a fifteenth-century bell and a seventeenth-century pulpit.

A famous personality connected with Gifford is the Reverend John Witherspoon (1722-94), who was born in the manse and emi-

The village of St Abbs

A view from Tantallon Castle towards Bass Rock

grated to America. He was one of the signatories of the American Declaration of Independence.

The village is a popular centre for walking, pony-trekking or motoring in the Lammermuirs, and there are many routes to suit all tastes. One interesting walk is the route on which the salted herrings were taken to the Border abbeys — The Old Herring Road.

Start this $15^1/_2$ mile (24.8km) walk at **Halls** in East Lothian, and walk over Watch Law to Beltondod. Continue over Bothwell Water and descend over Spartleton Edge past Gamelshiel Castle to the Whiteadder Reservoir. Walk to the western end of the reservoir and head south to Penshiel and beyond to the minor road. Proceed by Killpallet, pass the Mutiny Stones and descend to Dye Water — you are now in the Border Region. From Byrecleugh the way heads south over Watch Water to Wedderlie.

Another walk crosses the north-west corner of the Lammermuir Hills, starting at **Longyester**, just over 2 miles (3.2km) south of Gifford.

Walk on the track south, climbing above Sting Bank Burn to the shoulder of Lammer Law, where a quick dash west can easily be made to the summit, at 1,730ft (527m). Continue in a southerly direction, passing Crib Law and down to Tollishill. Just before the farm, bear left, and after a short distance head south skirting Cadam Law and Addinston Hill to Addinston and the A697. The distance of this walk is 10 miles (16km).

As both these routes are linear walks, arrangements have to be made for transport at the far end.

The A1 road bypasses **Haddington** to the north, but visitors should take the opportunity of looking round this fine eighteenth-century town. The large parish church of St Mary was built in the fifteenth century and has an open masonry crown similar to that of St Giles Cathedral in Edinburgh. In Lodge Street is the Jane Welsh Carlyle House. It is a restored eighteenth-century building, the home of Jane Welsh Carlyle, one of the greatest women writers of her time, and wife of Thomas Carlyle, the nineteenth-century historian and essayist.

The centre of Haddington has been designated a conservation area, and Court Street is a fine approach with its public buildings and avenue of lime trees. Other features include its Town House of about 1748, which occupies a key position in an irregular pattern of streets, and a three-storey cornmill at Poldrate with its undershot water wheel. Visitors will find a map on the walls of the Town House indicating the start of an architectural trail around the narrow side streets.

Other houses and gardens open to the public near to Haddington are Lennoxlove House and Stevenson House. The traditional seventeenth-century Scottish gardens of Haddington House are also worth a visit.

East Linton lies 5 miles (8km) along the A1 east of Haddington. It has a fine fourteenth-century bridge spanning the Linn, and a single street plan widening into two triangular areas, one decorated with a handsome cast-iron fountain. The town was craftsmen-built and now many of the old houses are being restored.

Just north of the town, the picturesque Preston Mill, a seventeenth-century riverside watermill, has been restored to its working condition by the National Trust of Scotland. Next to the mill is a small museum exhibiting old agricultural equipment. A short walk leads to the Phantassie Doo'cot which once held five hundred birds.

South of Haddington, the ancient village of **Athelstaneford** flies the Saltire flag of Scotland in the churchyard. The legend describes how Athelstane was inspired to vistory by the sight of a white cross of clouds against a blue sky above the battlefield. The area contains numerous forts. One, The Chester, NT 507 783, lies to the north-west. Although this circular two-ditched fortification has been extensively robbed of stonework, the remains are still impressive. It measures about 350ft (108m) in diameter within two massive ramparts with external ditches.

There are two museums in the area which visitors with more mechanical interests may care to visit. Just east of Athelstaneford is the Museum of Flight, with its nostalgic collection of aircraft, airships and engines. To the west, on the outskirts of the old coastal village of Aberlady is the Myreton Motor Museum, with its interesting collection of cars, lorries, motor cycles, bicycles and military vehicles.

The village of **Aberlady** is one of the oldest coastal settlements, with a cottage-lined main street and a fifteenth-century church with a fortified tower at the west end. Before the silting up of the harbour, Aberlady was the port for Haddington. Beyond the village lies the wide expanse of the Aberlady Bay Nature Reserve, a vital refuge for wildfowl. A mile (1.6km), east of Aberlady is Luffness Castle, a dramatic sixteenth-century moated castle which is still inhabited and sometimes open to the public.

Gosford House is situated between Longniddry and Aberlady, NT 455 785. The centrepiece of the Gosford estate is the Adam house, surrounded by parkland containing spectacular woods which were planted at the end of the eighteenth century. Gosford is the home of the Earl of Wemyss, and is noted for a celebrated marble hall and picture gallery. In the grounds there are ornamental waters with wildfowl.

Close by, the major attraction in **Gullane** is its extensive sandy beach, and for golfing enthusiasts, its two famous courses which include Muirfield, the venue for many an Open Championship. There is a coastal path to Aberlady. From the car park, take the cliff path to the left, from where spectacular views may be obtained along the Firth of Forth and towards Edinburgh Castle to Arthur's Seat. To the far west are the Pentland Hills, and in the middle of the Firth the island of Inchkeith can be seen.

In the neighbourhood, much work has been done by the local authority, and lately by the Forestry Commission, in stabilising and protecting the shifting dunes with laid brushwood and regular planting of marram grass. The latter has established a plantation of hardy Lodgepole Pine on the eastern headland of Gullane Bay. There

Dunbar Harbour

is a coastal path around the Black Rocks, the West Links, opposite Eyebroughy and Longskelly, that joins up with the nature trail at Yellow Craig.

Dirleton is a most attractive village and is enlivened by the remains of the thirteenth-century castle. The fortress, constructed at the end of the twelfth century by the first Baron de Vaux, was of the earth and timber type. It consisted of a wooden tower, other buildings of wattle and daub, and was surrounded by a ditch and earthworks. Access to good freestone in the thirteenth century led to the castle being massively rebuilt in stone. The castle has delightful gardens which are also open to the public.

The coastal park of Yellow Craig is reached by turning left at the end of the village street. There is a nature trail and a beautifully landscaped caravan site. Out to sea the rocky islets of Eyebroughy, Fidra — the model for R.L. Stevenson's *Treasure Island* — Lamb and Craigleith are the homes for countless colonies of seabirds. The latter isle supports the largest puffin colony in the Forth.

The ancient burgh of **North Berwick** has many amenities to offer the holiday visitor. An interesting harbour, a centre for yachting, fishing and skin-diving and a heated swimming pool. The town has a variety of accommodation, hotels and guest houses, and there are two golf courses, one on either side of the town. Overlooking the town, and a landmark for miles around, is the ancient volcanic trachyte plug of North Berwick Law, 613ft (187m). There is a convenient footpath to the top which affords expansive and wide-ranging views. A mile and a half (2.4km) out to sea is the famous volcanic island of the Bass Rock, with its sheer cliffs rising 350ft (106m). It houses a tremendous colony of gannets, as well as kittiwakes, shags, guillemots, fulmars, razorbills and herring gulls. Boat trips leave daily from North Berwick throughout the summer to the Bass Rock. However, permission is required to land.

Some $2^1/_2$ miles (4km) to the east stand the impressive ruins of **Tantallon Castle**, on a volcanic promontory protected on the seaward side by high cliffs. Immediately opposite, offshore, is the Bass Rock. The castle dates from the fourteenth century, but was altered and added to in the sixteenth century. It is of the courtyard type, and some of its features resemble those of a fourteenth-century French château.

Dunbar lies 9 miles (14.4km) to the east via the A198, A1 and A1087. The town has good road and rail communications with easily accessible beaches and the open Lammermuir Hills. The broad High Street of the town serves the needs of people in the surrounding countryside as well as catering for its many summer visitors. Along the eastern side of the street is the steepled seventeenth-century town house, which currently houses the Tourist Information Centre. Dunbar was the birthplace in 1838 of John Muir, who emigrated to the United States, and who inspired the setting up of the Sequoia and Yosemite National Parks. A plaque is erected on the wall of his house in the High Street.

Dunbar has been left an interesting legacy in the form of the old warehouse quarter, built when the town was a busy port. The area is a delight for the person who likes to explore narrow, steeply sloping streets. The ruins of Dunbar Castle stand overlooking the pictur-esque harbour. It was destroyed by Cromwell who used the stone to build the harbour quays. The harbour presents a colourful and interesting scene with boats of all types riding peacefully at anchor.

To the north of the town lies the expanse of Belhaven Beach, a mile in length, and approached by car with the access in West Barns, or on foot over the Biel Water. The Winterfield golf course is only minutes from the town centre, with a cliff-top walk from the castle to the west. The Dunbar golf course lies to the south-east of the town.

Two and a half miles (4km) south-east of Dunbar is the coastal park of White Sands and Barns Ness. The latter has the facility of a well-constructed and well-equipped caravan and camping site. Visitors may walk to Catcraig to view the restored massive stone limekiln, and at low tide to explore the foreshore and walk over the interesting sequence of seven limestones with accompanying fossils. Sea angling is excellent here, and from the camp site, which is protected by earth banks, there are magnificent views towards St Abbs Head, where the Lammermuir Hills reach the sea in rugged cliffs.

Inland there is a lovely circular trip for motorists, motor cyclists and keen cyclists who would like to be adventurous and explore the delightful Lammermuir countryside. From Abbey St Bathans, travel to Burnhouses on the B6355 and follow the Whiteadder valley to the Whiteadder Reservoir. Here the choice is either to continue on the B6355 to the attractive village of Gifford, (see p89-91) or bear right to follow the Whiteadder Water into the hills, past White Castle Fort, then descend to Garvald past Nunraw Abbey to the B6370. Continue through Stenton, and then take the lanes once more to Spott, twisting and winding, through Innerwick and on to Oldhamstocks. Keep on over Dunglass Common, descending to the valley of the Monynut Water and returning to Abbey St Bathans.

Musselburgh lies to the east and adjacent to Edinburgh. It has a

Sorting the catch, Dunbar

wide main street containing the sixteenth-century tolbooth. The present main road bridge carrying the A1 was built by John Rennie in 1807. Upstream is an ancient bridge still used by pedestrians and said to rest on Roman foundations. On the old bridge are traces of a gate used for defence when this was the main route.

Musselburgh is well-known for the Brunton Theatre Company which has an exciting drama season from September to March, plus the annual Christmas pantomime. This well-equipped theatre is situated in the Brunton Halls. There is usually a summer entertainment programme of variety concerts, musicals dance and drama.

Just south of the town, in the village of **Inveresk**, is an attractive group of fine listed buildings, including St Michael's Church. The gardens of Inveresk Lodge are open to the public throughout the year, and are under the care of the National Trust for Scotland. Between Musselburgh and Prestonpans is the site of the **Scottish Mining Museum** at Prestongrange. There is a visitor centre, steam locomotives and a Cornish beam-engine, plus the extra bonus of attractive views across the Forth.

8
EDINBURGH

To describe the vast range of attractions in and around Edinburgh in a single chapter is a difficult, if not impossible, task. Perhaps the best thing is to summarise some of the many things the visitor can see and do in this fine city and refer to further sources of information. Edinburgh is a city geared to the reception of visitors and you will find no shortage of literature or helpful people.

Scotland's captial city is founded on hills — volcanic plugs, the most dramatic of which, Castle Rock and Arthur's Seat, give the city its unique and splendid skyscape. From anywhere in the city centre or the surroundings you can see these strong outlines rising to dominate the view. At the centre lie the Royal Mile and Princes Street, dividing the old town and the new.

Edinburgh was originally named *Dunedin* — 'fortress on a ridge'. In the seventh century, the castle was re-fortified by the Northumbrian King Edwin, and the town was named after him as *Edwinesburg*. The modern name happily combines elements of both Celtic and Anglian origin.

As the **castle** is such a dominant feature in the city centre, and has been so important in its long history, it is right that the tour should begin there. The oldest surviving building is St Margaret's Chapel, dedicated to the wife of King Malcolm III and built in the late eleventh century. Near to it is Mons Meg, the castle's famous fifteenth-century cannon, used for many royal salutes in the past. It is not, however, the gun used daily (except Sundays) for the one o'clock time-check — an unusual signal and one that can be somewhat alarming the first time you hear it!

At the heart of the castle is Crown Square, all four sides of which hold interest. The north side is formed by the **Scottish National War**

Memorial, designed by Sir Robert Lorimer and dedicated in 1927. On the west side is the **United Services Museum**, opened in 1933. Further military mementoes can be found in the **Great Hall** on the south side of the square. Built in the early sixteenth century by James IV, it once housed meetings of the Scottish parliament, and is still used for banquets and receptions for important visitors to Edinburgh. There is a most interesting collection of weaponry and armour.

Finally, on the east side of the square are the **Royal Apartments**, including the little room where James VI of Scotland and I of England was born to Mary Queen of Scots. The view from its windows is impressive, with the castle rock dropping steeply away and the city of Edinburgh beyond. Nearby is the **Crown Room**, holding the Scottish Regalia — the crown, sceptre, sword of state and others.

The **Castle Esplanade** is the scene for the Military Tattoo held each year during the Edinburgh Festival — an event known worldwide for which tickets are sold out months in advance. There is a fine view south over the city to the Pentland Hills.

Edinburgh Castle is at the head of the **Royal Mile**, a truly historic thoroughfare. On the right-hand side, looking down, on the corner of Castle Wynd North, is a house with a cannonball embedded in the wall. The story that it was fired from the castle during the 1745 rising seems sadly not to be true — it marks the gravitation height of the water supply from Comiston Spring to Castlehill Reservoir, which sits just across the road and, with a capacity of over $1^1/_2$ million gallons, supplies the buildings of Princes Street and neighbouring areas.

On the same sides as the 'cannonball house' is the **outlook tower** and **camera obscura**. The first camera was installed over 100 years ago, but a more modern instrument replaced it in 1945 and on clear days it throws an image of Edinburgh on to a concave circular table; as it does so a commentary tells the history of some of the places depicted. There is a book and craft shop.

Just below the tower is **Mylne's Court**, originally built for the family of John Mylne, mason to Charles II. It was restored by Edinburgh University in 1971, the restoration winning a Saltire Society award, and now houses residential students. Across the road a little lower down is **Riddle's Court**. Note the turret staircase outside the building, and inside the fine painted ceilings. Nearby, Brodie's Close is named after the man whom Stevenson took as the model for Dr Jekyll and Mr Hyde — he was a town councillor by day and a burglar by night.

Lawnmarket (once Landmarket), as the name implies, was where produce was sold — milk, meat and vegetables could be bought here, and on Wednesdays a linen and wool cloth market was held. On the east side of the Lawnmarket is **Gladstone's Land**, a six-storey tenement built in 1620 for a merchant and burgess, Thomas Gledstanes. It has been restored as a typical home of the period, an added attraction being the seventeenth-century shop boots on the Lawnmarket. Gladstone's Land was one of the first properties to come into the care of the National Trust for Scotland in 1934.

Next down from Gladstone's Land is Lady Stair's Close, leading to **Lady Stair's House**, named after the widow of the first Earl of Stair. She died in 1731. The house belongs to the District Council and contains a fascinating collection of manuscripts and mementoes of three giants of Scottish literature — Burns, Scott and Stevenson.

Crossing the road to the west side, cross over George IV Bridge, completed in 1836. On the street corner are three brass plates set in the road, marking the site of the last public execution held in Edinburgh, when a murderer, George Bryce, was hanged here in 1864. Pass the statue of the fifth Duke of Buccleuch, and near the great front door of St Giles' Cathedral is the 'heart of Midlothian' — a design of cobblestones which marks the site of the **tolbooth**. Although the tolbooth was built to serve the purpose its name implies, to collect tolls, from 1640 onwards it achieved notoriety as a prison. Heads of victims of the scaffold were displayed on the north face of the building, which was demolished in 1817.

On the east side of the cathedral were the **Luckenbooths** (locked booths), built in the mid-fifteenth century to sell provisions and goods to the people of Edinburgh. They, too, fell to the demolishers in the early nineteenth century. The **cathedral** remains: St Giles, the High Kirk, church of the Knights of the Thistle. The oldest part, four massive pillars, goes back to 1120, but most of the building dates from the fifteenth century, the crown spire being completed in 1495. The Thistle Chapel, with its superb carved interior, was designed by Sir Robert Lorimer and built in 1911.

On the west side of Parliament Square is the **Signet Library**, built in 1815 for the Society of Writers to the Signet — the Scottish equivalent of solicitors and lawyers. The Upper Hall is a fine piece of interior design. This building was used for the inaugural procession of the Knights of the Thistle in 1911, and their processions still assemble there.

Parliament House was used by the Scots parliament from the time of its completion in 1639 until the Act of Union in 1707. It is a

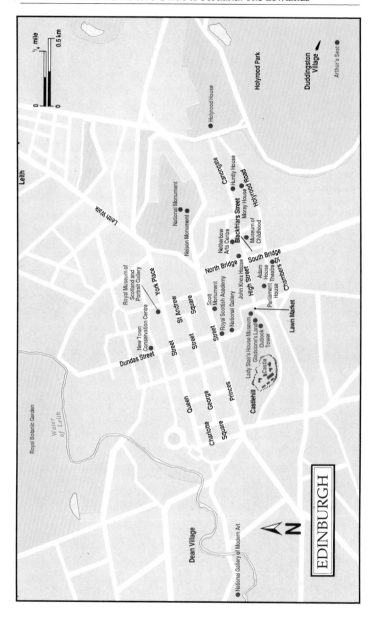

magnificent building with a hammerbeam roof and stained glass windows, still a busy place as it is used by lawyers from the adjoining courts for consultations with their clients and colleagues. The Laigh (or low) Hall was used by Oliver Cromwell as a stable. In Parliament Hall is a statue of Sir Walter Scott, who served as advocate and Sheriff of Selkirkshire for many years.

Opposite St Giles are **Edinburgh City Chambers**, where the sixty-four members of the City of Edinburgh District Council meet to conduct their business, with the Lord Provost in the chair. The building was completed in 1761, but was little used at first; it was intended to be a business exchange, but the merchants of the time preferred to conduct their business in the street! The chambers are eleven storeys high, one of the tallest buildings on the Royal Mile. In the courtyard is a statue of Alexander taming his horse Bucephalus, and within the arches facing the street are memorials to the dead of both world wars.

At the crossing of the Royal Mile and the South and North Bridges is the **Tron Kirk**, named after the weighing machine that stood on the site previously. The church was built in 1637 by order of Charles I, to house the congregation displaced from St Giles when the latter became a cathedral. The Tron Kirk was closed for worship in 1952, but it is hoped that the interior will eventually become a heritage and information centre for the city of Edinburgh.

Continuing down the west side of High Street, and crossing Blackfriars Street, you come to the **Museum of Childhood**, in Hyndford's Close. It has a large collection of historical toys, dolls, books and other items and also covers children's games, education and health. The museum was founded in 1955.

Opposite the museum is **John Knox's House**, dating from the late fifteenth century. It displays many interesting features, including its overhanging upper floors and an outside stair added in the sixteenth century. The house was saved from demolition in 1850, when the High Street was to be widened, and was then renovated at considerable expense. Knox, the great preacher, lived here from 1561 to 1572 and many items connected with him are on display.

Beside Knox's house, and contrasting nicely with it, is the **Netherbow**, the Church of Scotland's Arts Centre. Designed in the style of an Edinburgh town house, it was opened in 1972. It contains an art gallery, shop, a small theatre, audio-visual studio, and an excellent restaurant. In the street outside, brass plates mark the site of the Netherbow Port, one of the six entrances to the original town of Edinburgh. A bronze model of the port can be seen above the entrance to the Arts Centre, and inside the front gateway is the Netherbow Port Bell of 1621. The Netherbow was the point of entry for Prince Charlie in the 1745 rising.

High Street has given way to Canongate, originally a separate burgh owned by the canons of the Abbey of Holyrood. Much excellent restoration has been carried out here in recent years — note, for instance, Chessel's Court on the south side with its fine arcades.

Moray House, a little lower down, has a long history. It was built in 1628 for Mary Sutton, daughter of Lord Darnley and widow of the first Earl of Home. Charles I visited the house on a number of occasions, and Oliver Cromwell made his Scottish headquarters here in 1648. In May 1650 a party of notable people visiting Edinburgh for the marriage of Lady Mary Stuart to Lord Lorne took the opportunity to watch from the balcony the cart carrying the Marquis of Montrose passing on its way to Parliament House, where he was sentenced to death. In 1707, signatures were appended to the Treaty of Union in the gardens of Moray House. It is now a teacher training college.

On either side of Bakehouse Close, a property once owned by the Incorporated Bakers of Canongate, stand Huntly House and Acheson House. **Huntly House**, built in 1570, shows the projecting upper floors with plastered timber that were common in such buildings. On the exterior are four plaques which are said to answer criticism aroused by the building's fine architecture. One says 'As thou art master of thy tongue so am I master of my ears'. Huntly House was restored in 1932 and is now a museum of local history. Among the exhibits are a copy of the 1638 National Covenant and mementoes of the life of Field Marshal Earl Haig.

Acheson House is a little later in origin than Huntly House, dating from the 1630s. It was built for Sir Archibald Acheson, later a baronet of Nova Scotia and Secretary of State for Scotland. It was restored by Robert Hurd in 1937 and is now the headquarters of the Scottish Craft Centre. Craftwork from all parts of Scotland can be seen on display and purchased here.

Across the street is the famous **Canongate Tolbooth**, easily recognised by its large clock and turreted steeple. Built in 1591, it served as the council house and gaol for the burgh of Canongate. The clock dates from 1820 and replaced an earlier model. The tolbooth is now a museum with a collection of Highland dress and other interesting exhibits.

Next to the tolbooth is **Canongate Church**, dating from 1688. Prisoners captured by the Stuart army in 1745 at the battle of

Prestonpans were housed here. Notable people buried in the kirkyard include the economist Adam Smith, author of *The Wealth of Nations*; Mrs Maclehose, the original of Robert Burns' *Clarinda*; and the poet Robert Fergusson, whose headstone was paid for by Burns.

Approaching the foot of the Royal Mile, the gates of Holyrood Palace are ahead. On the right, before crossing Horse Wynd (which once led to the royal stables) is the **Holyrood Brewery**. Beer has been brewed here for over 800 years, firstly by the monks of Holyrood Abbey and later by the Younger family. The large brewery on the site today is owned by Scottish and Newcastle Breweries.

Holyrood Palace is the official residence of the Queen when she visits Edinburgh. The earliest parts date from 1530, but most of the building you see today was built by Robert Mylne, the king's mason for Charles II in 1671-6. Many of the state rooms are open to view when the Royal Family is not in residence. Perhaps the two finest rooms are the throne room, used for investitures, and the dining room, with its green and white Adam-style decorations. The state apartments contain French and Flemish tapestries and fine eighteenth-century furniture. When the palace is open to view, guided tours take place at regular intervals. There is a tea room in Abbey Strand.

On the south-east side of the palace, and predating it, are the ruins of **Holyrood Abbey**. It was founded in 1128 after King David I was charged by a stag while on a hunting trip in the area, which was then a forest. The king tried to grasp the stag's antlers but found himself holding a crucifix set between its horns. The crucifix stayed in his hand while the stag returned to the spring from which it had come. That night, in a dream, the king was bidden to make a House for Canons devoted to the Cross, and the Abbey of the Holy Rood (or cross) was founded as a result.

The abbey was badly damaged in the revolution of 1688. A new roof put up in 1758 was, unfortunately, incorrectly planned and collapsed not long afterwards. The abbey has changed little in appearance since that time.

Holyrood Park, which contains the palace, is a magnificent piece of open country to find in the heart of a city. It rises to 822ft at the summit of Arthur's Seat (an extinct volcanic plug), from where there are superb views in all directions, including a wonderful panorama of the city. There are coach tours around the park in summer, but for a more leisurely exploration, the walking is splendid.

On the south side of the park is **Duddingston Loch**, a bird sanctuary and nature reserve where many varieties of duck and

Edinburgh Castle

geese can be seen, especially in winter when they congregate here. **Duddingston village** has a twelfth-century church with, at its gate, 'jougs', the iron collar and chain once used to punish criminals.

Leave the old part of Edinburgh for the moment, to have a look at the 'new town' to the north of the castle, starting with the famous thoroughfare, **Princes Street**, and its fine gardens. The area between Princes Street and the Castle Rock, now occupied by the railway, was once a loch. The 'new town' was planned in 1767, following parliamentary approval for the extension of the city. It covers over 100 acres and is now a conservation area subject to strict planning controls.

The area was planned and laid out by James Craig, who was only 23 when he won the competition for the design. Perhaps the finest part of the new town is **Charlotte Square**, at the west end of George Street. The square was designed by Robert Adam in 1791. No 5 Charlotte Square is the headquarters of the National Trust for Scotland and No 7 has been opened by the Trust as an example of a house of the period; the rooms on the lower floors are furnished just as they would have been in the late eighteenth or early nineteenth century. The upper floors serve as the official residence of the Moderator of

A view over the city from Edinburgh Castle

the Church of Scotland, and No 6, next door, serves in a similar capacity for the Secretary of State for Scotland.

Returning to Princes Street, at the Mound is the **Royal Scottish Academy of Painting, Sculpture and Architecture**. Established in 1826, it has presented annual exhibitions ever since. Exhibitions run from May to August, followed by a special show for the festival in September. Nearby is the **National Gallery of Scotland**. As well as an important collection of painting by Scottish artists, there are many fine works by English and Continental masters ranging from the fourteenth century to Cézanne.

A stroll along the north side of the gardens leads to the **Scott Monument**, one of Edinburgh's best-known landmarks. It is a Gothic spire 200ft high erected in 1844 to the design of George Meikle Kemp. (A memorial room to Kemp can be seen on the outskirts of Peebles, on the A702 Edinburgh road.) In the niches of the monument are sixty-four statuettes depicting characters from Scott's books and poems. The statue of the writer himself is by Sir John Steell. The monument is open all the year round and the climb up nearly 300 steps to the top may be judged worth the effort for the views it provides. There is no shortage of good refreshment rooms nearby to revive you afterwards!

Princes Street Gardens can occupy a pleasant hour or two. As well as the fine floral displays, there is the oldest floral clock in the world, dating from 1903. Up to 25,000 flower and foliage plants are used in the display on the clock, which is changed several times a year. The hands measure 8ft and 5ft and when filled with plants weigh 80 and 50lb respectively. The quarters are marked by the emergence of a sprightly cuckoo.

Near the clock are two fine war memorials, one to the Royal Scots and the other erected by Americans of Scottish blood. Between the Ross Foundation and the open-air theatre is an eight-ton boulder from southern Norway, presented in 1978 by the Norwegian Army as a remembrance for the hospitality they received while based in Britain between 1940 and 1945. The open-air theatre stages shows and band performances during the summer and at festival time, and there are dancing sessions which the visitor is welcome to join.

Walking north from Princes Street along the west side of St Andrew Square, headquarters of banks and insurance firms, and across George Street, leads to Queen Street and the **Scottish National Portrait Gallery** founded just 100 years ago. It contains hundreds of portraits of famous Scots covering the past 400 years. In the same building is the **National Museum of Antiquities**, portraying the life of Scotland and the Scots from prehistory to the present times.

Down the hill in Dundas Street, at No 13a, is the **New Town Conservation Centre**, showing the work that has been done and is still going on, to conserve the new town. Guided walks start from here each week from May to September, and a pamphlet called *Four Walks in Edinburgh New Town* is available for sale.

To the east of Princes Street, above Regent Road, is Calton Hill, where there are several places of interest. The **Nelson Monument**, in the shape of a telescope, was completed in 1816. It is 108ft (33.48m) high and at the top is a time ball which descends each day at one o'clock GMT. The unfinished **National Monument** was designed as a copy of the Parthenon in Athens. Also here are the City Observatory and monuments to John Playfair, a noted mathematician, and the philosopher Dugald Stewart. In Old Calton Burial Ground is a statue of Abraham Lincoln.

South of High Street are further places of interest. In Forrest Road is **Greyfriars Kirk**, where the National Covenant was signed in 1638. The graveyard contains ornate tombstones and monuments to once-famous citizens of old Edinburgh. In Candlemaker Row nearby is the statue of the small dog known as Greyfriars Bobby, that stayed by the grave of its master John Grey for fourteen years. Bobby's collar can be seen in Huntly House, Canongate.

Chambers Street houses the **Royal Scottish Museum**, the **Edinburgh School of Arts** and **Adam House**, the theatre and conference hall for Edinburgh University. The Royal Scottish Museum houses collections devoted to archaeology, natural history, geology, technology, and science, with the exhibits ranging from primitive art to space travel. There are frequent lectures and films here.

On the northern edge of the city centre is the **Royal Botanic Garden** (car parking in Arboretum Road), with a very fine collection of trees and plants including superb shows of rhododendrons in season. The plant houses contain many rare and exotic plants and an exhibition hall covers all aspects of botany and horticulture. Across the road from the Botanic Garden is Inverleith Park, with a pond, children's playground, tennis courts, bowling greens and walks.

Leith Walk runs north-east from the city centre to the docks at Leith. On the way are two unusual attractions. The **Braidwood and Rushbrook Fire Museum** in McDonald Road contains a collection of uniforms, equipment and machinery associated with the fire service, and can be visited by arrangement with Lothian and Borders Fire Brigade.

Leith has served as port and dockyard for Edinburgh for centu-

A panorama of Edinburgh

ries. Cruise ships up to 35,000 tons gross can berth here, and the docks have a busy service running to the North Sea oilfields. Old buildings include **Trinity House**, dating from 1816 and **St Mary's Church**, Kirkgate, parts of which are fifteenth century. Lamb's House, a merchant's house from the early seventeenth century, was restored in 1958 and is now used as an old people's day centre. It is under the protection of the National Trust for Scotland and can be

visited by appointment —
contact NTS HQ in Char-
lotte Square for details.

The original village of
Leith began some 800 years
ago at the point where the
Water of Leith entered the
Firth of Forth. Much of the
waterway is now a pleasant
walk, the 4-mile stretch
through the city being especially interesting. The
river passes through **Dean
Village**, formerly a centre
for grain milling. At one
time there were seventy
mills on the Water of Leith,
and the measure for 1 pint
in Scotland was taken as
'three pounds Scots of water from the Water of Leith'.
Several of the old buildings
in Dean Village have been

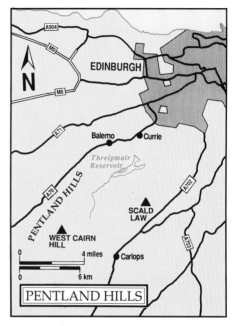

PENTLAND HILLS

restored and the riverside walk leads to St Bernard's Well, once a
favoured place for drinking mineral waters.

Follow the Water of Leith westwards out of the city, where
further upstream it passes near **Saughton Rose Garden** (on Balgreen
Road), open in the summer months. As well as the marvellous roses
there are dahlias, fine herbaceous borders, and a scented garden
developed for the enjoyment of blind people. Also near the Water of
Leith is the **Scottish National Gallery of Modern Art**, housed in a
classical building in its own grounds on Belford Road.

Off the A90, the road that leads to the Forth Bridge, is **Lauriston
Castle**, commenced in the sixteenth century by Sir Archibald Napier,
father of John, the inventor of logarithms. It has been considerably
extended, notably by the nineteenth-century banker Thomas Allan.
The castle is now owned by the city and contains fine furniture,
tapestries, and china. It is open daily except Fridays, and the grounds
include croquet lawns.

A walk south-westwards across Corstorphine Hill, a very pleasant wooded area, brings you to **Edinburgh Zoo**, open all the year and
a favourite attraction with children of all ages. The zoo covers 80

acres and its collection of animals, birds, reptiles and fishes is comprehensive. Young people are particularly well catered for at the children's zoo — almost a miniature farm, with ponies, calves, lambs, goat kids and lots of farm implements to play with.

Further west still on the A8, near Edinburgh airport, is **Ingliston showground**, where the Royal Highland Show is held over 4 days each June. The show features livestock of every kind and the recently completed exhibition hall holds machinery and other static displays. Other exhibitions are held at Ingliston throughout the year, and it also hosts regular motor racing meets for both cars and motor-cycles.

Edinburgh is especially well equipped for sport. Permanent facilities include the Commonwealth Pool at one side of Holyrood Park, and Meadowbank Stadium at the other. Both were built for the staging of the Commonwealth Games in 1970 and 1986, and both are open to visitors. As well as the Tartan athletics track, Meadowbank has indoor facilities for up to thirty different sports. A temporary membership scheme is available for visitors to Edinburgh looking for a workout on the squash courts, in the gymnasium, or at the golf driving range.

Another major facility of which Edinburgh is proud is the dry ski slope at Hillend, on the northern slopes of the Pentland Hills. It is open all year and facilities for grass ski-ing are also available. The ski tow and chairlift can be used by walkers to gain quick access to the Pentlands, from where there are splendid views over the city and the Firth of Forth.

Golfers are naturally well provided for; in Scotland's capital it could hardly be otherwise! Golf has been played in the Edinburgh area for at least 500 years and within the city boundary there are over twenty courses. Public courses can be found at Braid Hills, Carick Knowe, Craigentinny, Silverknowes and Portobello, and short-hole 'pitch and putt' courses at Inverleith Park.

There are many bowling greens, tennis courts (notably at Craiglockhart Sports Centre), and putting greens in Edinburgh. Pony-treks are organised from the Stables at Redford, Colinton. You can ice-skate at the Murrayfield Rink, watch greyhound racing at Powderhall — famous for its professional sprint races, though these are now run at Meadowbank — and enjoy boating and canoeing at Craiglockhart.

THE FESTIVAL

It would be impossible to end this brief survey of Edinburgh's attractions without mentioning the world-famous International

Festival, held over three weeks in August and early September and now the largest arts festival in the world. It includes music, opera, ballet, theatre, modern dance, poetry readings — every aspect of the arts is here. A major film festival is held concurrently with the main event; the military tattoo, already mentioned, is a notable event, and there is also the Fringe.

In recent years the Fringe has been threatening to surpass the main festival in terms of variety and number of events, if not quite in terms of quality. Up to 300 companies, amateur and professional, present shows of every possible kind in every possible setting from theatres, church halls and cinemas to the many open-air performances. Everywhere there seems to be a Fringe event happening; it is an extraordinary kaleidoscope of people and happenings, many of them apparently spontaneous.

The Pentland Hills

The Pentland Hills dominate the southern limits of Edinburgh, their long grassy slopes rising steeply to a number of prominent summits. The range stretches for some 15 miles (24km) in a south-westerly direction, and provides splendid hill-walking territory with spectacular views practically on the city's doorstep.

An attractive walk can be taken to the Bore Stane, East Cairn and West Cairn Hill, $14^1/_2$ miles (23km) in length. From **Carlops** on the A702, take the access road to the North Esk Reservoir and continue up to the Bore Stane. Bear left and ascend the slopes to the summit of East Cairn Hill, 1,839ft (561m). Descend to the pass, the Cauld Stane Slap, and proceed for another three-quarters of a mile (1.2km) to climb West Cairn Hill. Return to the pass and follow the Old Drove Road to Baddinsgill Farm. Turn left and walk down the path on the east side of Lyne Water to Stonypath. Bear left and follow the old road back to Carlops.

A 12 mile (19km) walk starts at **Currie** on the A70. Take the road past the church and proceed uphill on to the moor. Aim south-east and through the Maiden's Cleuch between Harbour Hill and Bell's Hill and descend to Glencorse Reservoir. Walk up the Logan Burn to Loganlea Reservoir and to The Howe. Continue to follow the stream, bearing right and up through the Green Cleuch between Black Hill and Hare Hill and by Bavelaw Castle. Proceed across Threipmuir Reservoir and down the minor road to Balerno. Turn right to Lymphoy and return to Currie.

9

NITHSDALE

F rom the rounded Lowther Hills in the north, which form the boundary between Dumfries and Galloway Region and Strathclyde Region, and the Solway Firth to the south, Nithsdale is a land of fascinating contrasts. On its winding journey to the sea, it is joined by swift-flowing tributaries from the Lowther Hills and the Penpont Moors. As the course of the Nith has been largely determined by the presence of basins of younger rocks, especially the Permian sandstones, it runs along a mature valley throughout its course. The Nith passes through an ever-changing countryside — a patchwork of gentle rolling uplands, wide wooded valleys, pastureland and rich coastal plains.

In northern Nithsdale, the B797 leaves the main A76 in the valley, ascends by a twisting route following the Mennock Water, and climbs the Mennock Pass to **Wanlockhead**, at 1,383ft (422m) the highest village in Scotland. This settlement, along with the neighbouring village of Leadhills, was a centre for lead mining until earlier this century. The eighteenth century saw the height of mining activity, with adits, tunnels, pumping engines, shafts, water courses, tramways and smelting mills. Mining for lead and zinc carried on until the 1930s, when the workings closed. The New Glencrieff mine was reopened in the 1950s, but closed at the end of that decade.

Wanlockhead is a unique settlement, rich in social history, with the evidence of a tremendous industrial enterprise still clearly visible. The houses of the village, many of them former miners' cottages, are set here and there without any proper planning. Today, visitors can spend a fascinating time at the Museum of Scottish Lead Mining. The visitor centre has a display of local minerals, and features outlining the history of lead mining. Visitors are taken on guided

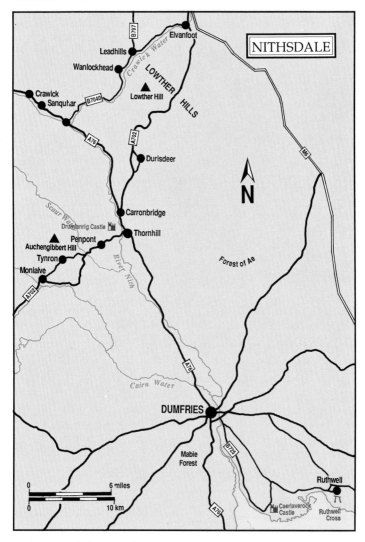

tours down the Loch Nell Mine, where a surprise tableau is suddenly revealed when extra lighting is switched on. They can also see period cottages, and walk along a visitor walkway to Pates Knowes smelt mill, part of the Open Air Museum.

Other attractions at Wanlockhead are the beam engine and the Miners' Library, founded in 1756, which was the second subscription library to be formed in Britain: the one at neighbouring Leadhills was the first.

The village of **Leadhills** lies $1^1/_2$ miles (2.4km) to the north-east along the B797. The mines, now closed, were mainly concentrated round the head of Glengonnar Water. Gold panned from the alluvial deposits was used in the Scottish regalia, and individuals still try their luck panning for gold in Shortcleugh Water. The Miners' Library was set up by the local poet Allan Ramsey (1686-1758), the son of a local lead mine manager, in 1741. The oldest circulating library in Britain, the building houses a valuable collection of eighteenth- and nineteenth-century books. At the northern end of the village is a memorial erected in 1891 commemorating William Symington, the inventor of steam navigation. In the local cemetery is the gravestone bearing the name of John Taylor, a miner, and the dates, 1637-1770. He died at the age of 133 years! There is a hotel, shop and post office, and bed and breakfast accommodation is available in the village.

The Leadhills and Wanlockhead Light Railway was opened by the Caledonian Railway Company in 1901. The line ran from the main line at Elvanfoot, and climbed to a height of 1,498ft (457m) at Wanlockhead. It closed in 1939. The line was the highest on British standard-gauge passenger railways. At the present time, the Lowthers Railway Preservation Society is planning and working on the construction of a narrow-gauge railway line on the existing track bed. It is hoped to operate a service with three stations on the $1^1/_2$ mile (2.4km) stretch between Leadhills and Wanlockhead, first with diesel and later with steam traction.

A 10 mile (12.5km) walk follows a section of the Southern Upland Way from Sanquhar to Wanlockhead. From the centre of Sanquhar walk up Leven Road and under the railway line. Climb uphill and follow the track to Dinanrig. Follow the right-hand road, and just before Bog, bear left and ascend the grassy slopes with Conrig Hill on the left. Descend to the ruined building at Cogshead by the Cog Burn. There is an alternative route from here, to avoid the April-May grouse nesting season, and during the grouse shooting season commencing on 12 August. The route goes northward above Cog Burn, heads over the north-west spur of Lawmill Knowe and swings round the valley of the Glensalloch Burn. Proceed through the forested area above Glenbuie Burn, cut round the head of Back Burn, through another patch of forest, and descend to Duntercleuch. From here the Way continues down the Wanlock Water to Wanlockhead.

For the main route, climb uphill and over the south-west shoulder of Lawmill Knowe, and proceed on a good path to the col west of Glengaber Hill. Follow the clear track down to the valley of the Wanlock Water and follow the route as above. The distance following this route is $7^3/_4$ miles (12.5km).

There is a private access road, over part of which is the line of the Southern Upland Way, from Wanlockhead to the top of Lowther Hill, 2,377ft (725m). The road is marked with coloured poles which is of considerable assistance to the walker in winter, and the upper slopes can provide fair ski-ing conditions at times. The summit is a conspicuous landmark, littered as it is by two huge golf-ball-like spheres in the area of the Civil Aviation Authority's radar station. There are extensive views from the summit across the surrounding high slopes and moorlands beyond to the Daer Reservoir. This high ground is often under cloud, often under arctic conditions, and frequently blasted by powerful winds. The area around the summit of Lowther Hill was once a graveyard for suicide cases. The distance of this walk is $3^3/_4$ miles (6km).

A $6^3/_4$ mile (10.8km) linear walk from Wanlockhead to Muiryhill follows a signposted path which ascends to the west of Stake Hill to meet the private road up Lowther Hill. After a short distance, leave the road and aim for the col between Lowther Hill and East Mount Lowther. Descend, and follow the valley of the Enterkin Burn to Glenvalentine. Continue south, climb over the spur and walk along the ridge. The way proceeds down to a minor road junction to Inglestone and beyond to Muiryhill. This is a well-known route through the hills. A party of dragoons escorting captured Covenanters was ambushed in the Enterkin valley by another band of Covenanters and some of their prisoners were released. A number of Bonnie Prince Charlie's soldiers came this way on their retreat from Derby.

Motorists can make a very pleasant circuit of the area by taking in the Mennock Pass, through Wanlockhead and Leadhills to Elvanfoot, and returning to the Nith valley by way of the Dalveen Pass, A702.

Returning to wooded, green Nithsdale down the Mennock Pass is particularly delightful when the heather and bracken on the hill slopes are changing colour. The A76 passes through Sanquhar on its way to Cumnock and Kilmarnock. The valley is open and the soil rich and red. Instead of bleak hill country supporting sheep there are now dairy farms. On entering **Sanquhar** from the south, a granite monument commemorates declarations read by two brave Covenanting leaders who challenged the king's authority. Richard Cameron was the first in 1680; he was killed a month later at the battle of Airds Moss. James Renwick was the second in 1685; he was tried and executed three years later.

Sanquhar was the original seat of the first Duke of Queensberry and was given royal burgh status by James VI. Although there is little of the castle to see nowadays, it played its part in battles against the English. The original tolbooth in the town was first used as a prison, but a handsome replacement attributed to William Adam was built in 1735 and still stands today in the High Street. Close by, with a projecting bow window, is the oldest post office in Britain dating from 1763, when a postboy service operated on horseback from Edinburgh.

From early times, coal mining was the town's livelihood, but all the mines closed down in the 1960s, and now the settlement depends on light industry established in the area. The town holds an annual Riding of the Marches ceremony in summer, the climax of its gala week.

There is a beautiful walk along the banks of Crawick Water, just outside the town. Turn right just before the clock tower on to a minor road, and proceed for approximately 2 miles (3.2km), to a small cottage called Plantainside. There is parking available here. Follow the route down through Moor Plantation to Crawick Water. There are bridges across the burn, and seats have been provided to view the surroundings.

Further south, the Nith valley narrows, and road, river and railway come together close by **Drumlanrig Castle**. This magnificent stately home built of pink sandstone is set in beautiful woodland, and is a fine Renaissance example of Scottish domestic architecture, now open to the public. The castle is built round an open courtyard, with a circular staircase tower in each inner corner. The immediate attraction is the graceful horseshoe-shaped staircase leading to the entrance hall. The interior contains richly decorated appartments, period furnishings and marvellous paintings. Drumlanrig also offers an adventure woodland play area, nature trails, picnic areas, a craft centre and tea room. A Countryside Ranger Service operates on the Drumlanrig estate, and rangers will be only too pleased to help and advise visitors. They are available to lead guided walks and school parties by arrangement. For further details ☎ (0848) 31555 or 315491.

The A76 continues south to Carronbridge, and from here the A702 leads up the Dalveen Pass to Elvanfoot. Leave the main road

Wanlockhead

$2^3/_4$ miles (4.4km) north north-east of Carronbridge, and bear right on a minor road to the village of **Durisdeer**, just over 1 mile (1.7km) ahead. The hamlet is dominated by the late seventeenth-century church, and contains the Queensberry mausoleum. The burial aisle is marble-floored, and contains a white marble canopy over the entrance to the vault of the first Duke of Queensberry. There is also a carved mural monument to the second duke and his wife. The churchyard contains the grave of the Covenanter, Daniel McMichael, shot at Lower Dalveen Farm by dragoons in 1685.

Take the track past the church for half a mile (0.8km), and then the left-hand turn when the track divides. Continue for 660yd (0.6km) to the site of an Antonine fortlet, NS 903048. The well-preserved remains lie above the line of the Roman road from Nithsdale to Clydesdale. Beyond the site the track, now called the Well Path, makes for the pass and descends to the valley of the Potrail Water.

Thornhill is an attractive village south of Carronbridge, with a wide tree-lined main thoroughfare overlooked by solid sandstone houses. A clear point of interest is the stately high column donated by the third Duke of Queensberry. Its crest carries his emblem, Pegasus, the winged horse.

Visitors may like to seek out the location of a mysterious four-teenth-century castle to the north-east of Thornhill. **Morton Castle**, NX 890 992, overlooks Morton Loch and is set against the backcloth of the Lowther Hills. Little is known about its builder, why it was built on that particular site and its subsequent history. The surviving remains consist of a two-storeyed hall block, attached to part of a turreted gatehouse at one end and to part of a large angle-tower at the other. It would appear that in its heyday the first floor had been a long and splendid room, lit by fine mullioned and transomed windows. The best point of access is from the A702 north of Carronbridge, NX 874 999, on a minor road. The castle is situated on the southern side of Morton Loch.

Just south of Thornhill is the site of Old Dalgarnock Kirkyard, with a beautiful granite cross erected in 1928 to the Nithsdale Martyrs. Fifty-seven names appear on it and a number of Covenanting families are buried here. The approach is from the B731, and the kirkyard is beyond Kirkbog Farm.

On the way from Thornhill to Moniaive, the A702 crosses the River Nith, and passes a fine tenth-century Northumbrian cross shaft in the field by the bridge. Beyond the village of Penpont, a minor road bears right to Tynron, and to the north rise the steep slopes of Auchengibbert Hill. The summit is crowned by the impressive ramparts of Tynron Doon Iron Age hillfort of the first millennium BC. In the late sixteenth century a tower-house was built on the north-west corner of the fort. Access is either to the west of the summit from the south or north-east, or from Clonrae Farm, circling round the hill to the top. It would be courteous to ask permission at the farm to view the hillfort.

The minor road continues to the attractive village of **Moniaive**, a convenient centre for the exploration of the valley of the Cairn Water, the quiet glen of Dalwhat Water, the hill roads over to The Glenkens, and beyond to the forests and mountains of the Galloway heartland. Moniaive used to be the terminus of the Cairn Valley Light Railway, opened in 1905 and closed down in 1945.

Just east of Moniaive, off the B729, is the historic fifteenth- to seventeenth-century house Maxwelton, the birthplace of Anna Laurie in 1682. The house and gardens are open to the public at certain times in the year.

Below Thornhill the Nith valley widens out again, and the river enters fine farming country, and an area associated with Robert Burns. At Ellisland Farm, NX 929 838, he made an attempt at farming by improving the ground and enclosing some fields, and had a farmhouse built by Thomas Boyd, a local architect and builder. Despite the hard life on unproductive land, and hours spent fitting out the cottage, Burns had time to create some of his famous works, such as *Tom O'Shanter*, *Auld Lang Syne* and *O, Were I on Parnassus Hill*.

The farm did not do well, so Burns decided to sell the lease and concentrate fully on his job as an excise officer. In November 1791, the family moved into a three-room apartment in Dumfries.

The farm at Ellisland, including a small museum and display, is open to visitors.

Dumfries is the regional capital, and has a great deal of character, enhanced by the River Nith. The river flows between wide banks and is crossed by two modern bridges and an old weather-worn fifteenth-century sandstone bridge. It is known as Devorguilla's Bridge, for it was at this point that the Lady Devorguilla de Balliol had the first bridge built, almost certainly of timber construction, in the thirteenth century.

Close by is the long, wide esplanade called Whitesands, once a great cattle and horse market and now a meeting place for buses and visitors to the Tourist Information Centre. From here it is just a short walk up narrow Friars' Vennel, one of Scotland's oldest streets, to the heart of the town with its busy shops and public buildings.

High Street is dominated by an attractive stone tower, the Midsteeple, which was completed in 1708, to act as a meeting place for the town council, as well as a courtroom and a prison. Stand clear and have a good look at the building, which appears to be leaning to one side. On an outside wall is a plaque denoting a table of distances, and a marker illustrating the ell — a Scottish measurement of 37in used by merchants. In fact, the Midsteeple was a focal point for cattle drovers and merchants. Nowadays it features as a centrepiece for the Guid Nychburis (Good Neighbours) festival, which combines the Riding of the Marches, and the crowning of a schoolgirl as Queen of the South.

Another prominent feature at the north end of High Street is the white marble statue of Robert Burns, Scotland's national poet, who spent the last 5 years of his life in Dumfries. The Globe Inn is approached through narrow Globe Close off the High Street, and the poet referred to the tavern as 'my favourite howff'. His punch bowl, toddy ladle and favourite armchair are preserved, but resist the temptation to sit in it, because you might be asked to pay for a round of drinks for everyone. Two small window panes in an upstairs room are inscribed with the poet's diamond stylus.

Burns died in 1796, and after a great funeral procession, he was

Drumlanrig Castle

buried in St Michael's churchyard. Eventually, friends and admirers felt that the bard's grave was totally unsuitable, and decided to launch a public subscription fund for a mausoleum. After many arguments and disagreements about the project, the domed temple-like structure was finally completed, and the poet's remains were laid in the mausoleum. In March 1834, before Mrs Burns was buried, a number of gentlemen were given permission to take out the poet's skull and made a plaster cast of it. The cast can now be seen in Dumfries Museum.

In 1987, the old town mill opposite Whitesands was converted into the Robert Burns Centre. The exhibition contains letters, manuscripts, personal belongings and relics, and the building houses a seventy-seat theatre that features an audio-visual presentation of the poet.

Other places of interest in Dumfries are the museum, which contains a camera obscura, the Old Bridge House Museum, and the ruins of Lincluden Collegiate Church on the banks of the Nith, founded in the early fifteenth century by the third Earl of Douglas. St Michael's churchyard abounds with interesting tombstones and memorials to the Covenanters who died in the 'Killing Time'. An interesting and informative booklet on the Covenanters, illustrating the Nithsdale Covenanting Trail, can be obtained from the Dumfries Tourist Information Centre.

Few tombstones of the Covenanting era were left untouched by Robert Paterson, a stone mason-cum-engraver, who spent his working life maintaining and re-cutting the memorials to the victims of the 'Killing Times'. He was the inspiration for Sir Walter Scott's *Old Mortality*. There are statues to him and his pony at Dumfries Museum and near The Holme, NX 645796, and another statue of him in Balmaclellan village.

In Dumfries, the Burns Walk may be followed along the banks of the Nith. Leave the A701 road and proceed down Nunholm Drive, where parking is available. The walk is about 2 miles (3.2km) long and is favoured by anglers and birdwatchers.

Whilst exploring Nithsdale, a journey should be made to the village church at **Ruthwell,** $6^1/_2$ miles (10.4km) east of Dumfries, to see the Ruthwell Cross. The key to the church is available at the modern house (NY100681) near the B724. This preaching cross is regarded as one of the two finest monuments of the Dark Ages in Europe, an outstanding example of Northumbrian sculpture; the other one is at Bewcastle in Cumbria. Dating from the seventh

Caerlaverock Castle

century, it stands 18ft (5.4m) high in a special apse in the village church.

The Anglo-Saxon sculptors probably used ideas from the eastern Mediterranean, as the cross is ornamented with Christian themes. The carved panels include *St John with the Eagle, John the Baptist, Christ in Glory* and *The Flight into Egypt*. The sides display vinescroll ornamentation with birds and beasts and is bordered with Anglian runes.

The B725 road runs close to the estuary of the Lochar Water, following the course of the river to Bankend, and then turning south to the solid red sandstone splendour of **Caerlaverock Castle**. Undoubtedly the finest castle in the district, it was built in the latter part of the thirteenth century and has later additions. It is the only triangular castle in Britain, with a double-towered gatehouse, fine living quarters and a water-filled moat.

Seawards, beyond the castle, lies the **Caerlaverock Nature Reserve** along the Solway Merse. The Wildfowl and Wetlands Trust has established a refuge covering many acres adjacent to the nature reserve. Every winter the entire population of barnacle geese, the largest of the native European black geese, flies down from Spitzbergen, far beyond the Arctic Circle, to the Solway Firth. Here visitors may watch not only the barnacles, but greylag, whooper and Bewick swans, oystercatchers, golden plovers and other waders. The refuge is also the home of the rare natterjack toad, which is easily recognised by the yellow stripe which runs from its nose to the rear of its body. The Trust has provided excellent facilities to view and photograph the birds, with an observatory, three towers and twenty hides.

The B725 continues north alongside the estuary of the Nith, where salmon fishermen use the huge frame haaf net standing in a line in the water. You may also be there when the tidal bore gathers momentum as it rushes up the channel. In former years, ships were able to sail up the River Nith and discharge their cargoes from North America, the Baltic and the West Indies at Glencaple and Kingholm Quay. Robert Burns worked as an exciseman in these ports.

North of Dumfries, via the A701 and left to Ae village, is the **Forest of Ae**. There are various paths in the forest, with parking facilities and a picnic site.

South-west of Dumfries, off the A710, is **Mabie Forest**, where there are several varied walks, one of which leads to the Forest Nature Reserve, with good viewpoints. There is a picnic site with car park and toilets.

10

SOLWAY COAST

Administratively, Galloway consists of the old counties of Kirkcudbrightshire (The Stewartry) and Wigtownshire, bounded on the east by the River Nith and its catchment area around the upper tributaries of the Urr Water. The Stewartry is a historical title, harking back to the time when the lands of the Douglases were forfeited in 1455, and the lordship was administered for the Crown by a steward.

A journey along the Solway coast draws together the fascinating Christian heritage of the area — its ancient remains, abbeys and castles. The long, indented coastline of Dumfries and Galloway extends from the north shore of the inner Solway Firth, round the estuary of the River Nith, to a series of bays increasing in size, and down to the Mull of Galloway, the southernmost tip of Scotland. Then north around The Rhins and Loch Ryan and on to Ayrshire.

A new heritage trail has been designated along the Solway coast westward from Annan to Stranraer. It is indicated by the blue-on-white symbol representing the Monreith Cross, one of the earliest Christian monuments in Scotland, which can be seen at Whithorn.

The Solway shores are perhaps more famous for their marshes, with sinuous channels uncovered at every low tide. There are gleaming mudflats treasured by the ornithologist and marine biologist. The wide sands of the Solway attract many who enjoy a seaside holiday, although parts of this region are not good for swimming. The eastern end of the Solway is swept by very fast tides and has ever-changing channels. Powfoot and Sandyhills Bay, Colvend, are safe at high tides, but it is dangerous to walk out over long stretches of sand to meet incoming tides.

The small village of **New Abbey** lies on the A710, 7 miles (11.2km)

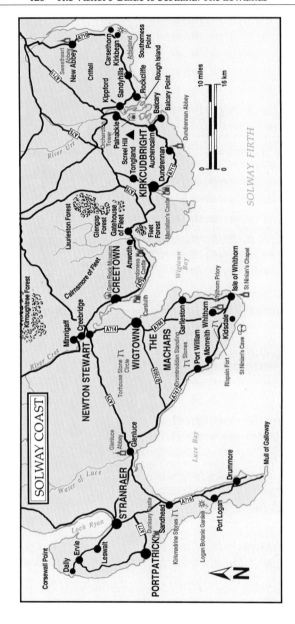

Mull of Galloway lighthouse

Sweetheart Abbey

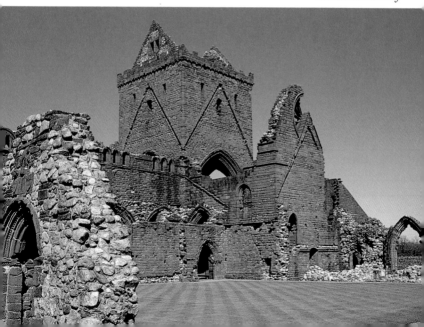

south of Dumfries. Here there is a fine water-powered corn mill from the late eighteenth century, with substantial alterations from the nineteenth century. A mill stood on the site during the Middle Ages, serving the monks at the nearby Cistercian monastery.

At the east end of the village are the impressive remains of **Sweetheart Abbey** (Dulce Cor). It was founded in 1273 by Devorguilla de Balliol in memory of her husband John de Balliol who died in 1268. It is the most romantic of the region's Cistercian houses, because of the story that she carried his embalmed heart in a casket wherever she went, and that the casket was buried with her on her death in 1290. The beautiful red stone building is of typical Cistercian cruciform shape, consisting of an aisled nave with square-ended transepts. The tower, with its battlemented parapet, contains traceried windows, and there are rose windows in the south-west gables.

Just north of the village stands Shambellie House, a Victorian mansion in the Scottish baronial style housing a Museum of Costume. Mr Stewart gave the collection to the nation in 1977, after he had spent many years gathering together items of historical clothing.

New Abbey is an excellent starting point for an ascent of Criffel 1,868ft (569m). This granite mass is a prominent landmark and there are expansive views of the Solway Firth to the south, and north north-east to the Moffat Hills.

Take the A710 south from New Abbey to the unclassified road on the right signposted to Ardwell Farm and park just before the farm entrance. This is $2^1/_2$ miles (4km) from New Abbey. Turn left to a farm track and proceed to another gate. Take the right turn just beyond and walk to the edge of the woodland. Ascend through the forest to a stile at the edge of the plantation. Head diagonally left, and climb up on a clear path to the summit. From the trig point and summit cairns, walk north for 1 mile (1.6km) to Knockendoch, and descend steeply to the south-east to the forestry fence. Return to the starting point. The walk covers $3^3/_4$ miles (6km).

Continuing along the coast road to the village of Kirkbean, a minor road leads to **Arbigland** estate, where the gardens are open to the public. It is an ideal family outing; a garden including rhododendrons and camellias, a sandy beach for the children, a toddlers play area and a tea room.

Close by lies the tiny harbour of **Carsethorn**, from which ships used to sail to Whitehaven and Liverpool. A little further south is **Southerness Point**, with one of the oldest lighthouses in Scotland. It was built in 1748-9 as a beacon by Dumfries Town Council, to guide ships in the difficult waters of the Nith estuary. Later, it was heightened and altered, closed down, and then re-opened and raised in height again. It continued operating until about 1936. Facilities for visitors include an 18-hole golf course, with fine panoramic views from the links, and the Southerness Holiday Village with a caravan and camping site. Don't forget, bathe only at high tide.

Opposite the Mersehead Sands lies **Sandyhills Bay** where there is a riding centre at Barend, a caravan park and a 9-hole golf course. A narrow road leads to Portling and Port O'Warren, where caves, once the haunt of smugglers, may be explored at low tide. At Sandyhills during the summer, you may see the Stake Nets which are in place to trap salmon with the ebb and flow of the tide.

There are some good walks in the Sandyhills, Rockcliffe and Kippford area. One of 3¹/₂ miles (5.6km) is on the Jubilee Path, which links Kippford and Rockcliffe. At the post office in Kippford turn left, climb steeply uphill and follow the signposted path to Rockcliffe. For the return journey there is an alternative route past Barons Craig into the forested area. Take the left fork, and descend down the steep path back to the post office.

From Sandyhills on the A710, walk down the lane to the sands, and westwards to the footbridge over the stream, the Fairgirth Lane. Head up to a path along the cliff edge, passing the Needles Eye, a natural rock arch on the shore below, and on to Portling. From here, follow the path above the high cliffs, passing interesting cliff formations such as the Cow's Snout. The best months to see sea birds are May, June and early July, with cormorants, herring gulls, lesser black-backed gulls, razorbills and fulmars frequenting the cliffs. On the cliff path and surrounding verges the wide variety of plants, wild flowers and gorse scrub attract small birds like the yellow hammer, linnet, whitethroat, stonechat and willow warbler. The wild flowers in turn, attract butterflies such as common blue, orange tip, meadow brown, small tortoiseshell and later on, the red admiral.

The path descends to a monument erected in memory of the schooner *The Schodner Elbe*, shipwrecked on 6 December 1866, and then climbs up to Castlehill Point overlooking the Urr estuary. Continue round the headland, down to the site of a Bronze Age fort, and along by the caravan site to Rockcliffe. This is a superb walk, with magnificent scenery and fine bird watching opportunities. You can either arrange to be picked up in Rockcliffe, or walk up to the main road, and catch the bus back to Sandyhills. The cliff path walk is 4¹/₂ miles (7.2km). **Note:** Strong boots are required, and take great care on the cliff tops.

The nearby lochs support a variety of ducks, and the rivers and mudflats have shelduck, curlews, herons and oyster catchers.

On the estuary of the Urr Water are the holiday villages of **Rockcliffe** and **Kippford**. The latter has a lively harbour and is a great yachting centre. The coastline in the vicinity offers an infinite variety of beaches, bays and inlets, some sandy, some rocky. From Rockcliffe, a signposted footpath, 550yd (0.5km) long leads to the summit of the Mote of Mark, a Dark Age defensive citadel, occupied in the fifth and sixth centuries AD. It was attacked in the early seventh century, and the main rampart was fired, causing the stonework to become vitrified.

Rough Island (NTS), is situated off the village of Rockcliffe. Access is by walking over the mud at low tide from Rockcliffe or Kippford. It is the nesting site of terns and oyster catchers, but you are asked not to visit the island in the nesting season of May and June, because it would be easy to walk on the nests in the shingle beach.

The River Urr rises in the Bogrie Hills and flows to just below Dalbeattie, becoming tidal on the outskirts of the town. From June onwards the river has a good run of sea trout and salmon through to the end of the season. There are also plentiful brown trout. The season extends from 25 February to 29 November, and permits and further information may be obtained from Tommy's Tackle Shop, Castle Douglas, or N. Parker, Dalbeattie.

The main road turns inland to cross the Urr near the granite town of Dalbeattie and then heads south as the A711. There is a caravan park at **Palnackie** with chalets, holiday caravans and facilities for touring caravans and camping. Palnackie is also the home of the World Flounder Tramping Championship. Contestants wade into the mud barefoot, attempt to feel the flat fish beneath their feet, and then spear them with a three-pronged spear.

One-and-a-half miles (2.4km), south of Palnackie and via the minor road, is the interesting **Orchardton Castle**. It is the only known round tower-house in Scotland, and can probably be dated from the fifteenth century. At one time there were a number of buildings associated with the tower lying a little distance away, most probably providing vaults, a large hall and other rooms. The occupants were able to enter the tower from the other buildings through what is now a window. The tower has thick walls, thus providing rather cosy rooms on each floor, and the tower top affords an excellent vantage point over the surrounding countryside.

The main road passes beneath the wooded slopes of Bengairn and near to the wide sandy bays of Orchardton and Auchencairn. Take the minor road from the village of Auchencairn along the edge of the bay to Balcary Bay where there is a car park. For a short walk, take the path beyond the hotel to the old tower, and on to Balcary Point, which is called Balcary Heughs. In former days this vantage point was used by smugglers signalling to boats offshore. There were many cargoes of brandy, silk and tobacco landed in the vicinity, despite the vigilance of Burns and his excisemen. Smuggling around the Solway coast was not defeated until well into the nineteenth century. The area around Auchencairn Bay is popular with bird watchers, and the best months for viewing are September to May.

Around Balcary Heughs, where there are splendid views across the bay, there are many patches of wild flowers — sea campion, English stonecrop, thrift, rock rose and ragged robin. A good time to visit is from May to early July when many sea birds nest on the cliffs, including razorbills, guillemots, kittiwakes, fulmars, herring, black-headed and the lesser and greater black-backed gulls. There is also a colony of cormorants on the rock outcrops.

A walk to Bengairn begins half a mile (0.8km) north of Auchen-cairn. Take the minor road on the left, and then second right, to ascend up through the forest to a gate. The track bears sharp right to a fork. Take the route on the left and continue past the ruins of Foresthill, through gates in the fences of sheep pastures, to the summit of Bengairn, 1,282ft (391m). The distance, returning by the same route, is 5 miles (8km).

For a longer, circular walk via Screel Hill, descend on a north-westerly bearing to a wall. Bear right past the immediate junction with another wall. Beyond, follow the wall as it turns sharp right to an old gate. Continue ahead to the large round cairn, and head right on a pleasant path to the pointed cairn, marking the summit of Screel Hill, 1,128ft (343m). The descent is via a zig zag path to the base of the rock outcrop, and then following a marked route to a wall and a tempting seat. Continue down the gated forest track to the main road at NX801545. Finally, there is a walk of $1^1/_2$ miles (2.4km) along the A711 back to the start.

The total distance from Bengairn and Screel is 7 miles (11.2km). Alternatively, the round trip, or just the ascent of Screel Hill, can be made from NX801545, where car parking is available.

From Auchencairn, the A711 heads inland, away from the coastal military training area, and passes through the village of **Dundren-nan**. The fine medieval remains of the twelfth-century Dundrennan Abbey exhibit some fine examples of medieval workmanship. It was founded as the daughter-house of Rievaulx Abbey in Yorkshire, and the later twelfth-century work closely follows the the style of architecture evident in other Yorkshire Cistercian religious houses. There are grave slabs in the chapter house and effigies in the nave and in the north transept.

'Cup and ring' marks are associated with Bronze Age people, who may have regarded them as having magical properties. In Scotland, Argyll and Galloway are the two main areas to locate these marks. There are over a hundred such sites listed in Galloway alone. The main form of pattern design is a simple cup-like depression surrounded by one or more continuous or broken concentric rings. One of the important sites is located south-east of Kirkcudbright near High Banks Farm, NX709489, in a field south-east of the farm. The farm track can be reached by minor road above Mutehill on the A711, or from the B727 east of Kirkcudbright.

The ancient town of **Kirkcudbright** is situated on the east bank of the River Dee, and is at the head of the deep sheltered river estuary. One of the picturesque points of interest in the estuary is St Mary's Isle, a finely wooded peninsula. The house on the island, now in ruins, was once the seat of the Earls of Selkirk.

Kirkcudbright, the capital of the Stewartry, was once an important seaport, well placed to trade with the transatlantic colonies; but its harbour was filled in many years ago. Close to the river is Castledykes, the site of one of the largest Scottish medieval castles. Close to the delightful public park of Moat Brae is the picturesque Greyfriar's Church. It has a notable and interesting history, first as a monastery, then as the parish church, afterwards as a school and now as an Episcopal Church of Scotland.

Close to the church are the substantial remains of MacLellan's Castle, a sixteenth-century tower-house. Despite its fortified appearance, the building was essentially a domestic one, with large windows, a number of stairs and a considerable number of heated rooms. The western part of High Street is the most ancient area of the town, with some very interesting houses. Broughton House is Georgian, with some good panelled interiors; it is now the Hornel Museum containing many of the artist's paintings.

The ancient building at the south end of the High Street is the tolbooth, the oldest portion of which was built in 1626. Look for the 'jougs', a kind of manacle to which wrongdoers could be fastened. It was at the tolbooth where the heads of the Covenanters, executed in Edinburgh, were put on display. Close to the tolbooth are several ancient houses with round 'pends', much loved by artists who draw inspiration from the old buildings and the scenery around the town. The fine building in St Mary Street houses the Stewartry Museum with an interesting, well-displayed collection of local antiquities.

The River Dee rises in the heart of the Galloway Hills and flows through Loch Dee, Clatteringshaws Loch, Stroan Loch and Loch Ken. The lower reaches of the river are excellent for sea trout and for brown trout. Salmon run from September to October and sea trout in June and August. Many of the best stretches are in private hands, but a few day permits are available from The Gun and Tackle Shop, Castle Douglas, and The Kenmure Arms Hotel, New Galloway.

Guided tours, which must be pre-booked, are arranged to the Tongland Power Station and Salmon Ladder, between the beginning of May and the first week in September. Tongland is the main control station of the enormous Galloway Hydro-Electric Scheme, built between 1931 and 1935. There is also the fine road bridge across the River Dee, built by Thomas Telford in 1804-8.

There are beautiful views from the rising ground above the town of Kirkcudbright, across the bay to the Solway, and also of the hills to the north. The countryside around is emerald green and farm-dotted, and the coast between Kirkcudbright and Gatehouse of Fleet is carved with coves and rocky promontories. This picturesque stretch of the Solway coast attracted the attention of famous novelists; Borgue was used in R.L. Stevenson's *The Master of Ballantrae* while Gatehouse of Fleet is the Kippletringan of Scott's *Guy Mannering*. John Buchan used the bleak hills of the Cairnsmore of Fleet as his setting for *The Thirty Nine Steps*.

Gatehouse of Fleet is another pleasant town full of character and surrounded by the wooded hills of the Fleet valley. Burns is reputed to have written *Scots wha hae wi Wallace bled*, in the town, and the Murray Arms Hotel will show you the room where the song was written. The town, founded as an industrial centre, is popular with visitors who enjoy its well laid out streets and spacious air. Nearby is the Fleet Oakwoods Interpretive Trail, which is a delightful way through fine broad-leaved woodland. There are other trails available, with a picnic area and Information Centre. The National Trust for Scotland property, Venniehill, is open to visitors.

The minor road leading north past the golf course heads on an attractive route into the hills towards the extensive forests of Glengap and Laurieston. Some $7^1/_2$ miles (12km), north of Gatehouse of Fleet, there are forest walks and a picnic site in the Laurieston Forest. The road continues to the village of **Laurieston**, and motorists and cyclists have the opportunity of exploring the superb river, loch and hill scenery of the Glenkens, perhaps returning via Castle Douglas. Another scenic circular route from Gatehouse of Fleet is to follow the valley of the Water of Fleet on the B796, then climb inland to follow the course of the old railway to Creetown. The return journey is on the A75 along the coastline of the Cree estuary and Fleet Bay to Gatehouse of Fleet.

The road westwards from Gatehouse of Fleet is a particularly beautiful section, passing the commanding pile of Cardoness Castle, the fascinating remains of the Cairnholy Chambered Cairns and the well-preserved, four-storeyed tower of Carsluith.

Recently installed floodlights have made fifteenth-century **Cardoness Castle** a striking landmark, a feature the laird Alexander McCulloch, would certainly not have entertained, as the fortress guards the approach to the Water of Fleet. The tower is strongly constructed to resist all but the heaviest assaults. Its features include thick stone walls, gun ports for hand-held firearms, and a stout entrance door protected by an inner iron gate or yett. The ground floor was used for storage, the main hall was on the first floor, the principal bedrooms were above the hall, and the upper two floors were taken up by lesser rooms and attics. A newel stairway in the south-east corner of the tower gave access to the upper floors.

For a short walk of about a mile (1.6km) to Trusty's Hill (NX589560), go just a short distance along the main road to the west where a minor road slants right to Anwoth. Proceed for three-quarters of a mile (1.2km) to a crossroads and the site of an old church. A track strikes east, becoming a footpath climbing to a wooded ridge. The tree cover clears, and there is a trig point bearing right marking the summit of a hill, 276ft (84m). This is an excellent vantage point for a sight of Trusty's Hill. Strike east and descend to a little glen, climbing up the other side to the ramparts of the fort. On the summit of this little hill, and with a commanding view of the valley and estuary, lie the remains of an Iron Age fort. Later on the defences were strengthened and the original fort entrance was extended. Near the southern gateway, and incised on a rocky slab, are fascinating Pictish symbols, comprising a Z-rod, a double disc, a beast, and a circle containing a human face with curved horns. These are Class 1 type Pictish symbol stones.

The **Cairnholy chambered cairns** lie on the southern slopes of Cairnholy Hill overlooking Wigtown Bay. The site is signposted from the A75, $6^1/_2$ miles (10.4km), west of Gatehouse of Fleet, at Kirkdale Glen. There is a car park at the lower site, from where there is a short walk up the farm track to Cairnholy II.

The A75 continues to hug the coastline of the Cree estuary to the village of **Creetown**, at which point the river begins to widen into

Rockcliffe

Wigtown Bay. On the way past Carsluith Castle, it is well worth scanning the estuary at the stopping point, NX485548, for at high tide, a favourite roosting spot of a large number of oystercatchers and some ringed plovers and turnstones can be seen. The Cree is another famous salmon river, and some fishermen have licences to net them at certain seasons in the estuary, using long net walls stretched on poles across the run of the tide. These stake nets are common, but the traditional method is by 'haaf' nets. These are held by men standing in line, and working their net up to their chests in the running tide.

When you reach the village of Creetown, spend some time in the Gem Rock Museum, which has a fascinating collection of gems and minerals from around the world. There are three display halls, a gemstone polishing workshop, a giftshop, tearoom and parking.

Newton Stewart lies on the west bank of the River Cree, just south of its confluence with the Penkiln Burn. Across the river is the older settlement of Minnigaff, on the old route followed by pilgrims en-route for Whithorn. Nowadays, modern travellers in the form of walkers and cyclists stay at the long-established youth hostel on the banks of the river. From Newton Stewart, routes lead north and north-east to the Carrick District of Ayrshire, the Galloway mountain heartland and the Galloway Forest Park.

Newton Stewart is a popular holiday town, consisting of a long principal street with the former town house. It does have a successful industry in the weaving of wool, particularly mohair. It is possible for visitors to visit a working mill at Creebridge, and see beautiful mohair scarves and rugs being woven. The Newton Stewart Museum has an extensive collection of historical treasures from the area. There is a Tourist Information Centre at Dashwood Square.

Three miles (4.8km) east of Newton Stewart off the A75, at Palnure, is the **Kirroughtree Forest Visitors Centre** with ample parking space. A number of well-marked walks start here, varying in distance from $1^1/_2$ miles (2.4km) to 4 miles (6.4km), including a separate bird watchers' trail.

A large area of ancient woodland, 4 miles (6.4km) north of Newton Stewart, is the location of the **Wood of Cree RSPB Nature Reserve**. It is open to the public at all times, and visitors are asked to keep to the trails which commence at the car park.

The River Cree has its source at Loch Moan in Glentrool Forest, and is joined by a number of major tributaries on its journey to Wigtown Bay. The river contains salmon and sea trout, as well as brown trout and grayling. For information concerning the availability of fishing, consult the Newton Stewart Angling Association. Permits are available from Galloway Guns and Tackle, Newton Stewart.

From Newton Stewart the main road, A75, leads westwards to Stranraer, and the A714 heads south into the large triangle of land called the Machars. This gentle part of Galloway, bounded by Wigtown Bay and Luce Bay, has none of the rugged hills or numerous lochs associated with the Galloway mountain heartland to the north. The rolling dairy farmland has witnessed many happenings since the earliest communities were established around six thousand years ago. Today, the story of these societies can be traced through conspicuous remains — grass-covered mounds, stone circles, inscribed stones, fortified settlements, abbeys, mottes and castles.

After the withdrawal of the Roman legions, this part of Galloway may have been evangelised from a diocese in England based at Carlisle. This is Ninian's country, where it is believed he established the first Christian Church in Scotland at Whithorn in the fifth century. Today, none of the early remains of the once powerful priory and cathedral of Whithorn survive, only the shell of the much-altered nave of the great twelfth-century church, which lay at the western end of the cathedral.

Before the re-organisation of local government in 1975, **Wigtown** was the county town. It had long been the capital of the area, a major burgh and a once busy port. The town grew up round a royal castle, and once possessed a great Dominican friary; the remains of both establishments have been obliterated. The ruins of the old church stand close by the present nineteenth-century church.

Today, the town's main street is flanked on either side by houses painted in different colours, impressive county buildings, and a bowling green and floral garden set in the middle of the main thoroughfare. Wigtown is widely known for the group of late seventeenth century 'Martyrs Tombs'. They commemorate the barbaric killing by drowning, of eighteen year old Margaret Wilson, and sixty-three year old Margaret McLachlan. The Martyrs' Stake on the edge of the salt flats marks the site of their execution. Three men were also hanged for refusing to renounce the Presbyterian faith in favour of the Episcopalian Church. Overlooking the town is the great nineteenth-century stone obelisk on Windy Hill erected in their memory.

Wigtown Bay is an important site for wintering wildfowl and waders, particularly oystercatchers, curlew, golden plover, and redshanks. Ducks begin to arrive from the end of August, the main species being mallard, wigeon, teal, pintail, shelduck and shoveler. Geese fly in from late November, mainly pinkfeet and greylag. They feed on the surrounding farm land during the day, and roost offshore during the night.

Secrets of the whisky distilling process are revealed on a visit to Bladnoch Distillery, situated just south of Wigtown on the A714. A guided tour explains the step by step distilling process, and ends with a taste of Bladnoch single malt — well worth a visit.

Just west of Wigtown, on the B733, is the site of Torhouse Stone Circle, NX382564, one of the best preserved sites in Britain, and the frequency of drumlins in the area provided easily-worked, rich agricultural soil for prehistoric settlers of the second millennium BC.

South of Bladnock, the B7004 leaves the A746 for a short journey to **Garlieston**. The village is set round the bay, and again the bowling green is squeezed in between the main street and the sea wall. In former days the village enjoyed a prosperous coastal shipping trade, even an occasional steamer excursion to the Isle of Man. Today, there is still excitement to be had in Garlieston, by trekking down to the Wigtown Bay Trading Post. In a huge converted grain mill is a true treasure trove of domestic delights — liquidated and salvaged household and commercial stock at great savings. Nearby are the sheltered gardens of Galloway House, first planted in the eighteenth century and open to visitors. Accessible from the gardens is a beautiful, secluded beach.

The broad main street of **Whithorn** runs between rows of houses, the centre occupied by the war memorial and parking spaces. Entrance to the ruins of the old priory, the archaeological 'dig', the museum and the visitor centre is under an archway decorated with the Royal Arms of Scotland. In early times this was the entrance which led from the main street into the monastic precinct. Today, Whithorn is a classic example of a medieval burgh with an unspoilt seventeenth- to nineteenth-century townscape.

St Ninian or Nynia arrived here in the fifth century, and is associated with the stone church, which was known as the Candida Casa, and generally translated as the White House. The name Whithorn is derived from the Old English, *hwit erne*, or White House. The gaunt ruin alongside the present parish church is part of the original great new church built in the twelfth century. In the sixteenth century, the wealth and splendour of Whithorn cathedral was

Kippford

Whithorn Priory

renowned throughout Galloway. Today, all that remains is the shell of the nave at the western end of the cathedral, which was the church in the Middle Ages. It retains some of its former richness in the shape of two finely decorated doorways and a number of tall pointed windows. All that remains of the eastern part of the cathedral is a series of vaulted rooms which formed a crypt below the church. The cloisters have entirely disappeared, and certainly many of the local farms and houses contain plundered stone from the site.

The 'dig' reveals the Whithorn story, a fascinating record of Early Christians, Anglo-Saxons and Vikings. The museum houses a fine collection of important early Christian carved stones. The Latinus stone, of the fifth century, is the earliest Christian memorial in Scotland. There are at least five examples of eighth- and ninth-century Northumbrian sculpture, and others belonging to a period of Viking or Anglo-Norse domination in the surrounding area, beginning in and progressing from the early tenth century.

A short distance to the south-east is the picturesque harbour of the **Isle of Whithorn**. It is not really an island now, but a small fishing port sheltered by a headland, popular with holidaymakers, and a fine centre for sea angling. From the car park at the harbour, signposts direct the visitor to St Ninian's Chapel. Long a place of pilgrimage, the small ruined chapel dates from AD1300. It was probably built to serve pilgrims travelling by sea to visit St Ninian's shrine at Whithorn. Many of the existing dressed stones were taken away by local inhabitants, particularly from its doorway and windows.

From the Isle of Whithorn, take the A750/A747, and then turn left down an unclassified road to **Physgill**. Follow the signposts from the car park at Kidsdale Farm and along the footpath down the wooded dell to the sea. Bear right, and walk along the stony strand to St Ninian's Cave, probably the secluded place to which St Ninian came for peaceful meditation. A number of cross-incised slabs in the Whithorn Museum came from this cave. The walking distance there and back is nearly 2 miles (3km).

There are two other interesting sites in the area. One is Rispain Fort, NX429399, which has a massive rectangular ditch with rounded corners, and inner and outer ramparts, and was probably a first/second century AD fortified homestead. The other is at Drumtroddan, where slabs of rock bearing cup and ring carvings, along with some standing stones, can be found.

From the Isle of Whithorn, the exposed nose of Burrow Head juts out into the sea, and the coastline with its fine cliff scenery streams away to the north-west, uncluttered by habitations, until the cliff-sheltered sandy bay at **Monreith** is reached. Look out for the otter memorial to Gavin Maxwell, the writer, who was a native of the area. The Luce Bay Shore Centre has interesting displays relating to the coastline. There are two beaches at the foot of cliff paths at Monreith village, and two beaches beside the golf course. Close to these latter beaches is the old chapel of Kirkmaiden, which is possibly the very first home of the Monreith Cross, now in Whithorn Museum.

The A747 refuses to part company with the shores of Luce Bay, but is checked for a few moments by the pleasantly situated seaside village of **Port William**, which is mostly set round the little harbour. The road quietly continues without interruption, keeping the sea alongside and affording lovely views across the bay to the raised outline of The Rhins and the Mull of Galloway. Almost reluctantly, it climbs inland by the Cock Inn and neighbouring caravan site to avoid the headland of the Mull of Sinniness. Auchenmalg Bay, below the Cock Inn, was a favourite landing point for smugglers; so much so, that a barracks was built to house fifty men and an officer to assist in the patrolling of that stretch of coastline.

Glenluce, situated close by the Water of Luce and straddling the A75, is the gateway to the remote open landscape of The Moors.

From here, adventurous motorists can tackle a variety of minor roads; one, for example, keeps British Rail's only line in the area company, as road and rail snake northwards over the lonely countryside.

Glenluce Abbey lies 1 mile (1.6km) north of the village close by the Water of Luce. The monastery dates from the thirteenth to the fifteenth centuries, and was founded as the daughter house of Dundrennan. There are only slight remains of the abbey church, but part of the east range was rebuilt in the fifteenth century, including the chapter house. The capitals of the doorway bear interesting carving, and the room is roofed with a ribbed vault supported by a central columned pier. The water supply system, with earthenware pipes and junction boxes, is very interesting and important. The abbey is under the care of the Historic Buildings and Monuments, Scottish Development Department and the National Trust for Scotland. For visitors interested in things mechanical, there is the Glenluce Motor Museum, with a display of vintage, classic cars and motor cycles.

Leaving behind the lowland area between Luce Sands and Loch Ryan, the long indented coastline of Dumfries and Galloway terminates in the knobbly peninsula of The Rhins. At the finger tip, the Mull of Galloway, bold cliffs point towards England, Ireland and the Isle of Man. Here, a lighthouse keeps watch over the area where nine tides meet.

The A715 passes two caravan and camping sites overlooking Luce Sands. From these locations the view looks out across the bay to the Machars and south to the Scares Rocks, the haunt of sea birds. South of the village of **Sandhead**, with its magnificent stretch of sandy beach, a minor road leads inland to the nineteenth-century burial chapel of Kirkmadrine, NX080483. On display in a glass-fronted recess, is a collection of the oldest Christian monuments outside Whithorn. Three of the stones date from the fifth century, and all have inscriptions in good Roman lettering. One stone, with a thicker encircled cross, has the message *Initivm et Finis* (the beginning and the end).

The A716, which passes close by Ardwell Gardens (open to the public), keeps a low profile close to the coastline until it reaches **Drummore**, the most southerly village in Scotland. It lies in a sheltered position at the foot of rising ground with fine views out to sea. From there the B7041 takes over for the final part of the journey, rising towards the tip of the peninsula. Close-cropped grass verges accompany you on the gentle climb to the lighthouse, which occupies a most impressive position at the end of a rugged promontory. On a clear day, the scene is truly magnificent, with views across to

St Ninian's Cave, Whithorn

Kintyre, Carrick, The Machars, Stewartry, Ireland and the Isle of Man. The lighthouse, built by Robert Stevenson in 1828, is 60ft (18m) high and is permanently manned.

Moving northwards, the exciting windswept western coastline of the Rhins of Galloway peninsula is a scenic mixture of clifftops and small bays. **Port Logan** is a peaceful spot, with a pleasant picnic area by the harbour. On the pier-head stands a sturdily-built lighthouse tower with a stone-slabbed conical roof.

At the north end of the bay is the famous Logan Fish Pond, originally created to provide the Logan Estate with fresh fish. The pond is a natural pool hollowed out from the rock, with an iron grill which allows the tide to enter and keeps the fish in. It is normally stocked with cod, pollack, coalfish, sea perch and plaice. In time the fish become very tame and can be fed by hand.

The Logan Botanic Garden lies a little way to the north via the B7065. The mild climate of the area and its proximity to the warming influence of the Gulf Stream has enabled a fine collection of plants from temperate regions of the world to be grown out of doors. There are magnificent rhododendrons, cabbage palms, tree ferns, a peat garden and a woodland area.

Fishing boats at Kirkcud-bright

From Sandhead, a twisting route via the B7042 and the A77 brings the visitor to **Portpatrick**. This neat seaside town is set around a steeply curving bay, protecting the picturesque harbour with its rocky entrance. In the mid-nineteenth century it had great hopes of being part of the official sea route to Ireland. Unfortunately, despite the expenditure of large sums of money on harbour improvements, and the advent of the railway, the project

Logan Gardens, Mull of Galloway

failed due to the coming of the steam packet, and the more sheltered harbour in Loch Ryan.

Today Portpatrick is a popular seaside resort catering for summer visitors, with many facilities such as guest houses, caravan and camping sites, and two golf courses. There is a small sandy beach, sea angling, and the 'Little Wheels' exhibition, a nostalgic toy transport and model railway display — a fascinating experience for all ages! There are exhilarating cliff walks in the area, for example, to the spectacular location of Dunskey Castle, perched on the sea cliff half a mile (0.8km) south of the town. Built in the sixteenth century, it has a superb defensive setting on a rocky promontory protected by steep cliffs on three sides. Access is via the cliff-top footpath which ascends from the old quarry at the south end of Portpatrick harbour.

Portpatrick is the starting point for the challenging Southern Upland Way, a long distance walking route of just over 200 miles (326km) across southern Scotland to the North Sea. The first section, from Portpatrick to the A764 via Killantringan lighthouse, makes an enjoyable walk of about $3^3/_4$ miles (6km).

North of Portpatrick, many narrow minor roads criss-cross the area, and it is well worthwhile exploring these quiet ways, where there is a different view round every corner. Go along the road past **Lochnaw Castle**, an early sixteenth-century tower house with nineteenth-century extensions which was the ancestral home of the Agnews, for a glimpse in season of the banks of magnificent rhododendrons. A short walk through the varied and charming woodland environment of **Aldouran Glen** near Leswalt is also enjoyable. It is preferable to park near to Glenhead Farm, NX006635 and walk towards Leswalt on the south side of the stream. Or follow the B78 north from Leswalt, ignoring the turning to Ervie and turning right. At the next junction bear left, and then first right, passing Knocktimm Farm. This road leads down to **Dally Bay**. The area is rich in bird life. Herring gulls, oystercatchers and cormorants can be seen. A walk of about $1^1/_2$ miles (2.4km) extends north from Dally Bay over fine coastal scenery and returns to the starting point. Further north, the lanes begin to peter out as they come towards the end of the land. But, a final excursion can be made, to **Corsewall lighthouse** at the head of the peninsula. Designed by Robert Stevenson, it was built to aid navigation to the Clyde. The lighthouse is permanently manned, and can be toured if the light keeper is available.

Returning towards Stranraer, a pleasant time can be had browsing around the **Soleburn Garden Centre** at Leswalt before the next part of the journey into Galloway's mountain heartland.

11
GALLOWAY FOREST PARK

S tranraer is the chief centre at the foot of Loch Ryan. Created a
burgh in 1596, it was originally a port and market town for the
rich agricultural region of the Machars and the Rhins. The town has
benefitted from a highly successful shipping trade to Ireland; it is
linked by rail to the north, and by the Euro-road, the A75, to the east.
Major airports are situated at Prestwick Scotland and Glasgow Abbotsinch. Stranraer is growing as a tourist centre too, and extensive
amenities have been provided, such as a leisure centre, paddling,
swimming and putting facilities, and a marine lake enclosed by a sea
wall. The area around the old castle has been cleared, colourful
flower beds set out, and seats provided.

The three-storeyed castle, with a parapet wall-walk and angle
turrets, was built around 1500 by the Adairs of Kinhilt, with modifications in the nineteenth century when an extra storey was added.
During that century, the castle saw service as a courtroom, a criminal
and debtors' gaol and a police station. It will soon be put to another
use — that of a visitor centre for the town.

Stranraer's livelihood suffered when the shoals of herring de-
parted from Loch Ryan, but its prosperity revived when the town
became the Scottish link in the Irish steam packet and ferry service.
This is a very important factor in the town's economy today, and
there are regular sailings from Loch Ryan to Larne. Sealink operate
a service from Stranraer to Larne and P&O Ferries sail from
Cairnryan to Larne. Both services take vehicles and passengers.

Stranraer Old Town Hall in George Street is now the local
museum, and to the west of the ferry terminal is Agnew Park, which
has a memorial to those who died when the ferry Princess Victoria
sank in January 1953. There are some interesting nineteenth-century

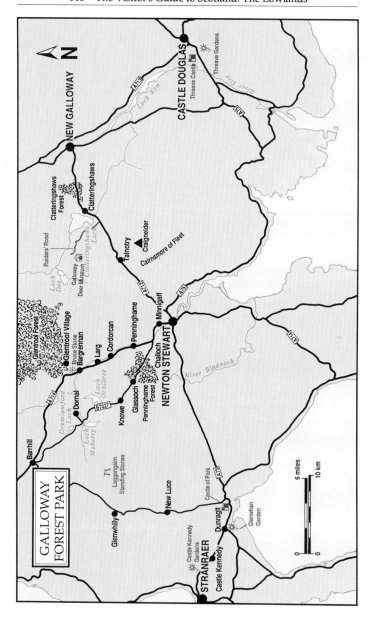

hotels in the town, particularly the imposing North West Castle Hotel, close to the ferry terminal, which was the home of Rear Admiral Sir John Ross (1777-1856), who searched the Arctic waters of Canada for the North-West Passage.

Just to the east of Stranraer are two places of interest that should certainly be included in a visit here: the Meadowsweet Herb Garden at Soulseat, and Castle Kennedy Grounds and Gardens. For the **Meadowsweet Herb Garden**, proceed along the A75, and turn right half a mile (0.8km) beyond the turning off the A751. The house is situated on a tongue of land in Soulseat Loch, and the gardens contain over a hundred types of herbs in individual beds.

Return to the main A75 and turn right. Proceed for half a mile (0.8km) and bear left, where the entrance to **Castle Kennedy Gar-** **dens** is to be found three quarters of a mile (1.2km) along the minor road to New Luce. The gardens lie in an attractive wooded setting, on an isthmus between Black Loch (Loch Crindil) and White Loch (Loch of Inch); a canal connects the two lochs. The ruin of Castle Kennedy lies at the eastern end of the isthmus, and Lochinch Castle can be seen in the parkland on the northern shore of White Loch.

Lochinch Castle is the home of the Earl and Countess of Stair, and was built in 1864 to replace the old Castle Kennedy, which was accidentally burnt down in 1716. The high ruined walls of the old castle stand close by the entrance to the gardens, which were laid out by the second Earl of Stair. He landscaped the grounds round the old castle, inspired by the gardens at Versailles. They are formal in style, with avenues which converge on a giant lily pond.

The castle, which is not open to the public, is surrounded by formal gardens, lawns and gravel paths. There is a sunken garden containing many species of tender plants and examples of large Eucalyptus trees. Visitors may take advantage of a choice of walks round the grounds and gardens.

From Castle Kennedy there is a choice of routes into the area known as The Moors, either turning left and taking the minor road to New Luce, or continuing eastwards down the A75, where there is an opportunity to visit **Glenwhan Garden** at Dunragit. This is a hilltop garden with spectacular views over Luce Bay. Numerous varieties of trees, shrubs, rhododendrons and azaleas grow in a natural landscape round two small lochans. The garden is signposted off the main A75 at Dunragit.

Just before Glenluce, an access track turns sharp left just before the main road goes under the old railway viaduct, and ascends to the tree-fringed **Castle of Park**. The sixteenth-century laird's house has been beautifully restored. Points of interest are the steep roofline, chimney stacks, crow-stepped gables, and the inscribed panel above the entrance door.

The rough triangle of countryside from Glenluce, northwards along the valley of the Water of Luce and the Cross Water of Luce to Barrhill in Carrick, south along the line of the A714 to Newton Stewart, with its base in the south bounded by the A75, is an area of outstanding natural beauty and interest. In the west, the twisting moorland road from Glenluce follows the railway northwards to Barrhill. There was a station at Glenwhilly, but it is now closed. The Portpatrick-Girvan railway, opened in 1877 and now running from Stranraer, is spectacular, particularly the Pinwherry-Pinmore-Girvan section. The next station north of Stranraer is **Barrhill** (see p168), which can be used by walkers as a starting point from which to explore the area east towards Glentrool Forest, and south towards the moorlands traversed by the Southern Upland Way. This remote countryside is a canvas of heather moors, afforestation, rough bent grasses, bracken-encroached old intakes, frisky burns and rushing rivers. The area is criss-crossed by ancient tracks and paths, and only two minor roads, the B7027, Barrhill-Challoch, and the unclassified route, Glenluce-Tarf Bridge-Glassoch, dare to cross its lonely interior. It was not always so, as indicated by much evidence of human impact on the landscape. During neolithic and Bronze Age times, when the climate was warmer, this upland region was colonised by people who found the area drier and more suitable than the dangerous, tree-choked valleys and lower slopes. Evidence of their occupation comes in the form of hut circles, standing stones, cairns, chambered cairns, dykes and defensive settlements. In medieval times, the ancient paths and tracks were followed by pilgrims en route to worship at St Ninian's shrine at Whithorn. They would pass the **Wells of the Rees**, NX229723, which are three domed drystone structures, $3^1/_2$ft (1m) high, each with a recess for a statue of the saint or of the Virgin, watching over a source of fresh water.

To the west of the Wells was a chapel site in an enclosure, and an example of a pagan holy place re-used for Christian purposes is the site of the **Laggangairn Standing Stones**, NX222716. These two prehistoric monoliths were inscribed with a cross, together with four small crosses at the angles. They were probably used by pilgrims as wayside crosses, or even as one of a series of Stations of the Cross.

Walkers may wish to strike off across the moorland from the Southern Upland Way to visit **Linn's Tomb**, NX243725. This is another Covenanting monument, a well-maintained, walled structure which has been restored from time to time. A rose bush grows inside the tomb. Every 3 years, a religious service is held at this spot.

This sparsely populated area is a challenge for hill walkers. The open, bleak terrain, devoid of clear landmarks, with afforestation and very wet sections, demands good map and compass skills.

Motorists can enjoy the triangular round trip by visiting historic Glenluce Abbey (see p 141) and the attractive waterfall and gorge called the Loups of Barnshangan, NX193651, accessible by track from New Luce; close by are the Caves of Kilhern, NX198644, a long cairn with four or five chambers and a passage. From Barrhill the twisting, up and down B7027 road to Newton Stewart passes several lochs containing numerous islands — Lochs Drumlamford, Nahinie, Dornal, Maberry, Fyntalloch and Ochiltree. The two larger islands on the latter may be crannog and castle sites. The isolated hamlet of **Knowe** once consisted of a school, a post office, a public house — The Snap Inn — and a corn mill. The little community had a nucleus of occupations that catered for all the needs of the inhabitants and of the farmers in the locality. In 1851 they included blacksmiths, a hand-loom weaver, a stone waller, and a miller. Today it is a useful stopping place for Southern Upland Way walkers on the long section of $17^1/_2$ miles (28km) from New Luce to Bargrennan. Overnight camping and bed and breakfast accommodation is available, and food is for sale at the building on the right, which was the old Snap Inn.

The River Bladnoch has its source at Loch Maberry, and flows in a south-easterly direction meeting a major tributary, the Tarf Water, and entering the sea at Wigtown. The river carries brown trout, sea trout and salmon. However, there are restrictions for most of the river; no worm fishing before 1 April and fishing for salmon is not allowed on Sundays. Permits are available from The Sports Shop, Newton Stewart, and day tickets are obtainable from The Tarf Hotel, Kirkcowan, and from Corsemalzie House Hotel, Port William. This hotel also has some free fishing for residents.

At Glassoch, visitors on wheels may like to turn right on to the unclassified road to Glenluce, probably the best bet if they don't mind forgoing Newton Stewart, and the hell-for-leather A75 Euro-Road. This delightfully peaceful route passes through wide stretches of afforestation, and close by an enchanting trio of lochs.

Returning to the B7027, the stretch between Glassoch and Challoch on the Newton Stewart road is the area for the Penninghame Forest Walks. The Forestry Commission own a number of lochs in this part of the country, and three of them, Loch Eldrig, NX 353667, and the neighbouring small stretches of water, the Garwachie and

Castle Kennedy

Spectacle Lochs, NX350689, can be fished for pike, perch, tench, roach and rudd. Day permits may be obtained from the Caldons Campsite, Glen Trool.

Extensive afforestation, often very tightly packed, covers the lower slopes of many of the higher Galloway hills. Much more forestry has been introduced on these thin, wet peaty soils, than on the more easterly rolling hills of the southern uplands. The Galloway Forest Park is the second largest forest in Scotland; in fact forests now cover some 24 per cent of the land area of Dumfries and Galloway.

From Newton Stewart the A712 road leads to New Galloway, while there is a choice of route northwards to Glen Trool, either on the A714, or by a leisurely and more verdant approach along the east bank of the River Cree. Above **Minnigaff**, there is an opportunity to stop off at the RSPB reserve at Wood of Cree, and follow the trail through the woods and past a number of attractive waterfalls in rocky gorges. The minor road hugs the forest edge before it crosses a river and enters the vast area of woodland to meet the bridge over the Water of Minnoch. This is an attractive parking area, with a picnic site and the start of a forest walk. Travelling on the main road from Newton Stewart, turn right at Bargrennan, passing the House O'Hill

Hotel, a comfortable stopping place for Southern Upland Way walkers, past the Merrick Caravan Park, to the forestry village of **Glentrool**. It has a school, shop/post office, and the Western SMT buses call here on the Newton Stewart to Girvan service.

The narrow road, which continues all the way up to the loch, gives a journey of sheer delight. The long narrow loch is overlooked by craggy hillsides and slopes clothed with a mixture of deciduous and coniferous trees. In fact, the deciduous woods fringe the road  and soften the impact of the larch and spruce right up to the car park. There are toilet facilities here, and a path leading up to the Bruce Stone, for an all-embracing view of the glen and surrounding hills. A most beautifully sited caravan and camping site has been established at Caldons by the Forestry Commission at the south-west end of Loch Trool.

The Forestry Commission has established a way-marked trail of $4^1/_2$ miles (7.2km), around Loch Trool, which can begin from Caldons or the Bruce Stone. It is recommended that stout shoes or boots are worn, as parts of the walk are rocky and muddy. The Commission's forest walks and trails are well way-marked, interesting and mostly suited to the walking abilities of the whole family. Excellent

Black Loch, Castle Kennedy

Highland cattle in Glen Trool

descriptive leaflets on the walks are available from Forestry offices, tourist offices and camp sites.

The A712 road from Newton Stewart to New Galloway, has a number of attractions to be enjoyed as it journeys through the forest. This is the Queen's Way, and at Talnotry, some $6^1/_2$ miles (10.4km) from Newton Stewart, car parking and picnic areas, a caravan and camping site, and forest trails can be found. Some good views of waterfalls, particularly after a downpour, may be obtained by walking the forest trails here.

On the hillside opposite the campsite is the monument to Alexander Murray. Born close by, this shepherd's son, who lacked formal education and suffered from continuous ill health, rose to become a Doctor of Divinity, and later Professor of Oriental Languages at Edinburgh University. This famous linguist died in 1813 at the age of 38 years.

Just beyond the monument is the wild goat park, NX498720. A number of areas in Galloway still have herds of feral goats, and as these animals damage young trees, a number have been captured and then set free in a prepared enclosure. Several of the shaggy, long-horned goats can usually be seen from the road, although they do blend in well with the rock and heather of the hillside. Further east along the A712 at NX518733, is the deer park. Roe deer are common in all the Galloway forests, while red deer can be seen in the central hill region, as well as in many of the forests and around their fringes.

During the summer months, the **Raiders' Road Forest Drive** is open on payment of a small admission charge. From the A712, opposite the Clatteringshaws Loch Dam, the track enters the forest alongside the Black Water of Dee, NX547752. This ancient road is reputed to be the route taken by cattle thieves, who used it to drive the rustled beasts into the fastnesses of the surrounding hills. Samuel R. Crockett, the Galloway novelist, was born not far away, and used the area as the setting for his novel *The Raiders*.

The old drove road passes through the forest where the Sitka spruce is king, although the Forestry Commission has planted broadleaved trees wherever possible to enhance the surroundings. The route accompanies the Black Water of Dee; there are picnic spots, regular stopping places, such as the picturesque otter pool, and points where short walks can be undertaken. The way swings round Stroan Loch, and continues on up to the A762 Tongland Bridge to New Galloway road. This is an excursion which should not be missed, as it affords an opportunity of experiencing a remote area, and being able to view its animal, plant and bird life. The distance from Clatteringshaws to the A762 is 10 miles (16km).

The **Galloway Deer Museum**, NX551763, overlooks Clatteringshaws Loch. The waters of the Black Water of Dee were impounded to create a storage reservoir for the Galloway Hydro-Electric Scheme. The museum is well worth visiting, for the Forestry Commission has set out interesting and informative displays relating to forest management, archaeology, geology, ecology and wildlife. Near to the museum, there is the reconstruction of a Romano-British homestead from around AD200-300. Just a short walk to the north there is a picnic area overlooking the loch, and close by is the site of another Bruce's Stone, NX552769. This one is in the care of the National Trust of Scotland, and it celebrates a victory gained near here by Robert Bruce, or by his brother, over the English in 1307.

After a journey down the A713 through the Glenkens, past the string of lochs and the river system associated with the Galloway Hydro-Electric Scheme, there are two items of interest for the visitor just outside the town of Castle Douglas. Impressively situated on an island in the River Dee are the very well preserved remains of **Threave Castle**. The fortress was the ancestral home of the Black Douglases, the most powerful of the Scottish nobility, whose ambi-

Glen Trool and the Bruce Memorial Stone

tions frequently clashed with the early Stewart kings. The castle, now under the care of the Historic Buildings and Monuments, Scottish Development Department and the National Trust for Scotland, includes the most complete medieval riverside harbour in Scotland. Access is from the A75, $1^3/_4$ miles (2.8km) west of Castle Douglas. Turn right to Kelton Mains Farm where there is a car park. A footpath of half a mile (0.8km), leads to the river jetty, from which a small boat ferries visitors to the island.

A short distance to the south are the **Threave Gardens**, created by the National Trust for Scotland and now a teaching garden. It is internationally recognised for its collection of plants and imaginative layout. There is an old walled garden, glasshouses, peat and woodland gardens, rose garden, herbaceous beds and borders, heath garden and formal garden. Threave Garden is 1 mile (1.6km) west of Castle Douglas, and is well signposted from the A75.

Walking in the Galloway Hills

Although the Galloway Hills lack the rugged nature of the Highlands, they are still wild and fairly remote. For the walker, the area represents a varied canvas of hills, rocky bracken-strewn slopes,

154

forests, lochs, and numerous rivers and burns. Clear paths in the area are few and far between, with the exception of the trail around Loch Trool, the path to Merrick and the Southern Upland Way to Loch Dee and Clatteringshaws. This cannot be stressed too strongly with regard to the care taken in the preparation for the hill walk and the equipment needed. A lovely sunny day might tempt you to go on to the hills in shorts and tee shirt, or jeans and sandals — but resist the temptation. Those inexperienced in mountain walking cannot comprehend the extremes of temperature and wind velocity between those met in a sheltered valley, and those at over 2,000ft (609m). A journey which is straightforward in fine weather ceases to be so if bad weather sets in or the mist descends. It is a good idea to leave details of your intended route with the police, hotel, landlady, camp warden, neighbour or friend.

This walk to Merrick, 2,770ft (843m) leaves from the higher car park north of the Bruce Stone in Glen Trool. Follow the attractive Buchan burn and go through forest to Culsharg. Bear slightly left and up to a forestry track. Cross the bridge, turn left, and ascend on a clear path to the slopes of Benyellery. On reaching a wall, head right to the summit of Benyellery, 2,360ft (719m). Follow the dyke (wall) for a short distance, then head for the cairn and trig point on the summit

Clatteringshaws Loch

of Merrick. A tremendous all-round view of the magnificent scenery is the reward.

Your basic equipment should be:
Good hill-walking boots with moulded rubber soles.
Windproof and waterproof anorak or cagoule.
Thick corduroy or woollen trousers or breeches, not denim jeans.
Woollen socks.
Simple first-aid equipment, and whistle.
Overtrousers, anklets or gaiters.
Spare woollen clothing, hat or balaclava, gloves.
Comfortable rucksack.
OS map and compass, and know how to use them.
Spare food and clothing.
A bivouac bag or large plastic sack could save your life in an
    emergency.
In winter, hot soup or hot drink in a flask.
An ice-axe could be your best friend.

For safety on the hills, follow the Mountain Code:
Think carefully before you go alone.
Leave written word of your route with someone responsible.
Plan within your capabilities.
Know the local weather forecast.
Watch the weather and adjust your plans wisely.
Be properly equipped.
Know how to use map and compass.
Know the mountain distress signal — six regular whistles/flashes a minute, repeated at one-minute intervals.
Know simple first-aid and the symptoms of exposure.
East a little from time to time to maintain energy.
Keep alert all day.
In the event of accidents or emergencies, locate the nearest telephone and dial 999, asking for police.

A descent can be made via the same route, but an alternative way is to descend on a south-easterly bearing to the south-west corner of Loch Enoch. Follow the fence past the Grey Man of Merrick, an outcrop of rock shaped like a face, or if wet follow the wall to the gate in the forestry fence. Continue along the forest ride crossing the Gloon Burn. Proceed on through the woodland to a track and on to the bridge. Turn left down the path to Culsharg, and thence to the start of the walk. The distance of this walk is 9 miles (14.4km).

A splendid, round trip hill walk can be taken to Lamachan, 2,350ft (716m) and Curlywee, 2,212ft (674m), among the most rugged of the Galloway range. From the car park by the Water of Trool in Glen Trool, walk towards Caldons camping area. Do not cross the bridge into the camp site, but continue alongside Caldons Burn, crossing a track and climbing gradually through the heather. A short distance beyond a forest ride, cross the Mulmein Burn at a convenient point, proceed across to the wall and walk by it for half a mile (0.8km) to a fence which crosses the path. Cross the fence, negotiate a way over the burn and head up the slopes of Cambrick Hill to the top. Walk towards the large cairn on the summit of Lamachan. Head eastwards, following the line of old iron fence posts to Bennanbrack; turn right and follow the posts down to the Nick of Curlywee. Cross the wall and climb steeply up to the summit of Curlywee. There is another magnificent view encompassing several lochs, the Cairnsmore Hills, Merrick, the Kells and Dungeon ranges. Descend to the White Laggan bothy keeping to the left of the Well Burn. The return is along the Southern Upland Way track round Loch Dee. Continue to the end of the track, and bear right following the Southern Way signpost, on the path alongside Glenhead Burn. At the next stile and marker post, follow the path through the forest to a track. Bear right, and keep to the forest trail back to the campsite and the Water of Trool car park. This walk covers a distance of 11 miles (17.6km).

If you want a change from hill walking, take the minor road towards Straiton to visit **Palgowan Farm**, NX373833, which is 4 miles (6.4km) north of Glentrool village. This working hill farm of 7,000 acres offers a guided tour round the farm, with many items of interest, such as, sheep handling, horncraft, stone dyking (walling), walking-stick making and skin curing. The all-in admission price includes tea and biscuits and the conducted visits last for approximately 2 hours.

The view from Merrick towards Loch Enoch

Bargrennan, Glen Trool Forest

White Laggan bothy

Loch Dee and the Rhinns of Kells, on the Southern Upland Way

The Southern Upland Way

This long distance footpath, officially opened in 1984, is the first official route in Scotland to run from coast to coast, and goes from Portpatrick on the west coast to Cockburnspath near the east coast. As the prevailing winds normally blow from west to east, the usual procedure is to walk that way, but this is a matter of choice. However, it should be pointed out that the western half of the walk is the more difficult of the two, crossing higher hills and exposed moorland.

The line of the long distance walk lies wholly within the area of southern Scotland covered by this book. It winds through Dumfries and Galloway Region and Borders Region, and passes through many of the districts previously mentioned. The Way is defined by distinctive waymarkers, often tall wooden posts bearing a thistle logo, and in certain places they have arms pointing along the direction of the route. It is possible, therefore, to join the Way at many points throughout the Southern Uplands of Scotland.

It is a tough challenge to any walker, bearing in mind the remote nature of the terrain, for there is bleak moorland lacking in landmarks, rolling hills and forested areas, so that planning and careful preparations are most necessary. This means taking into consideration such things as weather conditions, accommodation, transport, food supplies, and the availability of emergency accommodation if tiredness, or adverse weather, forces a change of plans. A lone walker should pay very special attention to all these points when circumstances require a careful judgement to be made. This advice is particularly relevant, as some sections of the walk are very long, and there is little accommodation and no shops. There are three basic shelters along the Way in the form of disused cottages, cared for by the Mountain Bothies Association. The fourth shelter, Polskeoch, is a memorial bothy built by soldiers of 32 Field Squadron RE, as a memorial from the son to his parents, Henry and Shirley Chalk, who were killed in a car crash. This bothy, which was an Army Community Work Project in liaison with the Countryside Commission for Scotland and the Dumfries and Galloway Regional Council, offers good shelter, a fireplace, toilet and running water, and was opened on 21 October 1986. The building was completed in seven weeks from scratch.

As a proportion of Southern Way walkers will be backpackers, a suitable mountain tent with a sewn-in groundsheet is strongly recommended. Campers should use recognised camp sites where they are available close to the Way. If random camping is practised due to deteriorating weather, campers should avoid forestry plantations, land near to grazing stock, and the grouse moors. Permission to camp should always be sought wherever possible. Tourist Information Offices can provide information on camping sites in their accommodation leaflets.

Details of the Southern Upland Way Walk:

Section	Places	Distance
1	Portpatrick-Castle Kennedy	13.5 miles (21.5km)
2	Castle Kennedy-New Luce	6 miles (9.5km)
3	New Luce-Bargrennan	17.5 miles (28km)
4	Bargrennan-St John's Town of Dalry	22.5 miles (36km)
5	St John's Town of Dalry-Sanquhar	26 miles (41.4km)
6	Sanquhar-Wanlockhead	8 miles (12.5km)
7	Wanlockhead-Beattock	19.7 miles (31.5km)
8	Beattock-St Mary's Loch	20 miles (32km)
9	St Mary's Loch-Traquair	11.9 miles (19km)
10	Traquair-Yair Bridge	9.4 miles (15.5km)
11	Yair Bridge-Melrose	7.5 miles (12km)
12	Melrose-Lauder	9.7 miles (15.6km)
13	Lauder-Longformacus	15.3 miles (24.5km)
14	Longformacus-Abbey St Bathans	6.9 miles (11km)
15	Abbey St Bathans-Cockburnspath	10.3 miles (16.5km)
	Total Distance:	204.2 miles (326km)

Locations of bothies on the Southern Upland Way:

Section	Name	Map Reference	O.S. 1:50,000 map
4	White Laggan	NX 467 775	77
5	Polskeoch	NS 684 019	77
7	Brattleburn	NT 016 069	78
8	Over Phawhope	NT 182 081	79

Army work camp, Polskeoch

Scaur Water near Polskeoch, on the Southern Upland Way

12

CARRICK AND KYLE

A little further along the road northwards from Palgowan Farm, is the border into that great amorphous area called Strathclyde Region. However, if the part of south-west Scotland described in this chapter is referred to as Kyle and Carrick, then travellers will not expect to see the valley of the Clyde round the nearest corner.

The road bifurcates at Rowantree junction (NX353903) with the left-hand route venturing through the forest and eventually becoming a narrow and quite exciting way through the Nick of Balloch. The road descends to the Stinchar Valley, and follows the river to the attractive village of **Barr**. The Water of Gregg joins the River Stinchar close by the 1787 bridge that carries the B734, on another twisting route called 'The Screws', past Penwhapple Reservoir to Old Dailly and Girvan. Just before Old Dailly is the imposing fifteenth-century **Penkill Castle**. It houses a truly splendid display of seventeenth- and eighteenth-century furniture, tapestries and paintings collected by the fourteenth laird, Spencer Boyd. Visitors are welcome, but applications to view the display should be made in advance by telephone. A minor route to the east of Barr follows the burn and ends after a mile (1.6km), at a picnic site in Changue Forest. There are walking routes along forest tracks past High Changue or through the Howe of Laggan to the Stinchar Valley. From the village of Barr another footpath climbs to Dinmurchie Loch, and continues as an ancient trackway to the ruins of Darley and up to the cairn on Cairn Hill. Dinmurchie Loch can also be approached by another forest track west of Changue. To the east, beyond the Lead Mine Burn, are a number of hill summits clear of forestry that afford good views of the major Galloway hills, including one called Haggis Hill.

Back at the Rowantree road junction there is a car park with a picnic site, and a cairn with a plaque commemorating David Bell, who wrote weekly cycling articles under the pseudonym 'The Highwayman' in the Ayrshire Post. A walk to Shalloch on Minnock commences from this point. It is also a good spot for a look at the complete range of hills to the east known as The Awful Hand.

The little hill road to Straiton is a leisurely way through forest and across wild moorland to visit the remote fastnesses of Loch Doon. The alternative from the south is a colourful route along the A713 from New Galloway, with the accompaniment of the glorious lochs and river scenery of the Glenkens towards Dalmellington.

Continuing along the hill road, the next point of interest is Stinchar Bridge. There is an attractive picnic spot here, with forest walks westwards to a fine waterfall and viewpoint overlooking the valley. A route on the right leads to Ballochbeatties, from where a forest track winds its way eastwards to Loch Doon.

From Stinchar Bridge the road winds through Carrick Forest and descends to the Water of Girvan. A side road travels east to Tairlaw, and follows the river round the base of the tree-clad hills of Glenthraig and Cairn Craig Dhu to the dam holding back the waters of Loch Bradan. The isolated knoll, Doon of Waterhead, NX437988, gives a good view of the reservoir and the neighbouring lochs of Derclach and Finlas.

Straiton village has a pleasant main street, often cheerfully lined with floral displays in borders, pots and window boxes. The village hostelry, the Black Bull, is dated 1766, and the church has some interesting memorial stones in the churchyard. On Craigengower hillside to the south-east is the monument commemorating Colonel Blair of Blairquhan who died at the Battle of Inkerman in 1854.

Blairquhan House, a Regency-style mansion designed by Robert Burn, is occasionally open to visitors during the summer months. It has a museum, and the house contains a good collection of furniture and paintings.

Just outside the village of Straiton to the east, at NS385052, a pleasant 5 mile walk climbs over Sclenteuch Moor towards Loch Spallander Reservoir. Beyond, the route heads along rough forest rides to an unclassified road at Whitehill, and down to Patna on the A713. A little further along the B741 towards Dalmellington is a pleasant forest walk. Leave the parking place, and follow the path upstream, passing a number of waterfalls as the Lamdoughty Burn flows down the glen.

Dalmellington was once one of the centres of iron and coal mining activity in the Doon valley. There are some interesting buildings (all public houses) along the High Street, and a short distance from the Square is the Cathcartson Interpretation Centre, housed in a line of weavers' cottages. The centre exhibits a display of mining, weaving, railways, and other fascinating examples of life and work in the surrounding district. Nearby, at Minnivey, the former colliery is now·the home of the Scottish Industrial Railways Centre. They are very active at Minnivey, and regular 'open days' are held with locomotives in steam.

A little south of Dalmellington, a minor road leaves the A713 and passes along the dam at the north end of **Loch Doon**. This massive sheet of water extends for nearly $6^1/_2$ miles (10.2km), and the little access road runs along the whole length of its western shore, with many opportunities to picnic and enjoy the magnificent scenery.

Loch Doon forms the border between Dumfries and Galloway Region and Strathclyde Region. It became a key part of the Galloway Hydro-Electric Scheme, which became fully operational in 1936. An interesting feature at the northern end dam is the salmon ladder constructed in an ascending spiral in a submerged shaft built against the dam.

Stone tools and weapons found along the shores of Loch Doon show that early people were living by the loch side as early as 6,000BC. Until 1935 **Loch Doon Castle** stood on an island in the loch, but the raising of the water level meant that the castle would be submerged. So, the structure was dismantled, stone by stone, and carefully rebuilt on the shore. The thirteenth-century fortress was of an unusual polygonal shape with eleven unequal sides and with fine ashlar masonry. The island, with the foundations of the castle on it, will be visible when the water level in the loch is low. It was a refuge for early people, judging by the find of nine tree-trunk canoes on the bed of the loch close by.

For anglers, Loch Doon can prove rather a daunting prospect, considering its vast size and remote surroundings. Nevertheless, the fishing is free, brown trout and char grow well and provide good sport. The best areas for fishing seem to be close to where the many small streams enter the loch. It is a fine area also for hill walkers, but the forested slopes and rugged terrain make it a difficult prospect, and walkers should be well prepared and equipped.

Now, it is time to sample the coastal part of Carrick, and continue northwards along the A77 from Stranraer. On reaching Finnarts Bay, the route strikes inland along the narrow wooded valley of Glen App, following the line of the Southern Upland Fault. It climbs over the heather moor, and does a wide swing round Glenapp Castle,

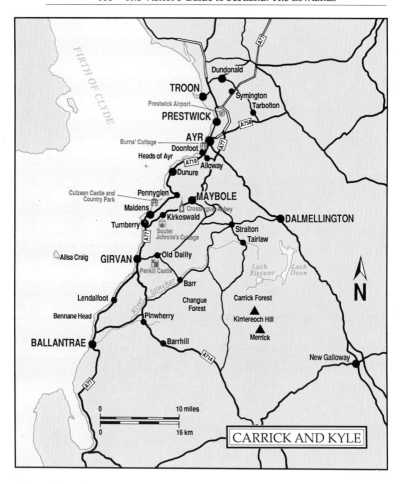

CARRICK AND KYLE

where the gardens are open to the public, before descending to the valley of the River Stinchar, well known for trout and salmon fishing.

Entering the town of **Ballantrae**, the gaunt ruins of Ardstinchar Castle dominate the river crossing, with the attractive eighteenth-century bridge now superseded by a more modern structure. The mouth of the river estuary is pushed southwards by a spit of shingle. Now a nature reserve cared for by the Scottish Wildlife Trust, it is the breeding ground for arctic, common and little terns, and is open to

Loch Doon

visitors, although access is limited during the summer. The church contains interesting memorials to two men, a gamekeeper and a postman, who lost their lives in blizzards, and in the churchyard is the Bargany Aisle, a memorial to Gilbert Kennedy. Once the haunt of smugglers in the eighteenth century, the harbour, with its stone-flagged quay, now welcomes only pleasure craft and fishing boats.

Just south of Ballantrae is an upland wedge of land, between the A77 and the coast, that seldom sees many visitors and provides an enjoyable walk. Cross the bridge over the River Stinchar, and take the minor road past the standing stones at Garleffin, NX087817. Continue climbing gradually for nearly 2 miles (3km) to a point where the road turns sharp left, and proceed straight on past Currarie Farm. A little further along, the path descends to the tiny cove at Currarie Port. For the return journey climb up from the Currarie Glen and head north-east along the cliff tops, past Dove Cove, and keeping to the right of Downan Hill, to a building and a farm track. There is a short alternative here, with a path making for the sea opposite Sgavock Rock, and doubling back to the farm road further on; or continue past Downan on the farm road back to Garleffin and Ballantrae. It is possible to vary the route, shortening the distance if so required. The distance for the route described is 8 to $8^3/_4$ miles (12.8 to 14km).

The main road heads north on the raised beach platform, with the former sea cliffs lying well back from the sea, until it approaches **Bennane Head**. Here, it is forced to cling precariously to the rocks as it inches round the headland. There is a grisly legend attached to this spot. In the fifteenth century a character named Sawney Beane and his gang of cannibals preyed on travellers in this part of Ayrshire. Eventually they were tracked down to a cave under Bennane Head. The pursuers were horrified to find human remains salted in barrels, or hanging up round the walls of the cave. From the lay-by, a gully gives access to the shore; climb over fallen rocks to reach Sawney Beane's cave.

As soon as you reach Lendalfoot, look out for two unclassified roads wriggling inland, one passing by the ruined fifteenth-century tower house of Carleton Castle with a motte close by, then over Moak Hill to Colmonell; the other following the Water of Lendal alongside a well-screened caravan park, to meet the A714 in $5^1/_2$ miles (8.8km). **Carleton Castle** is famed in a ballard as the seat of a baron who disposed of seven wives by pushing them over a precipice. But his eighth wife turned the tables and pushed him over.

At this point the road and railway keep very close company, and they compete athletically on their way down the valley towards **Barrhill**. This is an important meeting point for three lonely roads, and it is blessed with a station. There are other points of interest at Barrhill, namely the Martyrs' Tomb, a memorial to two Covenanters, and the waterfalls of Linn Dhu.

Continue north following the Duisk River to Pinwherry, past the sixteenth-century L-plan tower house and the junction with the A765 to the coast. Away on the moorlands to the east north-east is solitary Gleik Stone, NX217879. This tall, pointed tablet of stone contains strange bowl-shaped indentations on both faces, and it is interesting to note that the monolith lines up with particular landmarks in most directions — the gaps in the hills at Cairn Hill ridge to the east north-east; the Kirriereoch Hill-Merrick range to the east; and the prominent Knockdolian Hill to the west south-west.

Beyond Pinwherry, the A714 follows the River Stinchar and the Water of Assel to the head of the valley before it descends to Girvan. Just to the east of the road summit, which is tunnelled through by the railway, lies the very well preserved, impressive remains of the twelfth-century Dinvin Motte, NX200931. Its massive defences consist of two large U-shaped ditches protected by external earthworks. Walk for a short distance along the track leading off the north side of the main road, and then head uphill to the motte.

Back on the coast at Lendalfoot, the A77 renews its close relationship with the sea, and ultimately passes between the cliffs and a large standing outcrop of rock at Kennedy's Pass. Here, the presence of Old Red sandstone sedimentary rocks is reflected in the tumbled debris and sea stacks of the raised beach platform.

Girvan is the leading coastal resort in the south-west of Scotland, and extends along a bay with a good sandy beach, free of dangerous currents. The town is bordered by hills to the south and east; it faces west over the wide expanse of the Firth of Clyde to the commanding shape of the island of **Ailsa Craig**. Its dome-like shape attains a height of 1,108ft (338m), and is thought to be the basal remains of a volcanic vent, which created towering cliffs most of the way round. The granite has been cut through by dolerite dykes, and it is alongside these that the majority of caves are to be found. The red granite became famous for its use in top quality curling stones. Ailsa Craig is also well known for its vast and varied bird population. Although it is barren in appearance, the island is well-covered with flowers, noticeably on the upper slopes. The lighthouse, which has operated since 1886, is situated on a boulder strand on the eastern side.

It is worth attempting the clear path that zig-zags up to the ruins of a castle, which had three storeys and bears the coat of arms of the Hamilton family. The path proceeds below crags to tiny Garra Loch, and continues its airy way across great rock slabs, to swing round and up to the summit trig point. As can be expected, the view is panoramic and superb. A boat can be hired from Girvan, and there are regular day trips during the summer months. The crossing time is approximately one hour.

Girvan has a convenient car park beside the Tourist Information Centre in Bridge Street, just before the town centre traffic lights. Across the main road is the old kirkyard, with a memorial to Constable Alexander Ross, shot in 1831 in a riot during an Orangemen's march in the town. Other interesting stone slabs to be found there are believed to be medieval in origin with inscribed crosses, or possibly swords on them. Montgomerie Street contains the nineteenth-century North Parish Church, built in Early English Gothic style, with a slender spire soaring 149ft (46m) above the neighbouring roof tops. The church is well worth a look inside, for as well as being beautifully cared for, it has an artistic frieze and ceiling decoration illustrating the theme of the creation. The library is also in Montgomerie Street.

Dalrymple Street, which is the main shopping centre of the town, has some fine buildings, such as the McKechnie Institute built in Scottish Baronial style, where many important exhibitions are held. At the south end of the town visitors may be interested in the sixteenth-century chancel screen from Brougham Hall, Penrith, in St John's Scottish Episcopal Church. Duff Street leads to the sea front, passing on the way a number of single-storeyed dwellings, once the homes of hand-loom weavers.

For many years the town was an important fishing centre, and today there is still much activity around the picturesque harbour, as the fishing boats are always a centre of attraction for visitors. To the east of the promenade, there is the boating lake, a children's fun fair, putting greens and crazy golf. The beach pavilion beside the harbour is the venue for excellent family entertainment. The town has a modern heated indoor swimming pool, and a training pool for children. Other facilities include a bowling club with four greens, tennis, pleasure sailing and sea angling trips. There are many delightful parks, including the rose gardens in Victory Park. The Bargany Estate Gardens are situated 4 miles (6.4km) east of Girvan via the B734. There are azaleas in season, and attractive woodland walks and picnic areas.

There is good fishing from the pier at Girvan for plaice and flounder, and night fishing is good for rock cod. Just south of the town 'Horse Rock' is a popular spot, and at Bennane Lea, NX092859, deep water produces cod and pollack. Successful fishing can also be had from the rocks down from the lay-by south of Bennane Caravan Park.

Girvan hosts other attractions, such as the Folk Festival, which has been flourishing for more than a decade. The event is usually held over the May Bank Holiday weekend, and hotels in the town offer an inclusive package comprising accommodation and a weekend ticket for all events. There is also the Girvan Lowland Gathering, the town's answer to Highland Games held in other parts of the country. This is normally a one day event, usually held on the first Sunday in June. Also in June, there is a Civic Week with an exciting Gala Parade. A Girvan Golf Week is held during the autumn.

Girvan is fortunate in its location, having good attractive countryside close at hand. A $7^1/_2$ mile (12km) linear walk starts from the junction of the A77 and the A714 to the south of the town. Walk east to the track, passing over the railway, and proceed up the little valley to the north of Dow Hill. A little extra effort to reach the ancient fort on the summit, 517ft (158m), will be rewarded with fine views. Con-

tinue up the valley past Laggan Loch and descend to Barbae and Tormitchell in the Water of Assel valley. Take the road past the quarry, bear right and cross the stream to Dupin, and then climb steadily to meet a track coming up from Auchensoul. Descend to cross the stream, and walk uphill over the southern shoulder of Auchensoul Hill, and down to Barr. Afternoon teas are available in the village during the summer months.

North of Girvan, the A77 swings inland at Turnberry, and the A719 takes the short route to Maidens, passing the Culzean Country Park, before returning to its coastal way around the Heads of Ayr. The A719 route will be described first, followed by the places of interest along the A77 from Turnberry.

There are now scant remains of Turnberry Castle on the headland above Castle Port, but it was probably the birthplace of Robert Bruce in 1274. The lighthouse was constructed on the castle site and lit in 1873. **Turnberry** is a well-known name, famous for its international golf course.

By the side of Turnberry golf course, the village of **Maidens** has a fine sandy beach and picnicking sites. The breakwaters of the picturesque harbour stretch out into the bay, providing a sheltered haven for small craft. Look for the fine wall sculpture on the Bruce Hotel that depicts the well-known story about the patriot and the spider. Pony trekking/hacking is available at the Lands of Turnberry and at Maidens, offering rides on beautiful beaches and along country park trails.

Game fishing is available along the River Girvan, the River Stinchar and at the Blairquhan Estate. Loch fishing can be arranged at Loch Bradan, Loch Mochrum, Penwhapple Reservoir, Blairquhan Approach Loch and Snipe Loch. Remember, if you want to be alone amidst the wilds of Loch Doon, the fishing is free.

The A719 makes its way through the sandstone countryside east of **Culzean Castle**, as the hills push their steep wooded slopes seawards. Culzean (pronounced Culain), was originally a medieval tower house which was transformed into an elegant mansion in the late eighteenth century. It has many points of interest, including an oval staircase in its centre.

The castle is the property of the National Trust for Scotland, which also runs the Culzean Country Park as a partnership with the district and regional authorities. The original Home Farm was converted into a complex combining an information section, an exhibition wing, restaurant and other facilities. Paths fan out through the well-cared for woodlands and on to the clifftop, visiting attractive locations such as the Swan Pond, Happy Valley and the Deer Park. Other outside features include the Fountain Court, and the Walled Garden.

The ranger service provides wardening and information facilities, backed up by a varied programme of events, talks, films and guided walks. The study rooms are used by visiting schools and by the Young Naturalists Club, as part of an important educational environmental study programme. Car parks are to be found near the castle, the Country Park Centre, the Walled Garden and the Swan Pond.

From Culzean, the A719 suddenly takes a right-angled turn northwards at Pennyglen Lodge, and the direct route to Maybole, continues as the B7023.

From Pennyglen Lodge, the A719 begins to traverse westwards round the upland mass of Brown Carrick Hill. At Croy Brae, the so-called Electric Brae, motorists coming south feel they are on a downward slope, although in effect the road is going uphill. Many are keen to experience the phenomenon of a car apparently coasting up a hill — take care!

At Dunure Mains, an unclassified road descends to the fishing village of **Dunure**, with a fine little harbour overlooked by a small tapering light tower. Adjacent to the harbour, built on a promontory, is the cliff-top tower of Dunure Castle, which has a sixteenth-century beehive-shaped dovecote to the east.

The coastline assumes a rugged appearance in the impressive volcanic rocks at the **Heads of Ayr**. The 200ft (60m) high cliffs emphasise the wildness of the scene, and with care, a way down can be negotiated to the bay. A narrow minor road climbs over Brown Carrick Hill, from where splendid views can be obtained of the Isle of Arran, Ayr Bay, and north to the mountains of Ben Lomond and Stobinian. The little road descends to the B7024, and by turning left via Knockdon it is only a distance of 3 miles (4.8km) to Alloway, and the attractions of the Burns Heritage Trail. Alternatively, continue by country lane to the A77 and the B742, in order to explore the valley of the River Doon. The river flows past Cassillis House, which is overlooked by the ancient hill fort of Dunree. The road crosses the River Doon into **Dalrymple**, where there is a caravan site to the east of the village, and an attractive walk along the north bank of the river towards Skeldon House.

A little further along the coastal route the A719 passes the holiday camp complex, where an unclassified road leads down towards the sea, and there is a footpath along the shore edge to the ruins of

Culzean Castle gardens

Dolphin fountain, Culzean

Greenan Castle. The fortress now stands on the lip of the cliff which has been undercut by wave action. The main road leaves Carrick, crossing the River Doon at Doonfoot, and enters the district of Kyle and the county town of Ayr.

Back at Turnberry the A77 crosses the Milton Burn and turns inland towards Maybole. The first community on this route is **Kirkoswald**, where the 1785 thatched cottage of the village cobbler (Souter), John Davidson, is to be found. Both he and Douglas Graham of Shanter Farm were well known to Robert Burns, and both men were later to be immortalised in the poem, *Tam O'Shanter*. The cottage, under the care of the National Trust for Scotland, contains Burnsiana as well as contemporary cobblers tools. The ale house in the cottage garden has been restored, and has life-size figures of Tam, the Souter, the innkeeper and his wife, sculptured by James Thorn. Across the road lie the ruins of the old parish kirk, with the gravestones of John Davidson and Douglas Graham.

A few miles further on towards Maybole is the site of **Crossraguel Abbey**. This small Cluniac monastery dates from the thirteenth to sixteenth centuries and was a daughter house of Paisley Abbey. There is little to be seen of the thirteenth-century building work, but there are substantial remains of high architectural distinction, such as the abbey church, chapter house, dovecote, Abbot's Tower and refectory, plus an imposing castellated gatehouse.

Maybole, the capital of Carrick, slopes steeply down a hill, with the A77 frequently causing traffic problems as it cuts through the centre of the town. The castle, which dates from the sixteenth century, stands high above an intersection of streets, and features in the ballard of Johnnie Faa. See if you can spot the small window decorated with sculptured heads.

The red sandstone railway station, on the Ayr to Girvan line, stands high on the northern side of the town. Along the two unclassified roads running north from the station, one can obtain lovely views of the surrounding area. Beyond the Water of Girvan valley, the forests and foothills of Carrick rise up to the distant summits of Merrick and Shalloch on Minnoch.

The town has a number of substantial nineteenth-century buildings, including the post office, library, old parish church, west church, the Town Hall attached to the seventeenth-century tolbooth tower, and the Roman Catholic church. In Abbot Street are the fifteenth-century remains of a collegiate church founded by the Kennedys of Dunure. Returning to the High Street, look for the iron cross that marks the site of the mercat cross, and the traditional first meeting place of the parents of Robert Burns.

From Maybole the B7024 heads straight for Ayr, which is the centre of Burns Country. Within a radius of 12 miles or so, you can visit all the places where the National Bard of Scotland spent his early years and wrote some of his best loved songs and poems. The village of **Alloway**, where Robert Burns was born, has become a popular spot for visitors. The land o' Burns Centre, on the B7024 offers visual displays and an audio-visual presentation of the life and times of Burns, as well as picnic areas, a tea room and giftshop. Not far away, within easy walking distance, is Burns Cottage. The cottage, built by his father, William Burnes, in 1757, is a single storey dwelling with a reed thatch. It is a fine example of early eighteenth-century rural architecture, fortunately preserved due to its association with the poet. Robert Burns was born here on the 25 January 1759, and spent the first 5 years of his life in the cottage. The interior is divided into living quarters and kitchen at one end, a byre at the other, and is fitted with eighteenth- and nineteenth-century furniture and other domestic pieces.

Near to the Land o' Burns Centre, is the Auld Kirk, where Burns' father is buried, and his mother is commemorated below the two windows at the gable end.

A view from the road bridge gives a good picture of the Auld Brig o'Doon, NS322178. The Old Doon Bridge was the only bridge over the river in the neighbourhood of the village until Burns was 13 years old, when a bridge was built at Doonfoot in 1772 by his future father-in-law. Just beside the old bridge is the Burns Monument, which has nine Corinthian pillars each representing one of the muses. The monument and gardens are open to the public from April to September.

In **Ayr**, the A719 proceeds via Sandgate, and leaves over the New Bridge towards Prestwick Road, although it becomes the A79 after crossing the River Ayr. Wellington Square lies on the approach to Sandgate, and consists of a garden area surrounded by buildings. The central part contains a cenotaph, statues to various notables, and a memorial to John Loudon McAdam. You then come into Sandgate, where it widens due to a former tolbooth that once stood in the middle of the street. This thoroughfare contains banks, commercial premises and an attractive, well-designed shopping precinct; altogether, a fine architectural mix of eighteenth- to twentieth-century buildings. At the junction of Hope Street and Sandgate stands the town buildings and the town steeple. The town steeple was designed as part of the Assembly Rooms by Thomas Hamilton, and erected between 1827 and 1832. The slim, 230ft (70m) high spire, decorated with classical designs, is a very fine feature, but a better impression of it can be gained from the north end of the New Bridge.

Other locations in the area connected with Robert Burns are:

Mount Oliphant Farm — NS 357173

Tam O'Shanter Museum, Ayr — On east side of High Street

Leglen Woods — NS 388230

Lochlea Farm — NS 455301

Mossgiel Farm — NS 489286, Burns lived here for four years and wrote some of his finest works.

Mauchline churchyard — NS 497273

Mauchline, Burns House Museum, Castle Street

Mauchline, Nance Tannock's Tavern, Castle Street, (Back Causeway) NS 497274

Mauchline, Poosie Nancie's Tavern, Loudoun Street NS 498274

Mauchline — National Burns Memorial

Failford — Highland Mary's Monument. On the A758, Ayr to Mauchline road, $2^1/_2$ miles (4km) west of Mauchline.

Kilmarnock — Laigh Kirk NS 428379

Kilmarnock — Burns Federation Headquarters, Dick Institute, Elmbank Avenue

Newmilns — Loudoun Manse NS 527372

Irvine — Burns Club Museum, 'Wellwood', Eglinton Street

Kirkoswald — Laigh Park Farm, now called Park Farm. Farmed by Douglas Graham NS 223062

New Cumnock — Laight, Glen Afton NS 612117, the home of the poet's friend, John Logan.

❄ Close by stands the Auld Brig, a stone cobbled, four arched medieval structure that has withstood the ravages of time since the end of the fifteenth century. Its preservation is probably due to the fact that Burns wrote a poem about it. The Auld Brig was saved from collapsing into the River Ayr by being comprehensively renovated at the beginning of the twentieth century.

Turning left before the New Bridge brings you into Boat Vennal. Here is Loudoun Hall, one of the few examples in Scotland of a substantial town house of the early sixteenth century. It has been restored, and is now used as a cultural centre for local organisations. Along South Harbour on the left, are the walls of Cromwell's seventeenth-century citadel. Look for the corbelled turret of 'Miller's Folly' facing the harbour. John Miller was an eccentric Victorian businessman who made a fortune in India, and converted the Tower of St John's into a Gothic-style residence. Visitors may enjoy the activity in the South Harbour when fishing boats are unloading their catches. The Paddle Steamer *Waverley* has also docked there during the summer months when cruising along the Clyde coast.

Go past the swimming baths, complete with giant aquaslides, bear round to Cromwell Road and turn in towards St John's Tower. The tower is the remaining remnant of the great Burgh Kirk of St John the Baptist.

The Esplanade runs south alongside the long sandy beach. Ayr has $2^1/_2$ miles (4km) of golden sands, hence its popularity as the premier resort on the south-west coast of Scotland. Off the Esplanade is Craigweil Road, the location of Ayr's youth hostel. The building is a large, traditionally designed Scottish house, and it offers not only the usual hostel accommodation, but family rooms and conference facilities. It is a good place from which to explore the Burns Heritage Trail.

Having been refreshed by the invigorating sea breezes along the Esplanade, return to Sandgate, then along Newmarket Street to cross High Street, and enter the Kirk Port. Beyond the stone lych gate lies the Auld Kirk, a fine old church built in 1654 as compensation from Cromwell, who incorporated the Kirk of St John the Baptist within the walls of the citadel. Within the lych gate are a couple of mortsafes for protecting bodies from grave robbers. Robert Burns was baptised here, and the kirkyard contains some very interesting sculptured headstones.

High Street continues to a narrow section at the neo-Gothic Wallace Tower. The southern part of High Street contains the Tam O'Shanter Inn (of uncertain pedigree) now maintained as a museum.

Beyond this point, Alloway Street widens into Burns Statue Square, but the poet's statue has turned its back on Ayr, and appears to be looking wistfully towards Alloway and the days of his boyhood. Close by is the railway station, opened in 1886.

Ayr is famous for its beautiful parks and gardens, notably Belleisle, Rozelle and Craigie. South of the town, the B7024 to Alloway runs between Belleisle and Rozelle. The former contains golf courses, grounds and beautiful gardens. There is a pets corner and a deer park. The mansion now houses a hotel, and there is a cafeteria open to the public. The eighteenth-century mansion of Rozelle contains many items of local historical interest, especially military history. A stable block has been converted to form a number of exhibition galleries with money from the Maclaurin bequest. There is a continually changing programme of fine art exhibitions, and a convenient tearoom.

A little to the east, the River Ayr wriggles out its course in great loops edged with pleasant woodland surroundings. It is well worth exploring the area around the West of Scotland Agricultural College at Auchincruive, where the estate of the former Oswald Hall, built in 1767, sweeps down to the river. There is the attractive, three-arched bridge, NS388231, with unusual cutwaters, on the minor road to St Quivox, with the added bonus of a pleasant walk along the river bank. Soon it is hoped to implement a woodland trail linking the arboretum and the riverside gardens. To the east of Annbank, via the A758 and B742, lies Enterkine Wood, NS425241, which is a Scottish Wildlife Trust Reserve with natural deciduous woodland and a pond.

East of Ayr, the A758 Mauchline road passes to the south of **Tarbolton**. In the centre of the village is a two-storey house of considerable interest, the Bachelors' Club. The house has harled and whitewashed walls and a thatched roof, and the National Trust for Scotland have furnished it in the style of the late eighteenth century. The upper room contains a number of items connected with Burns.

Northwards from Ayr, the coastline consists of a number of raised beaches, dunes and wide areas of sandy foreshore. The town of **Prestwick** is the oldest recorded burgh in Scotland. Modern road requirements in the town resulted in the re-siting of the mercat cross, one of the best preserved in the south-west, to a site on a traffic island opposite the post office. In Kirk Street there are the roofless twelfth-century ruins of St Nicholas' Kirk, built by Walter, High Steward of Scotland.

Prestwick is a thriving holiday town, where the shore itself has 3 miles (4.8km) of glorious sand. Skirting this area are putting courses, crazy golf and three major golf courses. You can pass under the railway and walk across Old Prestwick golf course on a right of way to the shore. Continue southwards, turn inland at the end of the promenade, and proceed over the railway to the ruins of St Ninian's Chapel. Nearby is Bruce's Well, where Robert the Bruce, sick from a skin disease similar to leprosy, drank the water and found his condition was much improved.

The town is very much a family holiday setting, with many facilities for visitors. It is also very handy for pottering about the locality, providing a chance to keep off those main roads and to explore the variety of country lanes east of the town. One such excursion is to take the B739 from Monkton, pass under the A77 and proceed for 1 mile (1.6km), then turn left. For the next two turnings, bear right and then left to Underhills. Turn right here, and the **Barnweil Tower** sits on a hill to the south. This is a neo-Gothic tower, built in 1855 to the memory of William Wallace. On a clear day there is a superb view of the Ayr coast. The tower is open to the public by arrangement. Nearby is the ruined Barnweil Church, one of the oldest in Ayrshire; it was closed in 1673.

Continue to the B730, and northwards through the peaceful village of Craigie, bearing right to meet the A719. This is the eastern limit of the Kyle District, with the border running along the Cessnock Water. **Carnell House** is worth a visit. This is a sixteenth-century tower house with fine riverside gardens, which are occasionally open to the public.

Return south-west along the A719, then via the B730, crossing over the A77, and turning left into **Symington**. This is a most attractive village set round the beautiful twelfth-century Norman church, which was altered unsuccessfully in the eighteenth century. However, restoration in 1919 revealed the original oak ceiling timbers, and retained the north gallery. Symington is a good location for photographers, architects, and visitors who are just interested in villages, for there is a fascinating pattern of streets and buildings to study.

From the village centre, take the country lane north-west to **Dundonald**, where the main village street lies close to the castle. The ruins stand on an isolated hill, where the tower and much of the barmkin wall survives. The castle is currently being restored and is not yet open to the public.

From the village, a minor road runs through a small group of rocky hills and descends to Loans. Just half a mile (0.9km), south of

Dundonald, a path near the entrance to Hallyards quarry gives access for a walk along Dundonald Glen to Collennan Reservoir.

From Loans, it is just a short distance to the bracing holiday resort of **Troon**. Once a small fishing village, it has over 2 miles (3.2km) of sandy beaches stretching on either side of the busy harbour. The marina here is a hive of activity, and is popular with yachting enthusiasts, anglers and tourists. The sands slope gently down to the sea, and there are many rock pools full of interesting sea life. There is an interesting walk past the marina and picnic area, and along the Ballast Bank, which was a bank built up over many years using ballast unloaded from coal boats returning from Ireland. This is a good viewpoint, looking across to the bird sanctuary of Lady Isle and to the dramatic mountain outline of the Isle of Arran.

There is a good view over the town from the railway station, and the two interesting churches nearby, are St Meddans Church of Scotland, with the graceful spire, and St Meddans Roman Catholic Church with the very broad tower, plus a smaller stair tower. Look also for St Ninian's Episcopal Church which features oak doors and furniture displaying the trade mark of a carved mouse — the handiwork of Robert Thompson from Kilburn in North Yorkshire.

Troon is famous world-wide for its five superb golf courses, including the famous Royal Troon, the venue for the 1989 British Open.

Other attractions for visitors include crazy golf, bowling, tennis, trampolining, and a fine concert hall. On the edge of town is the Fullarton Estate, with beautiful grounds for walking, picnicing, and viewing the floral displays.

13

ISLE OF ARRAN

A rran, scarcely 2 hours journey from Scotland's industrial heartland, is an island of many attractions and great scenic contrasts.
It lies some 15 miles (24km) west of the Ayrshire coastline, and dominates the approaches to the Firth of Clyde and the entrance to Loch
Fyne. It is sheltered to the west by Kintyre, from which it is separated
by the Kilbrannan Sound.

The landscape of the northern part of the island is in marked
contrast to the southern part, principally due to the underlying
geological structures which give Arran a character of its own. The
island is 19 miles (30.4km) long from the Cock of Arran in the north
to Bennan Head in the south, and 10 miles (16km) wide from Machrie
Bay in the west to Corrygills Point in the east. Its 165sq miles (427sq
km), is split almost equally by the Highland Boundary Fault, giving
rise to geology and scenery akin to the Highlands in the north, and
to the Lowlands in the south.

The Isle of Arran is very accessible by roll-on roll-off ferry from
Ardrossan on the Ayrshire coast. From the south, via Carlisle, it is an
easy drive to Ardrossan, and the new high-speed electric train direct
from Glasgow takes only an hour. Visitors arriving by air at Prestwick Scotland Airport can reach Ardrossan by train, changing at
Kilwinning. From Glasgow Airport, the ferry train from nearby
Paisley is the best bet. The ferry sails to Brodick, the island's main
settlement, with five sailings per day, except Sunday which has four
sailings. Crossing time is 55 minutes. The service is operated by
Caledonian MacBrayne Ltd, who also run a seasonal service from
Lochranza, at the north of the island, to Claonaig in Kintyre for
vehicles and passengers. There is no service on this route from late
October to April. During the summer months, the last sea-going

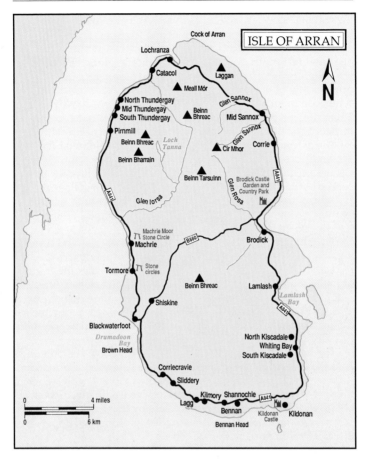

paddle steamer, the *Waverley*, runs day cruises and regular passenger sailings from Brodick and the Ayr coast around the Firth of Clyde. At Brodick, local bus services connect with the boat, and convey passengers on circular routes to the north and south of the island. In winter these services are limited, with no Sunday service. Car and bicycle hire is available, as is a good taxi service, which is very handy during the winter months. However, if remaining on the island for an extended stay, it is best to take one's own car or bicycle. The Tourist Information Centre at the Pierhead, Brodick, is open throughout the year, and will advise visitors on accommodation facilities, things to do, places to visit and transport arrangements.

Brodick has seen great changes during the last hundred years. At one time Old Brodick was situated on the north side of the bay, which was the entry point for goods, livestock and passengers. Close by, the original school at Rosaburn now houses the Arran Heritage Museum, comprising the old smithy, harness room, and two cottages. There are car parking spaces, a picnic area, and a tearoom. The museum is situated on the main road, the A841, just north of Brodick.

The entrance to Brodick Castle and Gardens (National Trust for Scotland) lies just $1^1/_2$ miles (2.4km), north of the Arran Heritage Centre, off the A841. The castle, which overlooks Brodick Bay, is backed by Goatfell, and surrounded by woodlands and fine gardens. It belongs to three main periods from the sixteenth to nineteenth centuries, although the earliest remains to be found in the present buildings date from the thirteenth century.

The interior of the house contains rich decorations and furnishings, and a large collection of Beckford's treasures. There is the long red gallery, with a row of austere straight-backed chairs; the gracious drawing room with a fine plasterwork ceiling and elegant furniture — look for the striking porcelain goose tureens, one of which carries an eel in its mouth, while the other holds a fish; and the part-panelled dining room situated in the sixteenth-century part of the castle, with its beautiful display of porcelain and silver.

The gardens at Brodick Castle are outstanding. The pond and woodland areas contain a comprehensive collection of rhododendron species, a sheltered walled garden is vibrant with colourful borders of herbaceous plants, and extensive well-manicured lawns are protected by trees and shrubs. Close by the pond garden is the Bavarian summer house, built about 1860, its ceiling and upper walls artistically decorated with pine cones.

A country park was established in 1980, with a Ranger Centre, providing several trails to a variety of interesting habitats. In the mixed woodland area there are many fine trees, including the rare Arran whitebeam, accompanied by a ground covering of wild garlic, dog's mercury, ferns and bluebells. It is a special thrill to spot the red squirrels, which are numerous here, and an opportunity to study the varied bird life, which includes the peregrine falcon and the buzzard.

Other facilities for visitors to Brodick include fishing, tennis bowling, boat hire, car hire, cycle hire, golf and pony trekking. There is a wealth of accommodation and a range of events over the season to suit every visitor.

The fine array of granite peaks in north-east Arran form the magnificent skyline that travellers see from across the Firth of Clyde, and in greater detail when approaching the island. The grey mountains are clustered around the highest point, Goatfell, 2,866ft (874m), and the serrated intervening ridges run out in all directions forming a splendid group of rugged summits. An evening sunset creates a wonderful silhouette of exciting dark outlines. The convenient composition of these mountains allows walkers to complete circuits of varying lengths, and the great glens of Rosa and Sannox effectively split them into two halves, which allows easy access to the heart of the group.

The popularity of these mountains has created problems with erosion, as thousands of walkers' boots have acted as agents of denudation, gouging out channels in paths, and grinding up the granite on ridge tops. This is particularly noticeable on the tourist path up Goatfell, and down the steep north-west ridge of North Goatfell, where the slopes are marked with surface sheets of light brown granitic gravel. With the exception of A'Chir and the Witch's Step, the ridges should not present any difficulty during the summer months, and will provide some very fine high-level walking. Where pinnacles and castellated tors exist, these can often be outflanked. However, during the winter months, these Arran mountains should not be underestimated. Mountain lovers will be impressed by the great rock faces, towering buttresses, and long extended slabs, or boiler plates of granite, dropping steeply into the glens.

The distances given for walks, particularly in the hills, can only be calculated approximately from the maps. Due to the nature of the terrain, a map mile may in fact be considerably more. Naismith's formula used for hill walking in favourable conditions, allows one hour for each 3 map miles, plus half an hour for every 1,000ft (305m) of ascent. Delays incurred because of bad weather are not included in the time allowed for reasonable stops.

Just south of the entrance to Brodick Castle is the start of the walk up Goatfell, NS012376, where there is a convenient car park. This is a straightforward route, crossing the exit drive from Brodick Castle, and climbing gradually through rhododendrons to reach the open hillside, dotted with boulders and juniper bushes. On reaching the east ridge at 2,070ft (630m), the Goatfell path heads up the boulder and scree slope to the summit, and the Corrie route bears right. Continue over Meall Breac, and descend left down the slope to the Corrie Burn. Cross over and follow the burn until the path leads left to the dwellings at High Corrie, and down the track to the road. The

The paddle steamer Waverley, *Brodick*

Brodick Castle gardens

⇐ *Brodick Bay*

distance of this walk is nearly 5¹/₂ miles (5.6km), and from Brodick Pier Head to the start of the walk is 2 miles (3.2km).

Another walk starts from the String road at NS004368, and descends on the unclassified road to the stream, continuing to Glen Rosa Farm. Beyond, follow the track above Glen Rosa Water to cross the footbridge over the Garbh Allt. There is a clear path forward which accompanies the burn up the valley, with the magnificent view of Cir Mhor in front, the surrounding ridges of Goatfell and Stacach on the right, and Beinn a'Chliabhain and A'Chir on the left. Follow the path as it gradually climbs up to The Saddle, on a route where the going can be very boggy in parts. From The Saddle, descend an eroded dyke in a north-west direction for a short distance, before veering to the right on a north-east heading. The descent is steep with loose stones at first, but then the route continues more gradually into Glen Sannox. Walk alongside the burn down the glen, and cross over to the remains of the former barytes mine. The derelict waterwheel lies close by a lovely, deep pool with overhanging willow, birch and rowan. Ahead lies the track, which goes past the burial ground and on to the main road. This walk covers nearly 8 miles (12.5km), and from Brodick Pier Head to the start of the walk is nearly 1¹/₂ miles (2.2km).

Because of its handy size, the whole of the inhabited part of the island can be viewed by the motorist in a single day. The A841 runs round the island, only leaving the coast in the north and south on its 56 miles (89.6km) round journey. Two minor roads also cross the island from east to west. The one across its waist is the B880 String road planned by Thomas Telford, and further south is the unclassified Ross road. In the far south, a short loop road leads to the seaside village of Kildonan.

Amongst the fourteen villages on the island, the communities of **Corrie** and **Sannox** lie to the north of Brodick. Corrie is a charming little seaside spot; it has a row of neat, colour-washed cottages with attractive dormer windows gazing out to sea. The cottages rest on the raised beach nestling beneath the former cliffs. Above Corrie there is a neolithic chambered tomb; a Bronze Age cairn and standing stones in Sannox; and Iron Age forts at North Glen Sannox and Mid Glen Sannox.

Corrie and Sannox welcome visitors and hope they will take part in the 'Corrie Capers', a week of events in August, which includes a round-Arran road race. The links of the Sannox golf course are to be found on the north bank of the Glen Sannox Burn, and there is the Sannox pony-trekking centre at Laimrig, Sannox.

Other Suggested Hill Walks in the Goatfell Area

Goatfell, 2,866ft (874m)
> From near Brodick Castle — Goatfell summit, along north ridge to North Goatfell, 2,659ft (818m). Descend north-west ridge to The Saddle, some scrambling required. Return down Glen Rosa. Distance: $10^1/_2$ miles (16.8km).

Goatfell from Corrie — High Corrie, Corrie Burn, Stacach, Goatfell, Meall Breac, Corrie Burn, Corrie. Distance: $5^1/_2$ miles (8.8km).

Cir Mhór, 2,618ft (799m)
> From Sannox — Glen Sannox, The Saddle, and a steep climb through rocky outcrops to the summit of Cir Mhór. Return same route. Distance: $6^1/_2$ miles (10.4km).

Cir Mhór from Sannox (Spring road) — Glen Rosa, The Saddle, Cir Mhór, south ridge to col, Fionn Choire, Glen Rosa. Distance: $10^1/_2$ miles (16.8km).

Glen Rosa to the Garbh Allt burn — Ben Nuis, 2,597ft (792m), Beinn Tarsuinn 2,706ft (826m), Beinn a' Chliabhain, 2,217ft (675m). Head north-west to lower part of Coire a' Bhradain and up south-east ridge of Ben Nuis. Continue along ridge past rock towers to Beinn Tarsuinn. Descend to Bealach an Fhir-bhogha and along ridge to Beinn a' Chliabhain. Descend from Cnoc Breac to Glen Rosa via the Garbh Allt burn. Distance: 10 miles (16km).

At North Sannox, a short stretch of road goes down to a most delightful picnic spot by the sea, NS015466. From here, a footpath follows the coastline to Fallen Rocks, Millstone Point, Laggan, Cock of Arran, Fairy Dell and Newton Point to Lochranza. In parts, it is a rugged, adventurous path, and involves boulder hopping, shore combing and bog dodging, but it is a good expedition and should not be missed. Visitors can walk to Fallen Rocks and Millstone Point, and return to the picnic area; walk to Laggan, and climb over the intervening moorland to descend to Lochranza; or go the whole hog, and follow 'Man Friday' on the trail round the coast.

The route from Sannox to **Lochranza** across the Boguillie was built in 1843, coming down Glen Chalmadale beneath the steep slopes of Torr Head. The road flattens out and runs along the strand by the river and by the side of Loch Ranza. The charming village is

The view from Goat Fell

Corrie

⇐ *Glen Rosa and Cir Mhór*

spread along the shore on both sides of the loch and was once one of the main fishing centres on the west coast of Scotland. The inner harbour is now used by pleasure craft that come in for shelter when there is a strong wind blowing from the west. The ruined thirteenth- or fourteenth-century castle, situated on the level spit, stands guard over the entrance to the loch. It was at one time thought to be a tower-house, but is now believed to have been a hall-house, which was similar to an English fortified manor house. The clues included a blocked-up doorway and a number of long arrow slits. The building was heightened in the sixteenth century to become a tower-house, with internal modifications and the main entrance sited on the south-west wall. It is possible to look over the castle by applying to the key holder, whose address is on a convenient notice board.

Steamers used to call at Lochranza, carrying goods, mail and passengers, and villagers were able to travel to Campbeltown in Kintyre to shop and conduct business. Sadly, the steamers ceased calling in 1957 and the old pier lies derelict, but Caledonian MacBrayne saved the day by starting a vehicle and passenger service, summer season only, across Kilbrannan Sound to Claonaig in Kintyre. Nevertheless, there is good tourist potential in that old pier and it would be very welcome to see it in use again.

Facilities for visitors include a 9-hole golf course and putting green, tennis courts, a caravan and camping site, and possibilities for many good walks in the area. There is a seasonal Tourist Information Centre at Lochranza and a wide range of accommodation, including an excellent youth hostel which has comfortable self-catering accom-modation for up to eighty people, with small rooms available for family use.

For a hillwalk from Lochranza which takes in Gleann Easan Biorach, Loch na Davie, Castles' Ridge, Creag Dhubh and The Boguillie, leave the main road near Ballarie and walk up the west side of the burn in Gleann Easan Biorach. As the glen opens out, the path deteriorates and can be wet. The little loch is unusual, as it has a watercourse issuing from both ends. Head east south-east from the loch, and ascend steeply over rough ground towards the rounded ridge to join the north-west ridge of The Castles (Caisteal Abhail). At this height, of about 2,200ft (670m), there are splendid views of the corries, rock castles and surrounding peaks. Bear left and follow the ridge down, keeping safely to the western side. The route curves over Creag Dhubh and over Sail an Im, and heads north over rough-ish ground. Cross over the Gleann Dubh Burn and head north-east towards the A841 at Boguillie. The distance is $5^3/_4$ miles (9.2km).

From Coillemore Point the main road hugs the coastline very closely down the west coast of the island to Machrie Bay. At the hamlet of **Catacol**, the 'Twelve Apostles' line the side of the road. This description is given to an attractive row of cottages built in the time of the eleventh Duke of Hamilton, to rehouse people displaced by later clearances in the north-west of the island. Just beyond, the road crosses the strath of Glen Catacol, and this is a favourite starting point for a wide choice of walks, to Loch Tanna, Gleann Diomhan, Beinn Bhreac, and to a number of other hills and lochs. Catacol has two hotels.

For an 8 mile (12.8km) hillwalk, take the path on the north side of the burn and walk up Glen Catacol. Bear left and ascend Glen Diomhan on an indistinct path on the left of the burn. Higher up you will pass a nature conservancy area, where two rare species of rowan are protected. There is access to the site if visitors wish to look at the trees. At the head of the valley bear right and walk westwards to the north summit of Beinn Tarsuinn, 1,819ft (554m). Continue south-west over a stony plateau, dipping slightly, and then rising to the southern summit of Beinn Tarsuinn, 1,717ft (523m). Walk west north-west to the head of Glen Catacol, and proceed down this very attractive valley, accompanied by the sound of rushing water, back to the starting point.

A little further south, beyond the headland of Rubha Airigh Beg, is another opportunity for hill walkers to explore the peaks of Beinn Bhreac and Beinn Bharrian and the beautifully situated Coire Fhionn Lochan — a jewel of a mountain lake.

From **Mid Thundergay** a signposted path points the way to Coire Lochan. Beyond the buildings of the settlement, pass through a kissing gate into open ground, and proceed to an access gate through the deer fence. Cross over the Lenimore Burn using the stepping stones, and bear right upstream. In parts, the route is boggy as it crosses and recrosses the burn. Keep alongside the southern bank as it cascades over ledges of rock. Soon the path reaches two cairns, and looking back there is a splendid panorama of Kilbrannan Sound, the Kintyre peninsula and beyond to the Paps of Jurs.

The Fhionn Lochan lies in a deep hollow, a typical glacial corrie surrounded by the enclosing arms of Beinn Bhreac, 2,334ft (711m). This is an idyllic spot with a great deal of atmosphere, where the crystal-clear water is edged by beaches of coarse granite sand. The distance, returning by the same route, is $3^{1}/_{4}$ miles (5.2km).

An 8 mile (12.8km) walk includes Coire-Fhionn Lochan, Beinn Bhreac, Beinn Bharrain, Glas Choirein and Pirnmill. Follow the route

Lochranza

Caledonian MacBrayne operate many ferry services around Arran

*Catacol: the Twelve Apostles (above);
looking towards Glen Catacol (below)*

for the previous walk to the col south of Meall Bhig. Bear right at the col and ascend the north ridge above Coirein Lochain to a minor top, 2,142ft (653m). Continue south on the stony whaleback ridge to the summit of Beinn Bhreac, 2,334ft (711m). Descend easily to the Bealach an Fharaidh, 1,882ft (574m), and climb the wide ridge to the north-east summit of Beinn Bharrain, 2,366ft (721m). The two tops of Beinn Bharrain have well-defined ridges enclosing the narrow recesses of Coire Roinn; both ridges offer exposed scrambling. Experienced hill walkers will delight in the descent of one of these ridges, before returning to Pirnmill alongside the Allt Goghlach. Ordinary mortals who wish to see another dawn, should re-trace their steps to the Bealach an Fharaidh, and descend the boulder-strewn slopes to the lochan in Glas Choirein. Follow the path on the north side of the burn, above a steep-sided ravine on the left, to the ladder stile in the deer fence. Follow the path to a stile, through some trees, and across the edge of a field to a house. Bear left, and walk down the track to Pirnmill. There is the promise of afternoon teas awaiting the tired walker arriving at Pirnmill. If you haven't arranged transport, it is another $1^3/_4$ miles (2.8km) back along the road to Mid Thundergay.

Once over the Iorsa Water, the land becomes lower in relief as one passes into the farming area of Machrie, Shiskine and Blackwaterfoot. The fields are now a mixture of improved grassland and arable land, bordered by distant low hills with slopes planted by the Forestry Commission. The Machrie Water enters the sea near the golf course (9-hole) at the junction with the little road that is a link to the B880. Along a track close by this turning is the late neolithic or early Bronze Age Auchagallon Cairn, NR893346. Although described as a stone circle, the monument is more likely to be a burial cairn surrounded by an interrupted ring of boulders. The larger stones lie on the west side, and the smaller ones on the east.

The immediate area was well favoured for settlement by early humans, and there is other evidence of their occupation in the form of chambered cairns, stone circles, hut circles and standing stones. A little further south, a sign directs the visitor to the Machrie Moor stone circles NR9032. Opposite is a small car park for three or four cars. The area contains a fascinating collection of neolithic and Bronze Age monuments, probably the most remarkable archaeological site on the island. All the principal sites lie close to the track leading to the derelict Moss Farm.

South of the Moss Farm track, the A841 bends inland in order to avoid the high ground of Torr Righ Mór, before returning to the mouth of the Black Water. The village of **Blackwaterfoot** was the port of Shiskine, another community which lies 1 mile (1.6km) away on the String road. At one time a sailing packet boat operated between Blackwaterfoot and Campbeltown, and towards the end of the nineteenth century the settlement began to develop as the main tourist centre in the district. There is a tiny, attractive harbour where a boat can be hired for sea angling trips.

North of the village, the coastline swings out to Drumadoon Point with a fine sandy beach in between. A walk to the King's Cave, NR884309, makes an interesting outing. Head north-west along the shore for half a mile (0.8km), and follow a grassy path which passes two rocky outcrops. Beyond a stile, ascend towards the rock pinnacle, and continue northwards along the foot of the impressive columnar cliffs to reach a wide grassy raised beach. The way climbs through sandstone outcrops to reach the King's Cave. It was reputed to be the hiding place of Robert the Bruce before he returned to the mainland. The cave contains some ancient, though now faint, rock carvings, thought to date back to early Christian or Viking times. One is of a large cross; the other is a human figure holding what appears to be a bow over its head. A return can be made up the steep path that climbs to the top of the cliffs, round the east side of The Doon and on to the summit of the Iron Age fort. Further on, continue along the perimeter of the golf course back to Blackwaterfoot. The distance there and back is $4^1/_2$ miles (6.4km).

The surrounding area can offer many facilities, including golf, trekking, tennis, river fishing and boat hire. A good range of accommodation is available.

Beyond Brown Head, the main road climbs away from the coast, and links the hamlets of Sliddery, Lagg, Kilmory, Shannochie, East and West Bennan. It crosses the two major streams flowing swiftly southwards from their moorland and forested recesses in this part of Arran. The southern coastline is a magnet for geographers and geologists, who come to study the extensive sections of raised beaches. Above the cliffs are the remains of duns and chambered cairns. The shoreline is an interesting mixture of rock dykes, boulders, caves, slabs, shingle and sand. Along the quiet Corriecravie strand, visitors should take the opportunity of walking by the sea to enjoy the wonderful variety of summer wild flowers, and to view curlews, black-headed gulls, eider, shags, cormorants, wheatears, whinchats and stonechats. You are also quite likely to spot seals just offshore.

Just past Corriecravie, a track leads directly, south of the road, to Torr a'Chaisteil Dun, NR922233. This Iron Age fort is typical of many

Pirnmill, with Kintyre in the distance

Standing stone at Machrie

Lagg Inn

Blackwaterfoot

hundreds of similar duns to be found in western Scotland. It consists of a single rampart wall enclosing a circular mound about 46ft (14m) in diameter, with an entry on the east side. The road descends to Lagg, sheltered by a garland of trees, with the Kilmory Water alongside the gardens of the attractive eighteenth-century coaching inn. Just beyond the bridge, a track gives access to Torrylin chambered cairn, NR955211. This Clyde-type cairn had a trapezoidal or rectangular mound containing at least four compartments. On investigation the mound was found to contain human skulls and other animal and human remains. Grave goods consisted of a fragment of a neolithic bowl and a flint knife. Further along the main road is a way up to Kilmory Church, and the prospect of a forest walk via Auchareoch and Aucheleffan farmsteads, returning to Kilmory.

Beyond Torrylin Cairn lies the sea, and although much of the immediate coastline is secluded and rocky, the longest and loveliest stretch of sand on the island is to be found here. East of Bennan Head, a loop road drops down to the sea at **Kildonan**. There are opportunities here for exploring the rocky strand as far as the Black Cave. The front at Kildonan is a pleasant spot with sandy sections between the rocky dykes running out to sea. It is a lovely spot for children, and there are sub-aqua facilities, self-drive cruise charter and boats for hire. At the end of the village are the ivy-covered ruins of Kildonan Castle. The fortress was given to John, the bastard son of Robert III, in 1406. Out to sea is the island of Pladda with its lighthouse, and to the right of it in the distance is the mass of Ailsa Craig.

The main road turns north again past Dippin Head and crosses over the Glenashdale Burn into **Whiting Bay**. The district has been inhabited since ancient times, with the chambered tombs of the Giant's Graves in forest clearings south of Glenashdale Burn, NS041248. Smuggling and the running of illicit stills were profitable sidelines in the eighteenth century, and outwitting the exciseman added spice to a hard life. In the early part of the nineteenth century, steamers brought visitors to Whiting Bay at the height of the tourist boom. Competition from road transport meant the end of sailing operations, and the pier was dismantled in 1964.

There are two attractive excursions from Whiting Bay. The first is the walk through Forestry Commission woodlands alongside the fast-flowing Glenashdale Burn to view the spectacular Glenashdale waterfalls, reached by a track alongside the golf course and a turning right at South Kiscadale. The main waterfall has two impressive drops, and from a railed area there is an excellent view of the cascades. Returning the same way, back to the centre of the resort, the total distance is $3^1/_2$ miles (5.6km). The second walk is to the Iron Age fort at King's Cross Point, NS056283, for lovely views of Holy Island, with its classical shape, columnar cliffs, and lighthouse.

Whiting Bay has a wide range of accommodation, and among the facilities are an 18-hole golf course, tennis courts, a putting green and a bowling green. Boats and cycles may be hired. The Isle of Arran Music Festival is held in March, and the Whiting Bay Fun Week in July.

Lamlash is the administrative, health and education centre for the island. The bay is dominated by Holy Island, called 'Eilean Molaise' after the Irish Saint who preached there about AD680. Interesting relics have been found in and around a cave on the island. Near the Saint's Cave is the 'Judgement Stone' or pulpit rock. It was in Lamlash Bay in 1263, that King Hakon assembled a great fleet of galleys prior to the Battle of Largs. After their defeat the remnants of the Viking fleet gathered before their final departure.

The present parish church of Kilbride was built by the twelfth Duke of Hamilton in 1884. It has a number of beautiful stained glass memorial windows, a carillon of nine bells and a fine two manual organ. The plainly visible spire of the former United Free Church is a conspicuous landmark, but the building is no longer used for church services. The ruined church of St Brigid in the Kilbride burial ground of Lamlash was built in the fourteenth century, but was damaged by fire during the English raid of 1406. The chapel walls and graveyard contain sculptured stones, the oldest dated 1603.

At one time Lamlash had a dye mill and a meal mill, but today it relies on farming and tourism, and allied to the latter there is a candle-making business, a mustard factory, and Arran Crafts handling hand-made goods produced on the island.

Facilities for visitors include an 18-hole golf course, tennis courts, bowling green, putting green, yachting, marine and sub aqua requirements, cycle hire, sea angling trips, and there is safe sea bathing.

From Lamlash towards Brodick, there is a fine picnic site on the brow of the hill at NS018333. It is a very pleasant spot with picnic tables set out in clearings amongst the trees.

For a 4 mile (6.4km) walk from here, cross over the road and walk towards a signpost, turning left along a line of conifers. Continue through bracken and along a heathery ridge of the Clauchland Hills to the cairn of Dun Fionn. This is a wonderful viewpoint looking south south-east to Holy Island, and north-west to Brodick Bay and its superb backcloth of jagged peaks.

Kildonan

Lamlash and Holy Island

Fishing boats at Lamlash

14

GLASGOW AND THE CLYDE VALLEY

Glasgow grew up as a settlement above the north bank of the Clyde, and according to legend has its origins in the sixth century as a community founded by St Mungo or Kentigern. The name Glasgow is probably derived from the Celtic language, meaning, 'a dear green place'.

Glasgow was granted a burgh charter in 1175 and throughout the Middle Ages, remained, despite its burgh status, a village settlement renowned for its cathedral and as a centre of learning. By the mid-seventeenth century, the city began to prosper from increased trade, particularly with the colonies, and in the eighteenth century was becoming an important centre for sugar and tobacco.

The nineteenth century saw the rise of the Industrial Revolution, and Glasgow became a prosperous place with the main manufacturing industries of textiles, chemicals and later, shipbuilding. The influx of thousands of immigrants from the Highlands and Islands and from Ireland gave ready access to cheap labour. The rapid growth of the city led to expansion to the north-west, and development on the south side of the river, which resulted in congested slums and general overcrowding.

This rich, overcrowded industrial sprawl of the Victorian era bequeathed to Glasgow a unique range of architecture, with a mixture of styles ranging from classical to baroque and Gothic. The city became Scotland's commercial capital, and huge sums were spent on spectacular building projects, particularly banks, churches and municipal edifices. They managed to blend together to form a comparatively harmonious townscape. John Betjeman described

Glasgow as the greatest Victorian city in Europe.

The energy and enthusiasm of the city fathers did not stop there. They rightly concluded that the teeming population deserved green open spaces and parks. Today, the legacy is of a greater number of parks per head of population than any other city in Europe. In fact, Glasgow District now includes more than seventy public parks. It also acquired an enthusiasm for the visual arts, music and theatre, and there is a splendid assembly of art galleries and museums all within easy reach of the city centre.

Glasgow was chosen to be Europe's 1990 City of Culture. The city has created an international platform to display both its achievements, and the culture of the region, and has hosted a numerous and wide variety of events and festivals.

At the heart of Glasgow is George Square the principal square in the city. It contains colourful flower beds and a number of statues, especially the tall column of the poet and novelist Sir Walter Scott. The square was laid out in the eighteenth century for the prosperous Glasgow merchants of that time. During the second half of the nineteenth century the Municipal Buildings and General Post Office moved to the site. The only survivor of the original buildings is the one now occupied by the hotel.

Queen Street Station has its main entrance in George Square, and services run to Edinburgh, Perth, Stirling, Dundee and Aberdeen, as well as on the main Highland routes to Inverness, Oban and Mallaig.

On the east side of George Square stands the magnificent **City Chambers**. It is a supreme example of Victorian confidence and prosperity, and it dominates that part of the square. The building has an ornate exterior, recently stone-cleaned, and a starkly imposing marble and alabaster staircase. There are painted ceilings and mosaic floors, a richly decorated Banqueting Hall, and a semi-circular Council Hall lined with mahogany and tapestries. There are guided tours at given times or by previous arrangement.

George Square also contains the Head Post Office on the southern side, and the **Merchants House** on the north-west corner. The latter building is now the home of the Glasgow Chamber of Commerce, and it contains many examples of the city's merchant past. Look for the golden sailing ship on top of the tower, a replica of one in Briggait where the Merchants' House once stood.

Just west of George Square is the Greater Glasgow Tourist Information Centre in St Vincent Place. Behind it is Royal Exchange Square, which is dominated by the imposing building of **Stirling's Library**. There is a spectacular view of its neo-classical façade,

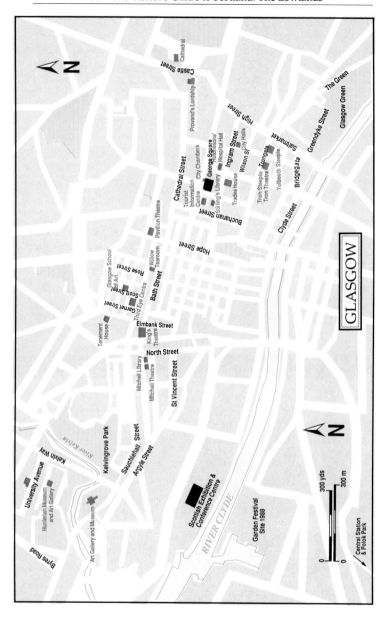

GLASGOW

Cathedral

Castle Street

Provand's Lordship

High Street

The Green

Glasgow Green

Greendyke Street

Saltmarket

Bridgegate

Cathedral Street

Clyde Street

George Square

City Chambers

Hutchesons'
Hospital Hall

Ingram Street

Wilson St

City Halls

Tongate

Tron Steeple/
Tron Theatre

Tolbooth Steeple

Tourist
Information
Centre

Stirling's Library

Trades House

Buchanan Street

Pavilion Theatre

Hope Street

Willow
Tearoom

Rose Street

Glasgow School
of Art

Scott Street

Bath Street

Third Eye Centre

Garnet Street

Tenement
House

Elmbank Street

King's
Theatre

North Street

Mitchell Library

Mitchell Theatre

St Vincent Street

Sauchiehall Street

Kelvingrove Park

Argyle Street

RIVER KELVIN

Kelvin Way

University Avenue

Hunterian Museum
and Art Gallery

Art Gallery and Museum

Byres Road

Scottish Exhibition &
Conference Centre

RIVER CLYDE

Garden Festival
Site 1988

300 yds

300 m

Central Station
& Polok Park

City Chambers, an example of Glasgow's fine Victorian architecture

guarded by the statue of the Duke of Wellington in front, from Ingram Street. The building stands in one of the few surviving Georgian squares, and is noted for its magnificently ornamented barrel-vaulted ceiling, which was originally the main hall of the Royal Exchange. The library was a private foundation in 1791, became a Glasgow Corporation Library in 1912, and moved to Exchange Square in 1954.

Glasgow Cathedral is about $1^1/_2$ miles (2.4km) north-east of George Square. It is easily reached by convenient buses from Central Station, Argyle Street, Hope Street and George Square. Car parking may be found in the immediate neighbourhood. Although the present building dates from the thirteenth to the fifteenth centuries, there has probably been an ecclesiastical institution on the present site since the late sixth century when St Mungo founded a church here.

The building really is a double church, with a rectangular nave, and the lower church lying below the choir of the cathedral. By the end of the fourteenth century the building was largely as it appears today, except for the erection of the Blacader Aisle in the lower church during the fifteenth century. The latter is one of the glories of medieval Scottish architecture, with a number of stone pillars, and the tomb of St Mungo. The west wall displays a beautiful modern Scottish tapestry designed by Robert Stewart.

During the troubles of the Reformation, the building was protected by the Glasgow Guilds, and although furnishings were damaged, the structure remained whole and roofed. The lofty nave is particularly impressive with a large quire screen, some ornate carving, and one of the finest post-war collections of stained glass windows to be found in Britain.

The Friends of Glasgow Cathedral plan a visitors' centre which will be the focal point of the new cathedral precinct redevelopment scheme. Close by the cathedral is the Necropolis, a Victorian cemetery containing an impressive array of ornate tombstones, mausoleums and monuments.

Just opposite the cathedral, on the corner of Macleod Street and Castle Street is the **Provand's Lordship**. This house of low ceilings and oak beams was built in 1471, and is now the oldest surviving domestic dwelling in the city centre. It was built as part of a paupers' hospital, probably as the manse for the cathedral clergy. It is now open to the public as a museum, and displays domestic interiors and articles from many periods in the city's history, plus a fine collection of furniture, paintings and pottery. The ground floor should be of interest to all children as it houses a tantalising assortment of goodies from an early twentieth-century sweet shop.

Continuing westwards along Cathedral Street you come to the residencies and faculty buildings of the **University of Strathclyde**. This institution was founded in 1795, with money bequested by Professor John Anderson of Glasgow University, whose interest lay in technical, vocational and evening-class education. From being the Royal College of Science and Technology, it became the University of Strathclyde in 1964. Over the years it has become well known for its lively department of arts and social sciences, and for its flourishing business school. Hidden away in a modern block of its city-centre campus is the Collins Gallery. This has become one of Glasgow's major venues for varied exhibitions of painting, sculpture, photographs and prints.

Walk south from the University of Strathclyde down John Street, cross Cochrane Street, and you come to Ingram Street. On the corner stands the recently renovated **Hutchesons' Hospital Hall** with its elegant classical façade, and statues of George and Thomas Hutcheson who founded this charitable institution for aged men and orphan boys.

In 1983 the building was acquired by the National Trust for Scotland as their regional headquarters. There is a visitor centre and a shop and the hall is a venue for meetings, dinners, concerts and conferences. The refurbishment of the building was completed in 1987.

Across Ingram Street to the left lies the **City and County Buildings**, a huge neo-classical structure built in 1842-4. The west front, facing Hutcheson Street, is graced by a splendid row of Corinthian columns. Looking back towards Ingram Street, there is a very good view of Hutchesons' Hall. Walk westwards along Garth Street to Glassford Street, and there you will see the **Trades House** with its fine Robert Adam façade dating from 1791.

Turn into Wilson Street and proceed towards Virginia Street, where there is a range of buildings built about 1817 which are recognised as fine examples of the period. During business hours it is sometimes possible to walk through Virginia Court to Miller Street. Here you will see grooves cut into the stone by cartwheels, as well as cobbles, flagstones and ironwork. All these visual effects consolidate the feeling of the early nineteenth century merchant city.

Walking east along Ingram Street brings you to Candleriggs on the right. Here is situated the **City Hall**, a building with excellent acoustics which has been the city's main large-scale concert venue up to now, but will soon be superseded by the new Concert Hall. The building also contains Glasgow's Ticket Centre — a computer-controlled Central Box Office for concert and theatre performances (☎ 041 552 5961).

Continuing south down Candleriggs brings you to Trongate, known as St Thenew's Gate until the Tron, or weighbridge, was set up. All Scottish burgh towns had such a facility in order to weigh the local produce or other goods brought in for sale. At this important crossroad is the **Tolbooth Steeple**, marking what once was the heart of the city's trading and business area. The tower, 126ft (38m) high, now stands alone, but resumes its full pride of place when it becomes the starting-point for the Glasgow Marathon. Close by is Glasgow's mercat (or market) cross, a sturdy, neat octagonal tower with a balustraded roof topped by a heraldic unicorn. The original market cross was demolished in 1659. Just along Trongate is the **Tron Steeple** dating from the late sixteenth-early seventeenth century, which was the remaining part of the original Tron Church destroyed

George Square, Glasgow

by fire in the late eighteenth century. The church was rebuilt away from the steeple and now houses the Tron Theatre.

From Glasgow Cross, stroll down Saltmarket, and turn left into

Glasgow Cross

St Andrew's Street to enjoy the fine view of St Andrew's Church built in 1756. The building houses an organ constructed by James Watt. Proceed down Turnbull Street and turn left at the bottom into Greendyke Street. The area between here and the river is **Glasgow Green**, the city's oldest public open space. This was common land as far back as 1178, where the ordinary citizens could graze their cattle and sheep. The Green was adopted by the city in 1662 as their first public park.

The Green is entered through a huge arch presented to the citizens of Glasgow by a local worthy a century ago. This spot is also the finish of the Glasgow Marathon. Walking along The Green you come to a striking red sandstone building built in 1898. This is the much-loved **People's Palace**, a museum devoted to the history of the city, and the social and industrial life of the people in the nineteenth century. It is a most entertaining place top visit, completely epitomising the spirit and character of the area. By 1990, the People's Palace will have new displays and exhibitions, and new facilities for visitors. To the rear, the soaring ironwork and glass of the Winter Gardens has been refurbished.

Across the road from the People's Palace, is the rather imposing, but strange-looking building of the **Templeton Business Centre**. Originally a carpet works, it was designed on the style of the Doge's Palace in Venice, but has recently been renovated to provide office accommodation. Walk across the Green and follow the River Clyde back to the Albert Bridge, passing on your way, Nelson's Column erected in 1807. There are two objects of interest nearby: the Doulton Fountain and an engraved boulder commemorating the invention of the steam condenser in 1765 by James Watt.

Leaving the Green, continue along Clyde Street with the High Court building on the right, and under the railway bridge to the Briggait indoor shopping centre, with its collection of small shops. Just beyond, on the corner of Bridgegate, is the **Merchants' Steeple**, all that remains of the seventeenth-century Merchants' House, which dominates the old Fishmarket area. This was originally the place where salt for curing fish was handled.

The next objective is the Jamaica footbridge and the sailing vessel *Carrick*, an old clipper which is the headquarters of the RNVR Club of Scotland. It still holds the world sailing record of 65 days for the twelve thousand mile journey from Adelaide to London.

Leave the cobbled walkway and turn right into Dixon Street and on to St Enoch Square. Here, the former site of the mainline railway station has been converted into a major shopping centre, a glass-covered complex which also has an ice rink. The neat underground station building has been conserved and is now used as a travel centre, adjoining the modern underground station. Affectionately known as the 'Clockwork Orange', the Glasgow Underground provides a rapid circular route around the edge of the city centre. The system has been completely modernised and the orange-coloured trains stop at fifteen stations on its circuit.

Walk northwards and turn into Argyle Street one of Glasgow's well-known thoroughfares. Buchanan Street, now mainly pedestrianised, has long been Glasgow's prime shopping street. It is linked to Argyle Street by a covered shopping mall, containing a variety of small shops. A short distance away to the west is **Central Station**, with its bridge spanning Argyle Street. This is known as the Hielanman's Umbrella, as it was once a favourite meeting place for the many highlanders who came to find work in the city. The station is a grand and imposing structure, a splendid example of Victorian railway architecture. Train services run from here to London and there are connections to the Clyde coast ports and to the Stranraer-Larne ferry to Northern Ireland. You can also catch a local train to Pollokshaws West for the Burrell Collection.

Sauchiehall Street is easily accessible by walking north up Hope Street. This is another of Glasgow's famous streets and the name is believed to come from two Scots words meaning 'a willow meadow', or *Sauchie haugh*. Running from West Nile Street to Blythswood Street, Sauchiehall Street is now a pedestrian precinct. North from Sauchiehall Street along Hope Street are the Pavilion Theatre in nearby Renfield Street, and a little further on the Theatre Royal and the Scottish TV Centre. Returning to Sauchiehall Street, beyond the shopping centre is the **Willow Tearoom**. If you have sampled afternoon tea at Betty's Tearoom in Harrogate, then you are in for another treat at Miss Cranston's emporium. This was a brilliant Art Nouveau establishment which Charles Rennie Machintosh designed for Miss Kate Cranston. Over the years all her tearooms were closed down, but the Willow has been rescued with replica Mackintosh furniture and the original Mackintosh façade has been restored. The tearoom is on the first floor above a jeweller's shop.

To the right in Rose Street, is the Glasgow Film Theatre, and a little further along Sauchiehall Street is the **McLellan Gallery**, which holds major exhibitions from Glasgow and abroad. Behind it in Renfrew Street, is the **Glasgow School of Art** designed by C.R. Mackintosh. The **Third Eye Centre** in Sauchiehall Street is a busy contemporary arts centre, with a variety of exhibitions including

Broomielaw, River Clyde, Glasgow

paintings, photography and sculpture. The Centre has a café and also houses a small theatre with a lively programme of plays, films, dance, music and poetry readings.

A steep climb up Scott Street and left along Buccleuch Street, Garnethill, beings you to No 145, a first-floor flat in a tenement house, now under the care of the National Trust for Scotland. The flat was restored by the Trust after its purchase in 1982 from the actress Anna Davidson, who had carefully preserved its contents. It is just like stepping into a world where time has stood still, a time capsule left by Miss Agnes Toward, who lived there from 1911 to 1965. The accommodation consists of a hall, parlour, bedroom, kitchen and bathroom, containing furniture, furnishings, box-beds and kitchen range. There are many domestic items and possessions of a lifetime, including letters, bills receipts and school books. A visit here will be a wonderful education for both children and adults.

After the steep descent back to Sauchiehall Street, turn right and follow the road over the M8. On turning left down North Street, look across to the leaning sandstone drinking fountain with four clock faces. The imposing building ahead, complete with a prominent copper dome, is the **Mitchell Library**, the largest public reference library in Europe. The western part of the building with its handsome façade and pillars, now houses the Mitchell Theatre, a café and meeting rooms.

Just across the M8 in Bath Street is the **King's Theatre**. Opened in 1904, it is the principal theatre in the city, and still retains its elaborate Edwardian interior. Famous actors and actresses of the past have played here, and amateur operatic societies and theatrical companies stage their productions in the theatre. Continue down Elmbank Street past Charing Cross Station, and turn left into Vincent Street. A short distance along on the right is the massive **St Vincent Street Church** designed by Alexander 'Greek' Thomson, and built in 1858. It is a remarkable building in the unique Egyptian-classical style, with many pillars and an interesting pinnacled tower topped by an elongated dome. Facing the church, in a contrasting style is the new **Britoil Building** opened in 1986. At the junction with Hope Street is the extraordinary building called the **'Hatrack'** — ten storeys high, but only three bays wide. Immediately adjacent, and again in contrasting style, is the **Scottish Amicable Building** covered with many tinted glass panels. Turn right at the road junction for the return to Central Station.

A good starting point to explore the western end of the city around Glasgow University, would be to take an underground train to Hillhead Station. From the station, walk up Byres Road to Great Western Road. Cross this very busy thoroughfare to the main entrance to the park and its **Botanic Gardens**. These have been on the site since 1842, but the most interesting feature is the Kibble Hothouse of 1873, a veritable glass palace containing a marvellous and unique collection of tree ferns, and plants from many parts of the world. Inside, a number of ornamental ponds are overlooked by sculptures, each by a different artist.

Return to Queen Margaret Drive, cross over the River Kelvin beyond the headquarters of BBC Scotland, turn right and proceed alongside the river on the **Kelvin Walkway**. The eventual aim is that the walkway should lead out along the upper reaches of the river and link up with the West Highland Way which starts at Milngavie (pronounced Mill-guy). Follow the river under the Great Western Road, past Kelvinbridge Station and through a tunnel under the road. Climb uphill into **Kelvingrove Park** to the statue of Field Marshall Earl Roberts. Walk south-west and descend to an impressive Victorian fountain, which commemorates the achievements of Lord Provost Stewart in bringing an abundant clean water supply from Loch Katrine to Glasgow.

Bear left on reaching the Kelvin Way, and turn right at the bottom along Argyle Street to the **Kelvingrove Museum and Art Gallery**. The building contains one of the finest municipal art collections in Britain, with seventeenth-century Dutch and nineteenth-century French paintings, and works from the Glasgow School. From the outside the building looks like a truly Victorian museum. A superb, red sandstone affair with ornate towers and sweeping stairways. It houses important collections in the fields of archaeology and natural history, as well as the decorative arts.

On leaving the Museum and Art Gallery, walk through the grounds towards the bridge over the River Kelvin, and rejoin the Kelvin Way up to the university. Turn left into University Avenue, and note the memorial gates to twenty-eight famous graduates, including Lister, Adam Smith and James Watt.

Glasgow University was founded in 1451, and moved to the west end of the city in 1870. The ornately spired, neo-Gothic tower which acts as the focal point of the university was designed by George Gilbert Scott and continued by his son John. A general guide and route plan of the university, may be obtained from the information office just off the quadrangle. Enter the campus by the gatehouse and walk round the main block of buildings. The Hunterian Museum is tucked away up a flight of stairs from the main quadrangle, and some of the highlights include Hunter's famous coin collection, and a superb geological display.

Across the road is situated the **Hunterian Art Gallery**; the present building was opened in 1980. The collection includes paintings by Rembrandt, Stubbs, J.M. Whistler and the 'Glasgow Boys'. The print collection, the largest in Scotland, contains over 20,000 individual items. Another treasure is the superb **Mackintosh House**, opened in 1981, which contains a reconstruction of Charles Rennie Machintosh's Glasgow House — high-backed chairs, cool white drawing room and a brilliant purple bedroom. The museum and art gallery should not be missed during a stay in Glasgow.

Walk down University Avenue to Byres Road and turn right to the starting point at Hillhead Station. The distance of this tour is 3 miles (4.8km).

Glasgow has a number of walkways which include a route along the former Forth and Clyde Canal into the city from Temple Bridge, NS549693, to Port Dundas basin, NS594667. The walking distance, there and back is 8 miles (12.8km). The return journey may be made by catching a Service 21 or 60 bus back to Maryhill Locks from Garscube Road.

The **Burrell Collection** is set in the delightful surroundings of Pollok Park to the south of the river. Sir William Burrell gave his priceless collection of art and other treasures to the city in 1944, having stipulated that the collection should be housed some miles away because of the danger of air pollution. Although the smoky atmosphere gradually cleared above Glasgow, it was not until 1967 that a suitable site was finally found. Opened by the Queen in 1983, this unique and varied collection is imaginatively displayed in a modern building with many glass walls and a supporting cast of warm-coloured Locharbriggs sandstone. The building has won many awards, and the collection now rivals Edinburgh Castle as Scotland's chief tourist attraction.

Nearby, in Pollok Park, is the stately mansion of **Pollok House** which is open to visitors. It has a fine collection of ceramics, silver, furniture and glassware, together with Spanish paintings by Goya, Murillo and El Greco. There is a demonstration garden, woodland trails, and a herd of shaggy Highland cattle.

Glasgow is easy to get out of to visit the wide variety of spectacular scenery and places of interest around the area. Westwards, at the mouth of the Clyde, is the **Muirshiel Regional Park**. It is an upland area south of Greenock, a beautiful landscape of moorland, river valleys, coastline and lochs. There are a number of visitor centres staffed by rangers, such as Cornalees, NS248722, which has a wildlife information centre, and a picnic site, with panoramic views looking out over the Firth of Clyde. Another visitor centre is situated at the head of the River Calder at Muirshiel. Here, patches of broadleaved and coniferous woodland hide nature trails and back on to bare heathery moors. This is fine bird-watching and hill-walking territory. To the south-east, **Castle Semple Water Park** near Lochwinnoch offers sailing, canoeing, rowing and sailboarding facilities. Northwards, there is a picnic site at Barnbrock Farm, BS356640. The RSPB has an excellent visitor centre off the A760, half a mile (0.8km) east of Lochwinnock village. The centre and shop are open daily, and there are special facilities for schools. (☎ (0505) 842663). Visitors can watch many species of wildfowl, such as great crested grebe, moorhen and mallard.

South-east of Glasgow, the River Clyde flows through a built-up and industrial landscape. However, the greening process began in the 1960s and 1970s with the transformation of an area of mining dereliction between Hamilton and Motherwell. The development of the **Strathclyde Park** meant relocating the river and constructing an artificial loch. The park now provides a large number of sporting and

The Burrell Collection, Pollok Park, Glasgow

Lohan, a statue from the Ming Dynasty

218

leisure activities. The visitor centre has information on nature exhibits, nature trails, local history, including the excavated remains of a Roman bath-house, picnic and play areas.

Only 8 miles (12.8km) from Glasgow is the **David Livingstone Centre** at Blantyre. Surrounded by parkland, and situated on the banks of the Clyde, the eighteenth-century tenement building, once part of a mill complex, displays a fascinating insight into a mill boy's dream and driving ambition to become a missionary.

Just south of Uddingston, and overlooking a wooded curve of the River Clyde, are the remains of one of the most imposing of Scotland's medieval castles, **Bothwell Castle**. Constructed between the thirteenth and sixteenth centuries, the walls and turrets of this red sandstone fortress make an impressive sight. During its early years it was beseiged, deliberately dismantled and rebuilt on a number of occasions. In the late fourteenth century, it was probably completed by Archibald 'the Grim', third Earl of Douglas, but was again partly dismantled in the fifteenth century. Today, the mighty round keep or donjon looks out over the rectangular courtyard, which is sur-

Hornby Castle portal — re-erected in the Burrell Collection

rounded by curtain walls and four flanking towers.

Travelling south towards Hamilton, the road passes over the Clyde at **Bothwell Bridge**. This was the site of the battle in June 1679, when the Covenanters suffered their worst defeat. They lost 400 dead and 1,200 captured by the forces of Graham of Claverhouse. A monument to the Covenanters can be seen at the north end of the bridge.

The town of **Hamilton** has a long and notable history. Originally called *Cadzow*, a name that goes back to the sixth century, its name was changed to Hamilton by a charter from James II in recognition of the great land-owning family. On the edge of Strathclyde Country Park stands a most remarkable building — the striking domed mausoleum built for Alexander X Duke of Hamilton, nicknamed, 'Il Magnifico'. The mausoleum was built in the mid-nineteenth century, and his ancestors were placed in its crypt. The duke was interred there in an Egyptian sarcophagus in 1852, but subsequent mining subsidence threatened the building, and the bodies were re-interred elsewhere. The mausoleum is open to the public and items of particular interest are its splendid dome, marble mosaic floor, bronze doors, and an unplanned chapel echo which lasts for fifteen seconds, making it acoustically unsuitable as a place of worship.

The town contains other places of interest which make it worthy of a visit. They include, the Hamilton District Museum in Muir Street, which contains an extensive transport section, and an eighteenth-century Assembly Room complete with a musicians' gallery. The Cameronian Museum on Mote Hill, just behind the District Museum, was once the Duke of Hamilton's riding school. It now houses the regimental museum of the Scottish Rifles, including relics of the Covenanting movement. The Old Parish Church in Church Street, designed in the classical style by William Adam was opened in 1734. At the front of the church stands the tenth-century, early Christian, Netherton Cross, a red sandstone slab decorated on all four sides. Also in the churchyard, on the east wall, is the 'Heads Memorial' commemorating four Lanarkshire Covenanters beheaded after the 1666 Pentland Rising.

From Hamilton, take the A72 Lanark/B7078 Larkhall road to the village of Ferniegair, and turn right into the **Chatelherault Country Park**. Another striking reminder of the Dukes of Hamilton is their eighteenth-century hunting lodge of Chatelherault (pronounced Shatellerow). The building is a fine example of Georgian architecture, designed in 1731 and recently completely renovated There is a visitor centre, parkland walks, and the wooded gorge of the River

Avon with the ruins of Cadzow Castle perched on the edge. The River Avon has worn its way through beds of sandstone, limestone and coal seams, and has created a paradise for flowers and wildlife.

The twisting A72 closely follows the River Clyde as it winds from side to side in a narrow valley. The river now passes through a landscape of woods, orchards and market gardens, and the road through a succession of interesting villages. There is **Dalserf**, with its parish church dating back to 1655, **Crossford**, with its wildlife reserve in the steep Nethan Gorge and the old weavers' village of **Kirkfieldbank**.

At Crossford, the road to **Craignethan Castle** turns right immediately before the Tillietudlem Hotel. The road has to negotiate a number of sharp steep bends on its journey across the valley of the Nethan. Work on the castle began in the 1530s for Sir James Hamilton, the illegitimate son of the first Earl of Arran. The castle occupies the tip of a promontory overlooking the Nethan Gorge.

Return on the same road across the valley of the Nethan and turn right at the first junction. Continue to the main A744, and take the unclassified road leading to Lesmahagow. Turn left at the first crossroads and proceed for half a mile (0.8km) to a track on the left. From here walk to the summit of **Black Hill** (National Trust for Scotland, NS832435). The summit contains a large Bronze Age round cairn, an oval hilltop fort enclosing the entire summit, and a later settlement defended mainly by double banks. From the 951ft (290m) high hilltop, there are magnificent views of the Clyde Valley and towards Ben Lomond and the Isle of Arran.

There are a number of other late first millennium BC hillforts to be found elsewhere in Clydesdale. These are Cow Castle, NT042331; Camps Knowe Wood, NT013228; Blackhill, Crawfordjohn, NS908259; Fallburn, NS961367. Continue left along the minor road to the B7018, and on down to the A72 once more. Just beyond Kirkfieldbank, the main road crosses over to the opposite bank of the River Clyde, and climbs steeply up to the town of Lanark.

Lanark is one of the oldest Royal Burghs in Scotland, and claims to have received a Royal Charter in 1140, although the earliest surviving one is from 1227. Many of the interesting and varied buildings in the High Street date from the eighteenth and nineteenth centuries, although they are often on the site of fifteenth-century buildings. At the foot of High Street, there are several examples of old passageways called wynds, which led to the vennels and closes of the town. St Nicholas' Church at Lanark Cross, built in 1774, houses what is said to be the oldest bell in Europe, first cast in 1110.

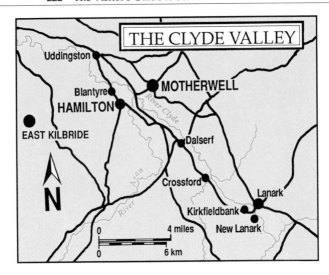

Lanark is noted for a number of ancient customs and the old tradition of checking the burgh boundaries continues as part of the Lanimer week celebrations. The climax comes in June with the crowning of a local schoolgirl as Lanimer Queen at the foot of Wallace's statue. Lanark Market (livestock) is one of Scotland's oldest and busiest and the main day is Monday.

In the Broomgate, the building with the crow-stepped gables adjoining Broomgate House is one of the oldest in Lanark, dating from 1640. At the east end of the town are the ruins of St Kentigern's Church, which was Lanark's parish church until the late eighteenth century. At one side of the domed chapel stands an obelisk commemorating the Lanark Covenanters. On Lanark Moor, south-east of the town, is the Lanark Country Park, with playing fields, boating, fishing, putting, an equestrian centre and picnic area.

From Lanark, follow the signs to **New Lanark**, descending steeply into the Clyde Gorge. Here, the river has quickened its pace through the narrow defile, and passes over a succession of spectacular waterfalls. The tremendous water power of these, the only cascades on the River Clyde, became the reason for the building of the village on a difficult site deep in a beautiful wooded gorge.

In 1784, Richard Arkwright, an English business man and inventor of the spinning frame, formed a partnership with David Dale a Glasgow merchant banker. Mills were erected on the edge of the river, and the water power used to drive the machinery. By 1799, the mills employed over two thousand people, mostly housed in stone-built tenements in the village.

In 1800, Robert Owen married Caroline Dale, and embarked on a series of social experiments during his time as a managing partner. Owen believed that people were affected by the conditions in which they lived and worked. He became a pioneer in education, putting into action ideas that had previously been only well-intentioned theories. The company provided a co-operative store, a nursery, a school, a counting house and an 'Institute for the formation of Character' — a form of Workers' Educational Association.

After the mills closed in 1968, the whole existence of the village was seriously threatened. However, a housing association and a conservation trust were formed to preserve this unique settlement. The local District Council purchased the tall mill buildings, small businesses were started, and the houses were renovated, all part of a massive programme of restoration. Today there is a mill and visitor centre which offers exhibition areas, gift shop and coffee bar.

From Caithness Row, a delightful way-marked trail leads into the **Falls of Clyde Nature Reserve**. The reserve takes in the whole of the thickly wooded gorge and all three of the waterfalls. The restored New Lanark dyeworks is the visitor centre run by the Scottish Wildlife Trust. The centre has an audio-visual show and windows looking directly over the Clyde — ideal for bird spotting.

From Lanark, the A73 travels over Hyndford Bridge to skirt round Tinto Hill, the highest hill in the Clyde Valley, 2,321ft (707m). It offers the finest viewpoint in Upper Clydesdale, from which the remarkably circuitous route of the Clyde from Lamington to Lanark can be observed. A footpath leaves Fallburn, NS964394, for the ascent of the hill, passing en route, Fallburn Iron Age hillfort. It is a superb walk to the top, where the summit area contains one of the largest Bronze Age round cairns in Scotland, measuring 135ft (43m) in diameter, by almost 20ft (6m) in height. The distance from Fallburn and back is 4 miles (6.4km), but with arranged transport, different return routes can be made over Scaut Hill to Broadlees or via Pap Craig to Millrig. There is a camping and caravan site close to Millrig at Wiston Lodge.

FURTHER INFORMATION FOR VISITORS

While every care has been taken in the compilation of these pages, opening times and circumstances can change from time to time. Please check locally. The publishers would be pleased to hear of any alterations or ammendments.

Abbeys

Dundrennan Abbey
A711, Dalbeattie to Kirkcudbright
Open: late March to end September, Sunday, 2-5pm, weekdays, 9.30am-7pm; beginning October to late March, Sunday 2-4pm, weekdays, 9.30am-4pm.

Glenluce Abbey
$1^1/_2$ miles (2.4km) north of Glenluce, off A75
Open: late March to end September, Sunday, 2-7pm, weekdays, 9.30am-7pm; beginning October to late March, Sunday, 2-4pm, weekdays, 9.30am-4pm.

Jedburgh Abbey
Open: April to September, weekdays 9.30am-7pm, Sundays 2-7pm; October to March, weekdays 9.30am-4pm, Sundays 2-4pm.

Melrose Abbey
Open: April to September, weekdays 9.30am-7pm, Sundays 2-7pm; October to March, weekdays 9.30am-4pm, Sundays 2-4pm.

Sweetheart Abbey
New Abbey, A710 south of Dumfries
Opening times as for Glenluce Abbey.

The following religious houses are open to view at all reasonable times: Abbey St Bathans Priory; Coldingham Priory; Cross Kirk, Peebles; Dryburgh Abbey; Kelso Abbey; Selkirk Abbey.

Accommodation

The holiday guides published by the Scottish Borders Tourist Board, East Lothian Tourist Board, Clyde Valley Tourist Board, Ayrshire & Burns Country Tourist Board, Dumfries and Galloway Tourist Board and Isle of Arran Tourist Board contain full lists of hotels and guest houses, self-catering accommodation, camping and caravan parks.

Castles and Towers

Borders

Ayton Castle
Off A1, 7 miles north of Berwick
Open: May to September, Sunday only, 2-5pm or by appointment.
☎ (08907) 81212
Admission charge.

Berwick-on-Tweed
Adjacent to railway station.
Open: all reasonable times. Free.

Bunkle Castle
On B6438, 8 miles north of Duns
Free. Ruin.

Branxholme Castle
On A7, 4 miles south-west of Hawick. Private residence, not normally open.

Fast Castle
On coast 10 miles north-west of Eyemouth
Free. Extraordinary cliff-top ruin, difficult access.

Ferniehurst Castle
Off A68, $1^1/_2$ miles (2.4km) south of Jedburgh
Open: May to October, Sundays 2-5pm; July and August, Wednesday and Sunday 2-5pm. Admission charge.

Floors Castle
Off A6089, 1 mile north-west of Kelso
Open: May, June and September, Sunday-Thursday; July and August, Sunday-Friday 10.30am-5.30pm (last admission to castle 4.45pm).

Greenknowe Tower
On A6089, $^1/_2$ mile west of Gordon
Free. Turreted tower house.

Hermitage Castle
Off A6399, 16 miles north-west of Langholm
Open: April to September 9.30am-7pm, Sundays 2-7pm; winter, weekends only. Admission charge.

Hume Castle
On B6364, 6 miles north of Kelso
Open: all year, Monday to Friday 10am-5pm, Sunday 2-5pm. Admission charge. Obtain key from Breadalbane Guncraft, below castle.

Neidpath Castle
On A72, 1 mile west of Peebles
Open: Easter to mid-October, Monday-Saturday 10am-1pm and 2-5pm, Sunday 1-5pm. Admission charge.

Newark Castle
Off A708, 4 miles west of Selkirk
Apply to Buccleuch Estates, Bowhill. Free.

Smailholm Tower
Off B6404, 7 miles west of Kelso
Free. Closed in winter.

Thirlstane Castle
Lauder, off A68
Open:Easter 2-5pm; July, August, Monday, Tuesday and Friday 2-5pm; May to September, Wednesday, Thursday and Saturday 2-5pm. Open Sundays 2-5pm.
Combined admission charge with Border Country Life Museum.

Tinnis Castle
Off B712, 9 miles south-west of
Peebles (Drumelzier)
Open: all reasonable times. Free.

East Lothian, Lothian
Dirleton Castle and Gardens
Off the A198, in Dirleton village.
Open: April to end September,
weekdays 9.30am-7pm, Sunday 2-
7pm; beginning October to March,
weekdays, 9.30am-4pm, Sunday, 2-
4pm. Admission charge.

Edinburgh Castle
United Services Museum
Open: daily 9.30am-6pm, Sunday
11am-6pm.

Hailes Castle
$1^1/_2$ miles (2.4km), south-west of
East Linton, by minor road
following River Tyne.
Open: as Dirleton Castle. Closed
Wednesday pm and all day
Thursday in winter. Admission
charge.

Luffness Castle
near Aberlady.
Open: by prior arrangement only.
☎ (08757) 218

Tantallon Castle
3 miles (4.8km) east of North
Berwick via A198.
Open: April to end September,
weekdays, 9.30am-7pm, Sunday, 2-
7pm; beginning October to March,
weekdays, 9.30am-4pm, Sunday, 2-
4pm. Closed Wednesday and
Thursday mornings in winter.
Admission charge.

Dumfries and Galloway
Caerlaverock Castle
Off B725, 8 miles (12.8km), south-
east of Dumfries.
Open: April to end September,
weekdays 9.30am-7pm, Sunday
2-7pm; beginning October to
March, weekdays 9.30am-4pm,
Sunday 2-4pm.

Cardoness Castle
A75, 1 mile (1.6km), south-west of
Gatehouse-of-Fleet.
Open: Easter to end September,
weekdays 9.30am-7pm, Sunday 2-
7pm; beginning October to March,
weekdays 9.30am-4pm, Sunday 2-
4pm.

Carsluith Castle
Beside A75, $3^1/_2$ miles (5.6km),
south-east of Creetown.

Comlongon Castle
Off B724, 8 miles (12.8km) west of
Annan.
Open: daily 10am-6pm. Admission
charge.

Drumcoltran Tower
1 mile (1.6km) north of
Kirkgunzeon, off A711

Dunskey Castle
$^1/_2$ mile (0.8km), south-east of
Portpatrick.
Ruins in dramatic cliff-top setting.

Gilnockie Tower
$1^1/_2$ miles (2.4km), north of
Canonbie, off A7.
View from outside only.

Hoddom Castle
Off B725, $2^1/_2$ miles (4km), south-
west of Ecclefechan.

View from outside only. Hilltop watch tower, $1/_2$ mile (0.8km) to the south. Countryside visitor centre is starting point for a number of easy riverside and woodland walks.

Lochmaben Castle
1 mile (1.6km), south of Loch-maben, on a promontory in Castle Loch. Off B7020, Annan to Lochmaben road. Castle Loch is a nature reserve. No restricted access.

Maclellan's Castle
In centre of Kirkcudbright
Open: April to September, weekdays 9.30am-7pm, Sunday 2-7pm; winter, weekends only.

Orchardton Castle
A711, south of Palnackie
Open: April to end September, weekdays 9.30am-7pm, Sunday 2-7pm; beginning October to March, weekdays 9.30am-4pm, Sunday 2-4pm.

Threave Castle
Signposted on A75 west of Castle Douglas. Car park at Kelton Mains Farm, small boat to island.
Open: April to September, weekdays 9.30am-7pm, Sunday 2-7pm; beginning October to March, weekdays 9.30am-4pm, Sunday 2-4pm.

Carrick and Kyle, Strathclyde
Culzean Castle and Country Park
(National Trust for Scotland)
On the coast, A77, A719.
Open: castle, Easter and end April to end August, daily, 10am-6pm; beginning to end April and beginning September to end

October, daily, 12noon-5pm. Other times throughout the year by appointment. Country park, all year, daily 9am-sunset. Visitor centre and shop, Easter, and beginning September to end October, daily 10am-6pm; end April to end August, daily 10am-6pm

Loch Doon Castle
A713, $1^1/_2$ miles (2.4km) south of Dalmellington on minor road to Loch Doon.
No restricted access.

Lochnaw Castle
5 miles (8km) north-west of Stranraer, off B7043. Now a hotel.

Isle of Arran
Brodick Castle and Country Park
(National Trust for Scotland)
North end of Brodick Bay, A841, 2 miles (3.2km) from Brodick Pier.
Open: Easter, daily 1-5pm; end April to beginning October, daily 1-5pm; end Easter to end April and beginning to mid-October, Monday, Wednesday, Saturday, 1-5pm. Admission charge.
Garden, country park, open all year daily 9.30am-sunset.

Glasgow
Crookston Castle
Brockburn Road
Open: April to September, Monday-Saturday, 9.30am-7pm, Sunday 2-7pm; October to March, Monday-Saturday 9.30am-4pm, Sunday 2-4pm. Closed Thursday and Friday in winter.

Haggs Castle
100 St Andrews Drive
Open: Monday to Saturday, 10am-
5pm, Sunday 2-5pm. (Closed 25
December and 1 January)
☎ (041) 4272725
Free admission.

Clyde Valley
Bothwell Castle
Uddingston, near Bothwell
From A721, junction 5 or 6 M74.
Open: April to September 9.30am-
7pm, Sundays 2-7pm; October to
March 9.30am-4pm, Sundays 2-
4pm. Closed Thursday pm and
Friday out of season.

Craignethan Castle
Up minor road from the A72 at
Crossford.
Open: April to September 9.30am-
7.30pm, Sundays 2-7.30pm. May be
open during winter. Please check
with Tourist Information Centre.

Hallbar Tower
Braidwood, Carluke. From B7056.
Open days arranged by Carluke
Parish Historical Society.
Contact Clyde Valley Tourist
Information Centre.

Country Parks

Chatelherault Country Park
From Hamilton, A72 to Ferniegair
Country park, open: dawn to dusk
all year. Visitor centre, open:
10.30am-5.30pm (6pm in summer)
all year except Christmas week.
House, open: 11am-3.45pm (4pm in
summer) all year except Christmas
week.

Dalzell Country Park
(RSPB reserve)
South of Motherwell, off A721
Woodland walks and picnic spots.
☎ (031556) 5624 (Reserve manager)

**Lanark Moor Country Park and
Lanark Loch**
East of Lanark, A73
Equestrian centre, boating, fishing,
picnic area.
Open: all year, amenities April to
September.
☎ (0555) 61853

John Muir Country Park
Near Dunbar
Open: all year
1,667 acre country park, extending
to the beautiful coastline around
Dunbar. Ranger service.

Strathclyde Country Park
Motherwell, M74 Junction 5, or
M74 Junction 4 and A723
Loch and surrounding park. Visitor
centre, watersports, picnic areas,
caravan and camping site.
☎ (0698) 66155

Forest Walks

**Cardrona Forest-Tweed Valley
Forest**
$3^1/_2$ miles east of Peebles on B7062
Three waymarked walks, 2, 3, $4^1/_2$
miles.

Craik Forest-Border Forest Park
Borthwick Water picnic place, on
minor road leaving B711 at
Roberton
Two waymarked walks, $1^1/_2$ and 3
miles.

Glentress Forest-Tweed Valley Forest
2 miles east of Peebles on A72
Four waymarked walks, 1, $2^1/_2$ 4, $4^1/_2$ miles.
Wayfaring course also available.

Thornylee-Tweed Valley Forest
$3^1/_2$ miles east of Innerleithen on A72
Informal walks in the forest.

Gardens

Borders

Bowhill
Off A708, 1 mile west of Selkirk
Grounds open end April to end August daily except Friday 12 noon-5pm, Sunday 2-6pm (every day when house is open).
Walks, woods and children's play area. Mountain bicycle hire from April to October.

Dawyck
Off B712, 8 miles south-west of Peebles
Open: daily 10am-6pm from beginning April to end September.
Small admission per car. Disabled access limited.
Arboretum, heronry and formal garden.

Drumlanrig
(See Historic Houses Section)
Grounds, shop and visitor centre, nature trail, adventure woodland, gift shop, tea-room and craft centre.

Floors Castle
Off A608, 1 mile west of Kelso
Open: daily 10.30am-5.30pm Easter weekend; May, June and September, Sunday to Thursday; July and August, Sunday to Friday.
Grounds open 10.30am-5.30pm.
Garden and coffee shop open 7 days. Admission charge.

The Hirsel
Off A697, 2 miles west of Coldstream
Open (grounds only): daily 10am-5pm all year.
Nature trails, spring flowers and visitor centre. Craft house and workshops. Suitable for the disabled.

Kailzie
Off B7062, $2^1/_2$ miles (4km) east of Peebles
Open: early April-mid-October 10am-6pm. Admission charge.

Manderston
Off A6105, $1^1/_2$ miles east of Duns
Open: mid-May-late September, Sundays and Thursdays 2-5.30pm.
Parties at any time of year by appointment. Admission charge.

Mellerstain
Off A6089, 3 miles south of Gordon
Open: Easter weekend and beginning May-end September daily except Saturday 12.30-5pm.
Admission charge.

Netherbyres
Eyemouth
For opening times enquire locally.
Eighteenth-century oval walled garden.

Priorwood
Melrose
Open: April, and beginning

November to 24 December,
Monday to Saturday 10am-5.30pm;
beginning May to end October,
Monday- Saturday 10am-5.30pm,
Sunday 1.30-5.30pm
Free (donation box for NTS).

Traquair
Off B7062, 7 miles east of Peebles
Open: Easter; Sunday and Monday
in May; daily from end May to end
September, 1.30-5.30pm; July and
August, daily 10.30-5.30pm.
Admission charge.

The Woodland Visitor Centre
Jedburgh
3 miles north of Jedburgh near
junction of A68 and B6400.
Open: Good Friday to end October.
April/May/October, Sunday,
Wednesday and Bank Holiday
Mondays; June-September open
every day, 10.30am-5.30pm.
Admission charge.
Facilities for wheelchairs.

Lothian
Haddington House Gardens
Sidegate
Open: all year, daily, dawn to
dusk.

Inveresk Lodge Gardens
(National Trust for Scotland)
A6124 south of Musselburgh, 6
miles (9.6km), east of Edinburgh.
Open: all year, Monday to Friday
10am-4.30pm, Sunday 2-5pm.
Admission charge.
The house is not open to the public.

Edinburgh
Holyrood Park
Laid out around Holyrood House
Extensive views from Arthur's

Seat; Duddingston Loch bird
sanctuary.

Princes Street Gardens
Edinburgh
Substantial floral displays including the oldest floral clock in the
world.

Royal Botanic Garden
Inverleith Road, Edinburgh
Open: daily, except 25 December
and 1 January, 9am-sunset, Sunday
11am-sunset.
Plant houses and exhibition hall
open: 10am (11am Sunday)-about
5pm. Gardens close 1 hour before
sunset during British Summer
Time.

Saughton Rose Garden
Gorgie Road, Edinburgh
Open: all year, daily, dawn-dusk.

Dumfries and Galloway
Arbigland Gardens
A710 Solway Coast road between
Kirkbean and Southerness
Open: May to September inclusive,
Sunday, Tuesday, Thursday,
2-6pm; House and garden open
last week in May and last week in
August. Admission charge.

Ardwell Gardens
Ardwell, Stranraer, off A716
Open: daily, beginning March to
end October 11am-6pm. Donation
requested.

Castle Kennedy Gardens
3 miles (4.8km) east of Stranraer,
off A75
Open: daily, Easter weekend to
September, 10am-5pm.
Gardens set between two lochs,

famous for rhododendrons, azaleas and magnolias.

Galloway House Gardens
South of Wigtown, A746 then B7004 to Garlieston
Open: daily throughout the year. Admission charge.

Glenwhan Garden
Off A75 at Dunragit, near Glenluce
Open: beginning April to end October, daily 10am-5pm. Admission charge.

Logan Botanic Garden
South of Stranraer, A716 and off B7065
Open: late March to end October (no animals allowed except guide dogs), daily 10am-6pm. Admission charge.

Meadowsweet Herb Garden
Soulseat Loch, Stranraer, off A75
Open: daily except Wednesday, beginning May to beginning September 12noon-6pm. Admission charge.

Threave Garden
(National Trust for Scotland)
Off A75, 1 mile (1.6km) west of Castle Douglas
Open: all year, daily 9am-sunset; walled garden and glasshouses, all year, daily, 9am-5pm; visitor centre, exhibition and shop, late March to end October, daily 9am-6pm; tearoom, late March to end May, daily 10am-5pm; restaurant, end May to end October, daily 10am-5pm.

Historic Houses

Borders
Abbotsford
Off B6360, 2 miles west of Melrose
Open: late March to end October, daily 10am-5pm, Sunday 2-5pm. Admission charge. Facilities for the disabled.

Ayton Castle
Off A1, Ayton
Open: mid-May to late September, Wednesday and Sunday 2-5pm.

Bemersyde
Off B6350, 4 miles east of Melrose
For opening times enquire locally.

Bowhill
Off A708, 1 mile west of Selkirk
Open: daily, beginning to end July 1-4.30pm, Sunday 2-6pm. Before 1 July and after 31 July the house is reserved for specialist educational courses and for school groups who are welcomed throughout the season by appointment.

Drumlanrig
Off A76, $4^1/_2$ miles (7.2km) north of Thornhill
Open: end April to end June, Monday to Saturday 1.30-5pm, Sunday 2-6pm; beginning July to end August, Monday-Saturday 11am-5pm, Sunday 2-6pm.

Manderston
Off A6105, $1^1/_2$ miles east of Duns
Open: Sunday and Thursday, mid-May to late September 2-5.30pm. Parties at any time of year by appointment. Admission charge.

Mellerstain
Off A6089, 3 miles south of Gordon
Open: daily except Saturday,
Easter weekend and beginning
May to end September 12.30-5pm.
Admission charge.

Monteviot House
Off A68, $3^1/_2$ miles north of
Jedburgh
Open: Wednesday only, early May
to late October 1.30-5.30pm.
Admission charge.
See also Lothian Estates Woodland
Centre under 'Gardens'.

Traquair
Open: Easter; Sunday and Monday
in May; daily from end May until
end of September.

East Lothian, Lothian
Gosford House and Policies
Off A198, between Longniddry and
Aberlady.
Open: June and July, Wednesday,
Saturday and Sunday, 2-5pm.
Visits at other times by appoint-
ment. Admission charge.
☎ (08757) 201

Lennoxlove House
Off the A6137, $1^1/_2$ miles (2.4km)
south of Haddington.
Open: Easter weekend and May to
September, Wednesday, Saturday
and Sunday 2-5pm. At other times
groups may visit by appointment.
Admission charge.
☎ (062082) 3720.

**Preston Mill and Phantassie
Doocot**
(National Trust for Scotland)
Off A1 in East Linton
Open: late March to end Septem-
ber, Monday-Saturday 10am-1pm,
2-5pm, Sunday 2-5pm; October,
Monday-Saturday 10am-1pm,
2-4.30pm, Sunday 2-4.30pm;
November, Saturday 10am-
12.30pm, 2-4.30pm, Sunday
2-4.30pm.
Phantassie Doocot a short walk
away. Key from mill.

Stevenson House
New Haddington, 2 miles (3.2km)
east of Haddington, via minor road
from centre of town.
Open: house and gardens, July and
first 2 weeks of August, Thursday,
Saturday and Sunday 2-5pm. At
other times by appointment.
Walled garden open to members of
the National Trust for Scotland all
summer. Admission charge.
☎ (062082) 3376

Haddington House Gardens
Sidegate, Haddington
Open: all year, daily dawn to dusk.
Admission free.

Edinburgh
The Georgian House
(National Trust)
7 Charlotte Street
Open: Monday-Saturday 10am-
5pm, Sunday 2-5pm

Gladstone's Land (National Trust)
Lawnmarket
Open: Monday-Saturday 10am-
5pm, Sunday 2-5pm

Lauriston Castle
Cramond Road South
Open: daily except Friday 11am-
1pm, 2-5pm; November to March,
Saturday and Sunday only 2-4pm.
☎(031 336) 2060

Palace of Holyrood House
Canongate
Open: April to October, Monday-Saturday 9.30am-5.15pm, Sunday 11am-4.30pm; November to March, Monday-Saturday 9.30am-3.45pm Guided tours, tearoom in Abbey Strand. Sometimes the palace is closed at short notice for state visits (usually for two weeks in late May and three weeks in late June/early July).

Glasgow
Pollok House
Open: Monday-Saturday 10am-5pm, Sunday 2-5pm. (Closed 25 December and 1 January). Free admission.
☎(041-632)0274

Provan Hall
(National Trust for Scotland)
Auchinlea Road
Open: all year. Free admission.
☎ (041-771) 6372

Provand's Lordship
3 Castle Street
Open: all year, Monday-Saturday 10am-5pm, Sunday 2-5pm (Closed 25 December and 1 January). Free admission.
☎ (041-552) 8819

Tenement House
(National Trust for Scotland)
145 Buccleuch Street, Garnethill (north of Charing Cross)
Open: January to mid-April, Saturday and Sunday 2-4pm; mid-April to October, daily 2-5pm; November to March, Saturday and Sunday 2-4pm.
☎(041-333) 0183

Dumfries and Galloway
Maxwelton House
Moniaive
Off the B729 near Kirkland.
Open: house, July and August, Monday-Thursday 2-5pm. At other times, by appointment only.
Garden, April to end September, Monday-Thursday 2-5pm. Chapel, April to September, daily 10am-6pm. Admission charge.

Museums and Other Places of Interest

Borders
Border Country Life Museum
Lauder
Open: Saturday, Sunday, Wednesday and Thursday plus national and local holidays, mid-May to end September 12 noon-5pm. Joint admission charge with Thirlestane Castle. Members of Museum Trust free.

Castle Jail
Jedburgh
Open: early April to end October, Monday-Saturday 10am-12 noon and 1-5pm, Sundays 1-5pm. Admission charge.

Chambers Institution
Peebles
See Tweeddale Museum.

Coldstream Guards Museum
Coldstream
Open: early April to end September, daily except Monday 2-5pm. Admission charge.

Eyemouth Museum
Open: April to late October,
Monday-Saturday 10am-12.30pm
and 2-5.30pm, Sunday 1.30-5.30pm.
Closed Wednesday except during
July and August. Admission
charge.

**Innerleithen, Traquair and Glen
Museum**
Innerleithen
Open: Easter to late October,
Wednesday 2-4pm, Saturday
10am-12noon, and by arrangement.
Admission by donation.

Jedburgh Woollen Mill
On A68, Bankend North, Jedburgh.
Open: 7 days a week 9am-5.30pm.
☎ (0835) 63585

Jim Clark Memorial Room
Duns
Open: early April to end September, Monday-Saturday 10am-6pm,
Sundays 2-6pm. Admission charge.

Mary Queen of Scots House
Jedburgh
Open: summer months, daily
10am-12noon and 1-5.30pm
(enquire locally for exact dates).
Admission charge.

Melrose Station
Palma Place, Melrose, Roxburgh
Open: all year. No admission
charge.

Museum of Old Ironmongery
Selkirk
Open: Monday-Saturday 10am-
5pm. Closed Thursday afternoon.
Admission by donation.

Scottish Museum of Wool Textiles
Walkerburn
Open: April to December, Monday-
Saturday 9am-5.30pm, Sunday
(April to November) 12noon-
4.30pm; January to March 10am-
4pm.

Selkirk Museum
(in public library)
Open: mid-May to mid-September,
Monday, Wednesday and Friday 2-
4.30pm; also Tuesday and Thursday in July and August. Free.

Tweeddale Museum
Peebles (Chambers Institution)
Open: all year, Monday-Friday
9am-7pm (closes Wednesday at
5.30pm). Free.

Wilton Lodge Museum
Hawick
Open: early April to end October,
Monday-Saturday 10am-5pm,
Sunday 2-5pm; early November to
end March, Monday-Saturday
10am-4pm. Closed Sunday.
Admission charge.

East Lothian
Glenkinchie Distillery
Pencaitland, East Lothian
Open: all year round. Visitors by
prior arrangement Monday-Friday
9am-4pm.
☎ (0875) 340333

Golf Museum
Gullane, Heritage of Golf, West
Links Road
Open: free all year by appointment.
☎ (08757) 277

Haddington Local History Centre
Open: Monday 2-6pm, Tuesday

10am-1pm and 2-7pm, Thursday
and Friday 2-5pm. Admission free.

Haddington Museum
Newton Port, Haddington
Open: Monday, Tuesday, Thursday, Friday 10am-1pm, 2-7pm,
Saturday 10am-1pm.
☎ (062082) 2531

Jane Welsh Carlyle Museum
Lodge Street, Haddington
Open: rooms and garden, April to
September, Wednesday, Thursday,
Friday and Saturday 2-5pm.
Admission charge.

John Muir House
High Street, Dunbar
Open: June to September, Monday,
Tuesday, Thursday, Friday and
Saturday 10.30am-12.30pm and
1.30-4.30pm. Admission free.

Macaulay Gallery
Stenton, Dunbar
Open: Monday, Tuesday, Thursday
to Saturday 12noon-5pm, Sunday
12.30-5pm. Closed all Wednesday.
☎ (03685) 256

Museum of Flight
East Fortune Airfield, near North
Berwick.
Open: end May to beginning
October, 7 days a week 10.30am-
4.30pm. Admission free.
☎ (062088) 308

Myreton Motor Museum
near Aberlady
Open: end March to October 10am-
6pm; end October to March 10am-
5pm.
☎ (08757) 288

North Berwick Museum
School Road, North Berwick
Open: beginning April to late
October, Monday-Saturday 10am-
1pm and 2-5pm, Sunday 2-5pm.
☎ (0620) 3470

Peter Potter Gallery Trust
Off Church Street, Haddington
☎ (062082) 2080

Scottish Mining Museum
Prestongrange, near Prestonpans
Open: Tuesday to Friday 10am-
4.30pm, Saturday and Sunday
12noon-5pm. Admission free.
☎ (031-663) 7519

Edinburgh
Art Centre
2-4 Market Street
Open: Monday-Saturday 10am-
5pm; June to September 10am-6pm.

Candle Carvery and Museum Shop
140 High Street
Open: 10am-5.30pm daily
☎ (031 225) 9566

Canongate Tolbooth
Open: Monday-Saturday 10am-
5pm (June to September, 10am-
6pm).

Edinburgh Wax Museum
142 High Street
Open: daily
☎(031 226) 4445

Glass Works
14-16 Holyrood Road
Open: Tuesday-Saturday 10am-
6pm

Huntly House
Canongate
Open: Monday-Saturday 10am-
5pm (June to September 10am-
6pm).

John Knox's House
High Street
Open: 10am-5pm. Closed Sunday.

Lady Stair House
Lawnmarket
Open: Monday-Saturday 10am-
5pm (June to September 10am-
6pm).

Museum of Childhood
High Street
Open: Monday-Saturday 10am-
5pm (June to September 10am-
6pm).

National Gallery of Scotland
Mound
Open: 10am-5pm, Sunday 2-5pm.

**National Museum of Antiquities
of Scotland**
Queen Street
Open: 10am-5pm, Sunday 2-5pm.

The Netherbow
High Street
Church of Scotland's Art Centre.

New Town Conservation Centre
13a Dundas Street
Open: Monday-Friday 9am-1pm,
2-5pm. Walks four times weekly,
May to September.

Outlook Tower Visitor Centre
Lawnmarket
Open: daily 9.30am-5pm

St Cecilia's Hall
Cowgate
Russell Collection of keyboard
instruments.

Scottish Experience Visitor Centre
West End, Princes Street
Open: daily 10am-6.30pm

**Scottish National Gallery of
Modern Art**
Belford Road
Open: 10am-5pm, Sunday 2-5pm,
or half an hour before sunset in
winter.

Scottish National Portrait Gallery
Queen Street
Open: Monday-Saturday 10am-
5pm, Sundays 2-5pm. Admission
free.

Dumfries and Galloway
Bladnoch Distillery Visitor Centre
Just south of Wigtown on the A714
Open: 10am-4pm Monday to
Friday, tours or by appointment.
☎ (09884) 2235

Broughton House
High Street, Kirkcudbright
Open: Easter to mid-October 11am-
1pm, 2-5pm. Closed Sunday
morning and Tuesday. Admission
charge.

Robert Burns Centre
Mill Road, Dumfries, $^1/_2$ mile
(0.8km) from town centre.
Open: April to September,
Monday-Saturday 10am-8pm,
Sunday 2-5pm; October to March,
Tuesday-Saturday 10am-1pm, 2-
5pm. Film Theatre open Tuesday-
Saturday. Films start 8pm April to
September, 7.30pm October to

March. Disabled access and
facilities.
☎ (0387) 64808

Burns House
Burns Street, Dumfries
Open: all year, Monday-Saturday
10am-1pm, 2-5pm, Sunday 2-5pm;
October to March, closed Sunday
and Monday. Admission charge.

Burns Mausoleum
St Michael's Kirkyard, Dumfries
The doors to the mausoleum are
normally locked, but the key may
be obtained on application to the
curator of Burns House nearby.

Carlyle's Birthplace
(National Trust for Scotland)
Ecclefechan
Open: late March to end October,
daily 12 noon-5pm. Admission
charge.

Creetown Gem Rock Museum
Creetown, signposted from A75
Open: 9.30am-6pm each day
(summer); 9.30am-5pm October to
March.
☎ (0671) 82357

Deer Museum, Clatteringshaws
A712, 6 miles (9.6km) west of New
Galloway
Open: daily, 10am-5pm Easter to
mid-October.

**Dumfries and Galloway Aviation
Museum**
Heathhall Industrial Estate,
Dumfries
Open: Saturday and Sunday, Easter
to October 10am-5pm. Admission
charge.

**Dumfries Museum and Camera
Obscura**
Church Street, Dumfries
Open: Monday-Saturday 10am-
1pm, 2-5pm, Sunday 2-5pm;
October to March, closed Sunday
and Monday.

Ellisland Farm
Holywood Road, Dumfries
Off A76, 6^1/$_2$ miles (10.4km) north-
west of Dumfries.
Open: all year, 10am-1pm, 2-5pm.
☎ (038774) 426

Galloway Farm Museum
The Queen's Way, New Galloway
Opening times, contact Tourist
Information Centres.
Admission charge.
☎ (06443) 317

Glenluce Motor Museum
Glenluce
Open: daily, beginning March to
end October 10am-7pm; beginning
November to end February, 11am-
4pm, but closed Monday, Tuesday.
Admission charge.

**'Little Wheels' Toy Transport
Display and Model Railway**
6 Hill Street, Portpatrick
Open: Easter to end October, 6
days a week (not Fridays); July/
August every day. Group viewing
by arrangement.
☎ (077681) 536

Moffat Museum
The Neuk, Moffat
Open: Easter, and mid-May to end
September, 10.30am-1pm, 2.30-
5pm, Sunday 2.30-5pm. Closed
Wednesday. Admission charge.

Museum of Scottish Lead Mining

Wanlockhead
Off A74 at Abington (B797) or
Elvanfoot (A702)
Open: visitor centre, daily 11am.
Last entry 4pm. Lead mine (guided
tours), daily 11am-3pm. Period
cottages (guided), daily 11.30am-
4.30pm. Open Air Museum, $1^1/_2$
miles (2.4km) walkway. Admission
charge.

New Abbey Corn Mill

A710 south of Dumfries
Open: late March to end September, weekdays 9.30am-7pm,
Sunday 2-7pm; beginning October
to late March, weekdays 9.30am-
4pm, Sunday 2-4pm. Closed pm
Wednesday and all day Thursday.

Newton Stewart Museum

Open: end March 2-5.30pm, beginning May to end September,
Monday-Saturday 2-5.30pm; July
and August, 10am-12.30pm, 2-
5.30pm. Sunday opening July to
end September 2-5pm. Admission
charge.

Old Blacksmith's Shop Visitor Centre

Gretna Green
Open: daily, January to February
10am-4pm; March to May 9am-
5pm; June to September 9am-8pm;
October to December 9am-5pm.
Admission charge.

Power Station Museum

Tongland Power Station and
Salmon Ladder, Kirkcudbright
Open: beginning April to end
August, Monday-Saturday.
Guided tours, four a day. To book,
☎ (0557) 30114, or contact Tourist
Information Centre, Kirkcudbright.

Shambellie House, Museum of Costume

New Abbey, A710 from Dumfries
Open: mid-May to mid-September
10am-5.30pm, Sunday 12noon-
5.30pm. Admission free.

Whithorn Excavation

Centre of Whithorn, south of
Newton Stewart A714, A746
Open: Easter to end October 10am-
5.30pm daily.

Carrick & Kyle, Strathclyde

Burns Cottage

B7024, north end of Alloway
Open: Easter Sunday 10am-5pm;
April and May, Monday-Saturday,
9am-7pm, Sunday 10am-7pm;
beginning June to end August,
Monday-Saturday 9am-7pm,
Sunday 10am-7pm; September and
October, Monday-Saturday 10am-
5pm, Sunday 2-5pm; November to
March, Monday-Saturday 10am-
4pm.

Land O'Burns Centre

B7024, Alloway
Open: all week. January to May
10am-5pm; June and September
10am-5.30pm; July and August
10am-6pm; October and December
10am-5pm.

Isle of Arran

Isle of Arran Heritage Museum

Rosaburn, Brodick
Open: May to end September,
Monday-Saturday. (October by
arrangement). Admission charge.
☎ (0770) 2636

Clyde Valley

New Lanark
Unique industrial village, sign-posted from all major routes.
Access to village at all times (New Lanark Conservation Trust)
☎ (0555) 61345
Visitor centre open: 10am-5pm every day ☎ (0555) 65876

Glasgow

Annan Gallery
130 West Campbell Street
Open: Monday to Friday 9am-5pm, Saturday 9.30am-12.30pm.
☎ (041-221) 5087

Burrell Collection
Pollok Country Park
Open: Monday-Saturday, 10am-5pm, Sunday 2-5pm. Closed 25 December and 1 January. Free admission. ☎ (041-649) 7151

Charles Rennie Mackintosh Centre
870 Garscube Road
Open: Tuesday, Thursday and Friday 12noon-5.30pm, Sunday, 2.30-5pm, or by appointment.
☎ (041-946) 6600

Glasgow Art Gallery and Museum
Kelvingrove Park
Open: Monday-Saturday 10am-5pm, Sunday 2-5pm. (Closed 25 December and 1 January). Free admission. ☎ (041-357) 3929

Glasgow Print Studio
128 Ingram Street
Open: Monday-Saturday 10am-5.30pm. ☎ (041-552) 0704

Glasgow School of Art
167 Renfrew Street

Escorted tours when staff available.
Open: Monday-Friday 10.30-11.30am, 2.30-3.30pm, term time only. ☎ (041-332) 9797

Glengoyne Distillery
Lang Brothers Limited
100 West Nile Street, Glasgow
Guided tours, Monday-Friday 10.30am, 11.15am, 12 noon, 2pm, 3.15pm.
Parties over ten must book in advance. ☎ (041-332) 6361

Hunterian Art Gallery
Glasgow University
Main gallery open: Monday-Friday 9.30am-5pm, Saturday 9.30am-1pm.

Hunterian Museum
Glasgow University
Open: Monday-Friday 9.30am-5pm, Saturday 9.30am-1pm. Free admission. ☎ (041-330) 4221

Mackintosh House
Open: Monday-Friday 9.30am-12.30pm, 1.30-5pm, Saturday 9.30am-1pm. Charge for the Mackintosh House on weekday afternoons and Saturday mornings. Other areas free.

McLellan Galleries
Sauchiehall Street
Opening times vary for each exhibition. ☎ (041 227) 5699

The Mitchell Library
North Street
Open: Monday-Friday 9.30am-9pm, Saturday 9.30am-5pm.
☎ (041-221) 7030

**Museum for the 602
(City of Glasgow) Squadron**
Queen Elizabeth Ave, Hillington
Open: Wednesday and Friday 7.30-
9.30pm, first Sunday of each month
2-5pm.

Museum of Education
Scotland Street School
Open: Monday-Saturday 10am-
5pm, Sunday 2-5pm. Free
admission. ☎ (041-552) 8819

Museum of Transport
Kelvin Hall, Kelvingrove
Open: Monday-Friday 10am-5pm,
Saturday 10am-10pm, Sunday
12noon-6pm.

People's Palace Museum
Glasgow Green
Open: Monday-Saturday 10am-
5pm, Sunday 2-5pm. Closed 25
December and 1 January. Free
admission. ☎ (041-554) 0223

**Regimental Museum of the Royal
Highland Fusiliers**
518 Sauchiehall Street
Open: Monday-Thursday 9am-
4pm, Friday 9am-4pm. (Closed
public holidays.) Free admission.

Rutherglen Museum
Open: all year daily, Monday-
Saturday 10am-5pm, Sunday 2-
5pm. (Closed 25 December and 1
January) Free admission.
☎ (041-647) 0837

Scottish Design Centre
72 St Vincent Street
Open: Monday-Friday 9.30am-
5pm, Saturday 9am-5pm.
☎ (041-221) 6121

**Scottish Exhibition and
Conference Centre**
North bank of the Clyde at
Stobcross Quay
☎ (041-248) 3000

Stirlings Library
Queen Street
Open: Monday, Tuesday, Thursday
and Friday 9.30am-8pm, Saturday
9.30am-1pm, 2-5pm. Closed
Wednesday. ☎(041-221) 1867

Third Eye Centre
350 Sauchiehall Street
Open: Tuesday-Saturday 10am-
5.30pm, Sunday 2-5.30pm. Free
admission. ☎ (041-332) 7521

Clyde Valley
Biggar Gasworks
Open: beginning July to beginning
September, Monday to Saturday 2-
5pm, Sunday 11am-5pm.

The John Buchan Centre
Broughton, 6 miles (9.6km) from
Biggar
Open: Easter to mid-October 2-
5pm.

**Gladstone Court, A Victorian
Street**
North Back Road, Biggar
Open: Easter to October, Monday-
Saturday 10am-12.30pm, 2-5pm,
Sunday 2-5pm.

Greenhill Covenanters House
Burn Braes, Biggar
Open: May to mid-October, daily
2-5pm.

Hamilton Cameronian Museum
Town centre, behind District
Museum

Open: Monday-Saturday 10am-1pm, 2-5pm.

Hamilton District Museum
Town centre
Open: Monday-Saturday 10am-12 noon, 1-5pm.

Hamilton Mausoleum
In the former grounds of Hamilton Palace.
Guided tours only — booking essential.
Open: Easter to September, tours at 3pm every day, also 7pm Saturday and Sunday in July and August; September to Easter, tours at 2pm Saturday and Sunday only.

David Livingstone Centre
Blantyre, off A724, north-west of Hamilton. On the banks of the River Clyde.
Open: all year, Monday-Saturday 10am-6pm, Sunday 2-6pm.
Admission charge. ☎ (0698) 823140

Moat Park Heritage Centre
Biggar, on A702, 28 miles (44.8km) from Edinburgh
Open: March to October, daily 10am-5pm, Sunday 2-5pm.

Puppet Theatre
Biggar
Shows and guided tours daily including Sundays.
Open: March to mid-January except 2 weeks early October.
Please book in advance. Monday-Saturday 10am-5pm, closed Tuesdays, Sunday 1-5pm.
☎ (0899) 20631

Nature Reserves

Barefoots Marine Reserve
Eyemouth coastline
Information from: Lawson Wood, Tighnamara, Pocklawslap, Eyemouth TD1 5AX
☎ (08907) 50741

Bass Rock
Off North Berwick.
Daily sailings (weather and conditions permitting) May to September.
World famous gannetry and bird sanctuary. ☎ (0620) 2838

Duns Castle
Off A6112, 1 mile north of Duns
Scottish Wildlife Reserve/Duns Castle Trust.
Permits and further information from: The Warden, W. Waddell, 26 The Mount, Duns.

Falls of Clyde
(Scottish Wildlife Trust Reserve)
Visitor centre open: 1-5pm Saturday and Sunday all year except January. Also 11am-5pm weekdays, Easter to October.
☎ (0555) 65262

Ken/Dee Marshes RSPB Reserve areas
On west side of A713, New Galloway to Castle Douglas road, and from A762 on other side of valley. The reserve lies at the north end of Loch Ken.
Open: by appointment with the warden.
☎ (06445) 236

St Abb's Head (Scottish Wildlife Trust/National Trust for Scotland) 3 miles north of Eyemouth
Open: all year
Further information from: The Ranger, Ranger's Cottage, Northfield, St Abbs. ☎ (08907) 443

The Wildlife and Wetlands Centre
Caerlaverock, 8 miles (12.8km) south of Dumfries. Signposted from A75 at Dumfries. From Carlisle and Annan follow Solway Coast Heritage Trail (B724 and B725).
Open: daily from mid-September to end April 9.30am-5pm. No dogs allowed in the refuge. Admission charge. Limited access for disabled visitors. Special rates for parties booked in advance. ☎ (038777) 200

Wood of Cree, RSPB Reserve
4 miles (6.4km), north of Newton Stewart, on minor road from Minnigaff.
Access at all times. Marked walks, impressive waterfalls. Warden. ☎ (0671) 2861

Yetholm Loch
(Scottish Wildlife Trust)
Open: by permit only. Further information from: Scottish Wildlife Trust, 25 Johnston Terrace, Edinburgh EH1 2NH
☎ (031 226) 4602

Nature Walks
Countryside rangers operate a programme of guided walks throughout the summer along the five nature trails listed —
Yellowcraig, Barns Ness, River Esk at Musselburgh, Longniddry, Bents and John Muir Clifftop Trail.

Contact Tourist Information Centres.

Farm Visits
Palgowan Farm
4 miles north of Glentrool Village
2-hour guided tours including tea and biscuits.

South Bank Farm
East Bennan, Kildonan, Arran
☎ (077082) 221

Parks, Gardens and Zoos

Bellahouston Park
Ibrox, Glasgow
Open: daily, end April to August 8am-10pm; September to April 8am-5pm. Free admission.
☎ (041-427) 4224

Botanic Gardens
Glasgow
Off Great Western Road
The Kibble Palace, Open: 10am-4.45pm (4.15pm in winter)
Main glasshouse, Open: Monday-Saturday, 1pm-1.45pm (4.15pm in winter), Sunday, 12 noon-4.45pm (4.15pm in winter). Gardens open daily 7am-dusk. ☎ (041-334)2422

Eastwood Butterfly Kingdom
Rouken Glen Park, Giffnock
Open: late March to beginning November, every day from 10am. Facilities for school parties (20 or more). ☎ (041 620) 2084

Edinburgh Zoo
Corstorphine Road
Open: daily 9am-6pm (dusk in winter). ☎ (031 334) 9171

Glasgow Zoo
Calderpark
Open: all year, daily 10am-5 or
6pm. ☎ (041-771) 1185

Linn Park
Cathcart, Glasgow
Open: daily 7am-dusk. Free
admission. ☎ (041-637) 1147

Pollok Country Park
Glasgow
Park always open.
Demonstration and display garden
open: daily, Easter to September,
Monday-Thursday 8am-4pm,
Friday 8am-3pm, weekends 8am-
6.30pm; October to Easter 8am-
4pm. Free admission.
☎ (041-632) 9299

Rosshall Park
Crookston, Glasgow
Open: April to September, daily 1-
8pm; October to March, daily 1-
4pm. Free admission.
☎ (041-882) 3554

Victoria Park
Whiteinch, Glasgow
Fossil Grove Building, open:
Monday-Friday 8am-4pm,
Saturday and Sunday pm only.
Park open daily 7am-dusk. Free
admission. ☎ (041-959) 1146

Public Buildings

City Chambers
George Square, Glasgow
Guided tours, Monday, Tuesday,
Wednesday and Friday at 10.30am
and 2.30pm (subject to functions).
Free admission. ☎ (041-221) 9600

Glasgow Cathedral
Castle Street, Glasgow
Open: April to September,
Monday-Saturday 9.30am-7pm;
October to March, Monday-
Saturday 9.30am-4pm, Sunday 2-
4pm. Free admission.

Hutchesons' Hall
(National Trust for Scotland)
158 Ingram Street, Glasgow
Visitor centre open: Monday-
Friday 9am-5pm, Saturday 10am-
4pm. Shop, Monday-Saturday
10am-4pm. Free admission.
☎ (041-552) 8391

The Stock Exchange
Nelson Mandela Place, Glasgow
Open: Monday-Friday 10am-
12.45pm, 2-3.30pm. Visitors'
gallery. ☎ (041-221) 7060

Edinburgh
Scottish Whisky Heritage Centre
358 Castlehill, The Royal Mile
Open: 7 days, 10am-5pm; summer
season 9am-6.30pm.
☎ (031-220) 0441

The People's Story Museum
Canongate
Open: Monday-Saturday,10am-
5pm; June-September, 10am-6pm;
during the Edinburgh Festival,
Sundays, 2-5pm.

**The High Kirk of Edinburgh, St
Giles' Cathedral**
High Street
Open: 9.30am-5pm, Monday-
Saturday. Sunday worship 9am,
11am, 6pm, 8pm.

City Chambers
High Street
Open: 10am-3pm, Monday-Friday,
when council business permits.

Parliament House
Parliament Square
Open: Tuesday-Friday, 10am-
4.30pm.

Scott Monument
East Princes Street
Open: beginning May to end
October weekdays, 9am-6pm;
beginning November to end April,
9am-3pm.

Fruit Market Gallery
29 Market Street
Open: Monday-Saturday, 10am-
5.30pm. ☎ (031-226) 5781

Sport and Recreation

There is a wide variety of sports
and recreation facilities in the
Scottish Lowlands. Angling is
widely available throughout the
region, as are golfing facilities, but
unfortunately space does not allow
for full details to be given here.
Also available are: boat hire and
sub-aqua (Arran); bicycle hire;
riding; ice skating (Glasgow and
Edinburgh); skiing (dry slope in
Edinburgh); and watersports.
There is also a good selection of
sports centres and swimming
pools. For details contact the
Tourist Information Centres listed
below.

Tourist Information Centres

Abington
Little Chef Service Area, A74
northbound. ☎ (08642) 436

Ayr
39 Sandgate
Open: all year. ☎ (0292) 284196

Biggar
High Street. ☎ (0899) 21066

Brodick
Isle of Arran
Open: all year. ☎ (0770) 2401/2140

Castle Douglas
Markethill. ☎ (0556) 2611

Coldstream
Henderson Park. ☎ (0890) 2607

Dalbeattie
Car park. ☎ (0556) 610117

Dunbar
The Town House
Open: all year. ☎ (0368) 63353

East Linton
Pencraig Layby, A1 (southbound)
Open: summer only
☎ (0620) 860063

Edinburgh
Waverley Market
Open: all year. ☎ (031-557) 1700

Eyemouth
Auld Kirk. ☎ (08907) 50678

Galashiels
Bank Street. ☎ (0896) 55551

Gatehouse of Fleet
Car park. ☎ (05574) 212

Girvan
Bridge Street. ☎ (0465) 4950

Glasgow
St Vincent Place. ☎ (041-204) 4400

Gretna
Annan Road. ☎ (0461) 37834

Hamilton
Road Chef Services, M74 north-
bound
Open: all year. ☎ (0698) 285590

Hawick
Common Haugh. ☎ (0450) 72547

Jedburgh
Murray's Green
☎ (0835) 63435/63688

Kelso
Turret House. ☎ (0573) 23464

Kirkcudbright
Harbour Square. ☎ (0557) 30494

Lanark
Horsemarket
Open: all year. ☎ (0555) 61661

Langholm
High Street. ☎ (03873) 80976

Maybole
Culzean Castle and Country Park
☎ (06556) 293

Melrose
Priorwood Gardens
☎ (089682) 2555

Moffat
Church Gate. ☎ (0683) 20620

Musselburgh
Brunton Hall
Open: summer only
☎ (031-665) 6597

Newton Stewart
Dashwood Square. ☎ (0671) 2431

North Berwick
Quality Street
Open: all year. ☎ (0620) 2197

Peebles
High Street. ☎ (0721) 20138

Prestwick
Boydfield Gardens. ☎ (0292) 79946

Prestwick Airport
☎ (0292) 79822

Sanquhar
Tolbooth. ☎ (0659) 50185

Selkirk
Town Centre. ☎ (0750) 20054

Southwaite
M6 Service Area (northbound)
Cumbria. ☎ (06974) 73445/6

Stranraer
Port Rodie car park. ☎ (0776) 2595

Troon
South Beach. ☎ (0292) 317696

All centres are open for the Easter
weekend and then from May-
October, except for Jedburgh,
Dumfries, Dunbar, Edinburgh,
Lanark, Hamilton, Glasgow, Ayr
and Brodick which are open all
year.

Travel and Transport

The District Travel Guides give
comprehensive timetables for all
public transport services to, from
and within the Scottish Lowlands.
It is available from the various
listed Tourist Boards and Information Centres.

FERRIES
P&O Ferries
Ferry Terminal
Cairnryan, Stanraer DG9 8BR
☎ (05812) 276

Sealink
Sea Terminal
Stranraer DG9 8EJ
☎(0776) 2262

Glasgow
☎ (041 204) 2844

Caledonian Macbrayne
Govrock (0475) 33755
Brodick (0770) 2166
Ardrosson (0294) 63470

BUSES
Western Scottish Omnibus Ltd
Whitesands, Dumfries
☎ (0387) 53496

Borders Regional Council Transport
Department of Roads and Transportation
Newtown St Boswells
Borders
☎ (0835) 23301

Lothian Region Transport
Waverley Bridge Transport
    Information Office
☎ (031 556) 5656
Details of coach tours and Touristcard

Lothian Region Transport Enquiries Office
14 Queen Street
Edinburgh
☎ (031 554) 4494

Scottish Omnibuses
Bus Station
St Andrew's Square
Edinburgh
☎ (031 556) 8464

Buchanan Bus Station
Glasgow
For routes to the north, north-west and east
☎ (041 332) 7133/9191

Anderston Bus Station
Glasgow
For more southerly routes
☎ (041 248) 7432

Travel Centre
St Enochs
For travel within Greater Glasgow
☎ (041 226) 4826

Scottish Citylink Coaches
Buchanan Bus Station, Glasgow
☎ (041 332) 9644

Strathclyde's Buses
Larkfield Garage, Glasgow
☎ (041 423) 6600

Clydeside Scottish Omnibuses Ltd
4 Gordon Street, Paisley
☎ (041 889) 3191

TRAINS
British Rail, Scotrail
Edinburgh
☎ (031 556) 2451

British Rail, Scotrail
Glasgow
☎ (041 332) 9811

British Rail
Central and Queen Street Station

24-hour passenger enquiries
Glasgow
☎ (041 204) 2844

Glasgow Underground
Travel Centre
St Enochs
☎ (041 226) 4826

AIRPORTS
Glasgow Airport, Abbotsinch
☎ (041 887) 1111

Prestwick Airport, Clyde Coast
☎ (0292) 79822

TRAVEL ON THE ISLE OF ARRAN
Arran Transport and Trading
The Pier, Brodick
☎ (0770)2121

Bannatyne Motors
Blackwaterfoot
☎ (0770 86) 277

A.C. Hendry
Cir Mhor
Glenrosa, Brodick
☎ (0770) 2274

Useful Addresses

Scottish National Tourist Board
23 Ravelston Terrace
Edinburgh
☎ (031 332) 2433

Scottish Borders Tourist Board
Murrays Green
Jedburgh
☎ (0835) 63435

Dumfries and Galloway Tourist Board
Whitesands
Dumfries
☎ (0387) 53862

Ayrshire and Burns Country Tourist Board
39 Sandgate
Ayr
☎ (0292) 284196

Clyde Valley Tourist Board
Horsemarket
Lanark
☎ (0555) 2544

East Lothian Tourist Board
Quality Street
North Berwick
☎ (0620) 2197

National Trust for Scotland
5 Charlotte Square
Edinburgh EH2 4DU
☎ (031 226) 5922

City of Edinburgh Advance Reservations Dept
Waverley Market
3 Princes Street EH2 2QP
☎ (031 557) 2727

City of Edinburgh Recreation Department
27 York Place
EH1 3HP
☎ (031 225) 2424

Automobile Association
269 Argyle Street
Glasgow
☎ (041 221) 8152

Waverley **Paddle Steamer**
Anderston Quay
Glasgow
☎ (041 812) 0101

Clyde Marine Cruises
31 Broomielaw
☎ (041 221) 8702

Project Ability
McIver House
Cadogan Street, Glasgow
Information about facilities for the
disabled.

Resource Centre for the Blind
276 St Vincent Street
Glasgow

Youth Hostels

Abbey St Bathans
Duns, Berwickshire TD11 3TX
☎ (03614) 217, bookings only.
Phone after 5pm, or between 8am
and 9pm, or 12noon-1pm.
Open: beginning May to end
October.

Ayr
Craigweil Road,
Ayr KA7 2XJ
☎ (0292) 26232
Open: mid-February to end
October.

Broadmeadows
Old Broadmeadows, Yarrowford,
Selkirk TD7 5LZ
Open: March to end September.
☎ (075 076) 262

Coldingham
The Mount, Coldingham,
Berwickshire TD14 5PA

☎ (08907) 298
Open: mid-March to end September.

Edinburgh (Bruntsfield)
Bruntsfield Crescent,
Edinburgh EH10 4EZ
☎ (031 447) 2994
Open: all year.

Edinburgh (Eglinton)
18 Eglinton Crescent,
Edinburgh EH12 5DD
☎ (031 337) 1120
Open: mid-April to beginning
December.

Glasgow
11 Woodlands Terrace,
Glasgow G3 6DD
☎ (041 332) 3004
Open all year.

Kendoon
Dalry, Castle Douglas,
Kirkcudbrightshire DG7 3UD
Open: mid-May to end September;
Friday, Saturday, Sunday at Easter;
and Saturday until mid-May.

Kirk Yetholm
Kirk Yetholm, near Kelso,
Roxburghshire TD5 8PG
Open: mid-March to end September.

Lochranza
Isle of Arran KA27 8HL
☎ (077083) 631
Open: mid-March to end October.

Melrose
Priorwood, Melrose,
Roxburghshire TD6 9EF
☎ (089 682) 2521
Open: March to end October;

closed November; open weekends, Friday, Saturday in winter. Closed every Tuesday from beginning March to late March and beginning to end October.

Minnigaff
Minnigaff, Newton Stewart, Wigtownshire DG8 6PL
☎ (0671) 2211
Open: late March to end September.

Snoot
Roberton, Hawick, Roxburghshire TD9 7LY

Open: mid-March to end September.

Wanlockhead
Lotus Lodge, Wanlockhead, Biggar, Lanarkshire ML12 6UT
☎ (0659) 74252
Open: mid-March to end September.

Whiting Bay
Isle of Arran KA27 9QW
☎ (07707) 339
Open: mid-March to end October.

Information for Overseas Visitors to Britain

Tourist Offices

Can help with most travel information. Many will book
accommodation, and it is often worthwhile writing to
those listed in this book before you depart.

Currency/Credit Cards

The units of currency are pounds (£) and pence (p). Most
major credit cards, especially VISA and MASTERCARD
(Access), are widely accepted. Money can be changed at
banks and at *bureaux de change* in major cities.

Driving Regulations

1) Speed limits: built-up areas 30mph (48kph)
   approach to built-up areas 40mph (64kph)
   motorways 70mph (113kph)
   dual carriageways 70mph (113kph)
   a 'de-restricted' sign (black diagonal stripe on
   white background) actually indicates a maximum
   speed of 60mph (97kph).
2) Age restrictions: drivers must be over 17.
3) Driving is on the left-hand side of the road.
4) The wearing of front and rear seat belts is
   compulsory.
5) Fuel: many fuel stations are self-service. The
   opening times vary, but many stay open until
   about 8pm and some for 24 hours. Lead-free petrol
   is now widely available.

Car Hire

The major car rental groups (eg Hertz, Avis etc) operate from most cities and airports. There are also many smaller firms, and large garages often hire cars. Details of these and many other services are to be found in the local classified telephone directories (*Yellow Pages*).

Public Transport

Provision varies greatly from area to area, and it is best to check locally where you are staying. Tickets for long-distance travel are available from railway/bus stations. For shorter journeys tickets are available on buses, and sometimes on trains.

Banks

Generally open from 9.30am-3.30pm, but some stay open later and some open on Saturday mornings.

Shops, Post Offices etc

1) General opening hours are 9am-5.30pm, but many supermarkets and some smaller shops stay open later.

2) Most provisions can be obtained from super-markets, but many specialised smaller shops (eg bakeries, butchers) are also available.

3) Stamps are available in 1st and 2nd class for letters/postcards. They can be purchased at post offices and some shops (eg newsagents).

Telephones

Most public telephones take all coins from 2p to £1. Phone cards are also available from post offices (there are separate phone boxes in which to use these)

Climate

The British weather is changeable throughout the year!
The warmest months are generally July and August, but
June and September can be drier. Generally, the west is
warmer and wetter and the east colder and drier; the
north is colder than the south. However, these variations
are fairly small. A good mixture of clothes is advisable.

Emergencies

Phone 999 (free) for police, fire and ambulance services.

Religion

Church of Scotland, Presbyterian, Episcopalian, Roman
Catholic and various other religions are practiced in
Scotland.

National Holidays

Banks, post offices and many shops close for several days
at Christmas and for 2 days at New Year; also Good
Friday, Easter Monday, May Day Holiday (first Monday
in May), Spring Holiday (last Monday in May) and Late
Summer Holiday (last Monday in August).

Pets

Quarantine requirements are very long, so visitors do not
usually bring their pets.

INDEX